Historical Criticism and the Challenge of Theory

Historical Criticism and the Challenge of Theory

EDITED BY

Janet Levarie Smarr

UNIVERSITY OF ILLINOIS PRESS
Urbana and Chicago

This book is printed on acid-free paper.

Library of Congress Cataloging-in-Publication Data

Historical criticism and the challenge of theory / edited by Janet
  Levarie Smarr.
        p.   cm.
    Includes index.
    ISBN 0-252-01965-2 (cl). — ISBN 0-252-06270-1 (pb)
    1. Historical criticism (Literature) 2. Literature and history.
  3. Literature—History and criticism—Theory, etc. I. Smarr, Janet
  Levarie, 1949– .
  PN98.H57H56 1993
  801′.95—dc20   92-17293
                                                              CIP

Contents

Janet Levarie Smarr

Introduction

Recent developments in critical theory have brought about intense debate and confusion concerning the basic aims and methods of a historical criticism of literature, or the kinds of relation possible between literary and historical study. Deconstruction's decentering of the subject, crossing paths with Marxist theory, has led to an ongoing discussion about the nature of the writing subject: about whether it melts away into the social, or maintains a space of its own from which to contest social structures. Moreover, by linking with Lacanian psychology through its emphasis on language and the social construction of the subject, deconstruction has provided a possible meeting point for Marxist and psychological theories, once seemingly incompatible. At the same time, the combined influence of Derrida and Lacan in treating reality as something that can be perceived or dealt with only in and through linguistic constructions has undermined our notions about the very social structures and histories to which the subject was in some views giving way.

As these examples make obvious, deconstruction has not acted alone in opening up the question of what the historical criticism of literature can be. Attempts to connect historical approaches with anthropological or psychoanalytic ones have further shifted our expectations of what history might mean. Feminism has led to analyses of the constructed and interested nature of histories; and the increasing study of non-Western cultures has multiplied perspectives to an extent where any totalizing reintegration or sense of center seems impossible.[1]

This volume contributes to our understanding of the possibilities of a historical criticism of literature and of the issues involved by offering an array of examples of historical literary study embedded in self-reflective commentary about their assumptions and methods. The

introduction reviews some of the issues at stake and addresses one
modest and practical, but also problematic, solution, emerging from
recent publications, to the question of how to do historical criticism.
The views I express here are not meant to represent or sum up those of
the other contributors, nor to find a tidy compromise among their
positions, but rather to join in their conversation from my own perspective.

History used to mean the hard facts to which one could turn in order
to support softer interpretive work. In recent years, this view of history
has been profoundly challenged. The attack, led by writers such as
Foucault and Hayden White, claims that "facts" as such do not exist in
an objective way but are determined by the historian's subjective purposes.
One finds what one is looking for. We had all heard the old phrase that
history is written by the winners; but its implications had been left
unexplored. One could still feel that there was a real, objective account
to be gotten at beyond the self-interested versions of the story. Now the
existence of facts awaiting our discovery is disputed. History, White has
suggested, is constructed rather than discovered. It has thus become as
soft, subjective, textual, and interpretive as the literary criticism that
had hoped to find there a solid foundation.

The textuality of history does not necessarily imply a free-wheeling
subjectivity, however. After all, there do seem to be things that most
people feel they have a right to say they "know" in some more objective
sense: for example, that Spenser published the first books of the *Faerie
Queene* in 1590; or that Boccaccio and Petrarch met several times and
corresponded until the end of their lives. No one will seriously argue
with these "facts." The questions remain as to what we can do with
them and whether there are other sorts of facts that might prove more
interesting for the purposes of interpretive work. Nonetheless, we can
still plausibly argue that interpretations that contradict these facts are
somehow wrong.[2] Most of us, including the "new" historicists, still
appeal to historical data in this way. Even Derrida, arguing against
what he perceives as misunderstandings of his work, has commented:
"It is totally false to suggest that deconstruction is a suspension of
reference. . . . But to distance oneself from the habitual structure of
reference, to challenge or complicate our common assumptions about it,
does not amount to saying that there is *nothing* beyond language."[3] Or
as Lentricchia comments, "*Il n'y a pas de hors-texte* must not be read as
positing an ontological 'nothing' outside the text."[4]

The chief problem seems to be not so much a loss of facts (an
invalidation of factuality) as an *embarras de richesses*. So many new
areas of inquiry have become part of history (besides social, economic,
political, and intellectual histories, we now have also histories of popu-

lar culture, of institutions, women's history, family history, leading into a kind of psychological history that promises to heal the divisions between Freudians and historicizers, etc.) that one does not know which way to turn for relevant material. Everything is potentially relevant; and there is a resulting sense of arbitrariness about the choice of "facts" to be related to a particular text. Greenblatt's use of historical anecdotes to be "read" and connected with literary texts has been accused of just such arbitrariness, but the problem is more general.[5] Thus Leigh DeNeef writes, criticizing old and new historicisms alike: "In such a discursive scene, any and all history can only be the provisional effect of a certain arbitrary cut, a referential context willfully privileged at the expense of and by excluding other contexts."[6] Since order is never possible without exclusions, there seems to be no escape from this problem for the critic seeking a practicable project.

How wide a circle do we draw? Are we to see a text as embedded in a particular moment consisting of the events, moods, and tensions of a particular year, or decade, or in the larger sweep of the century, or an even larger sweep such as the Christian Middle Ages or Capitalist Era, or all of these at once? Does the author's life matter, when we can know something about it, or should we forget about authors and consider the cultural institutions or structures that produced both the authors and the diachronically shifting meanings of their works? If one wants to write about Shakespeare's plays, does one need to analyze the group of people among whom he lived and worked, or the institutions of the theaters, the inns of court, and the court, or the current affairs and concerns of London more generally, or all of the known world's social, political, economic, religious, intellectual, and other concerns insofar as these have bearing on the words of the text? Do we have to know everything in order to say anything at all? Since that is impossible, is historical criticism a futile effort?

Lentricchia has suggested that we replace a totalizing history with multiple "histories."[7] So too Greenblatt, declaring himself "increasingly uneasy with the monolithic entities that my work had posited," calls it "important to resist the integration of all images and expressions into a single master discourse."[8] But if historical context turns out to mean whatever random collection of facts a particular scholar, following his or her personal interests, has managed to collect in years of reading, does this produce any sensible results? Does it give us anything resembling knowledge or explanations? Are some areas of fact more relevant than others, at least for a particular text? How can we tell? Is there any rational, structured, or principled way to limit how much we need to know in order to explain a text? Is that even what we are trying to do?

Or if history is as "soft" and rhetorical as literature, are connections between the two fields not to be thought of as "explanations" at all? But, then, what can motivate such connections? What can they show?

Recent approaches within both history and literary criticism make possible a new movement toward each other. For while the New Historical critics have turned from New Criticism and structuralism toward a revived interest in history, and have drawn on historians such as Foucault to provide fresh projects and directions for their thinking, simultaneously historical theorists have turned toward literature and literary theory to open new perspectives on their own field. Thus, for example, Hayden White has drawn from Northrop Frye the notion of a few basic myths or stories of which all other tales—including historical narratives—are displaced versions, or in terms of which all other tales are told.[9] La Capra meanwhile has urged his colleagues to consider how works of literature, not just in their documentary but in their "work-like" or performative aspect, are—or should be—a natural part of historical study, one that opens for the historian a way into the field of unrealized possibilities from which events have emerged.[10] Derrida's deconstruction of insides and outsides makes the old polarity of text and context blur. Even historians who do not specifically turn to literature have opened up the study of history to its possible inclusion. Thus, the Annales school, broadening historical study from political and diplomatic studies to an interdisciplinary "sciences humaines" and from particular events to long-term "mentalités," has inspired work like Darnton's, which attempts to access mentalities of the past through analyses of folktales or through reader responses to Rousseau's novels.[11] The implications are that history and literature help to explain each other and share the common field of our experience. Rather than a sharp demarcation between the study of history and the study of literature, one sees more and more a gradual merging across their common spaces, for which *culture* seems to be the favorite composite term.

Certainly, the constituted definition of separate disciplines is under attack. Cohen's essay in this volume, as well as his *Historical Culture,* aims at a deconstruction of the term *history* insofar as the term becomes reified in a way that makes possible the notion of history as an agent. History cannot "show" or "prove" anything or "direct" us in any way. Appeals to "history"—and "real history" is a frequent object of appeal in attacks on deconstruction[12]—are idolizing prayers to the empty name of a god who does not exist. But if one cannot neatly sum up one set of phenomena as history, neither, as Sinfield argues, can one really talk sensibly about "Literature," although the term is often used in order to exclude whatever one does not want to have to consider.[13]

The study of history deals increasingly with the symbolic constructions of reality, including its own. The struggle for power is in large part
a struggle over the control and production of images, terms, and meanings.
Thus analysis of literary texts helps us to understand a history that is
already a kind of fiction too; and the very power of those historical
fictions makes possible the power of literature, literary criticism, and
theory to work for change. Picking up the phrases of "cultural poetics"
and "social text," which indicate this merged field of history and
language, Carolyn Porter concludes her essay "Are We Being Historical
Yet?": "For I share with at least some new historicists the view that it
ought to be possible, once we are licensed to explore the horizonless
field of the social text, to produce not only a cultural poetics—as
valuable as this might be—but, more ambitiously, a 'cultural critique.'"[14]

Recent essays reviewing the nature of historical criticism have come
to realize that history is one of the terms rhetorically at stake. Certainly
feminism has been one source of this awareness. Thus Judith Newton
remarks: "In this case, writing feminist work into the history of 'new
historicism,' as I intend very briefly to do, may mean participating in
the definition of what 'new historicism' is going to mean.... This
difference ... makes for other differences in what 'history' looks like,
makes for differences in what is included as 'history' in the first place."[15]
A deconstructionist on the defensive can produce the same awareness:

> At issue, then, "is the process of recognition and even of naming with
> respect to various approaches to history. One important question facing
> us is that of the type of research that should be called intellectual history,
> indeed that of the type of research to be recognized as historical." Helgerson,
> like many new historicists, seems perfectly confident in deciding that
> some of the work he reviews is historical and that some is not; he is even
> more confident in deciding that that which is not historical is of question-
> able critical value.[16]

One cannot have a definition without exclusions; thus the arguments
over definitions—and the arguments for leaving these definitions
open—are all fraught with political implications for the various excluders
and excluded.

Changing concepts of the nature of history obviously change the
practice of historical criticism. One major way in which the meaning of
historical criticism has shifted in the last ten or fifteen years is from a
search for the contemporary meanings of the text based largely on
intellectual history (the meanings of nature to Alain de Lille, Montaigne,
or Wordsworth, for example) to the embedding of the text in a social
history based on the study of power relations understood in more

modern terms. This shift is partly, I think, an attempt to make history more useful. By turning to an analysis of class or institutional relations, one might find something to say to a larger portion of society and thereby escape marginalization in the corner of the merely academic. In some cases, this could be simply a matter of which kind of history one will do, of which other texts will represent the "context" of history: instead of reading Chaucer with Boethius, let us read him with accounts of peasant uprisings; instead of reading Spenser with Plato, let us read him with discourses on the troubles in Ireland. To the extent that its aim is either to illuminate the literary text with historical discourses, or to enlighten the social situation with literary insights, this criticism offers nothing really new. To the extent, however, that the conceptual framework of text and context is broken down to reveal the ubiquitous interplay of social and symbolic activities, the shift is both intellectually and politically significant and certainly works against the very possibility of separating academic from political interests.

There is a further potential, again not entirely new, when the shift to a social focus combines with a shift of interest from the "representative" or "documentary" to the "rhetorical" or "worklike" function of discourse.[17] In this case, one is looking not for meanings but for social effects, or potential effects, of the text. Dollimore, while encouraging this kind of project, warns against too sharp a distinction between the two kinds; for "effectivity is both decided and assessed in the practice of signification. If we ignore this then we are likely to ignore also the fact that the socio-political effects of literature are in part achieved in and through the practice of appropriation [of meanings]."[18] Newton has this clearly in mind as well, for her struggle to redefine history and historicism is part of the feminist struggle; "male" constructions of history have had social and economic effects of exclusion for women and "women's" history.

Besides this shift in kinds of history, the same recent decades have seen the shapes of history redefined, from development or some such unifying theme to a more random series of changes without necessary direction.[19] "Shouldn't we get gradually used to looking at intellectual history as a multifarious, intricate mixture of strands, to which encompassing concepts have only the slightest relevance? Why not investigate the reciprocal *independence* of disciplines, their irregular growth, their whimsical interaction, their irreducible obsessions? . . . After so much coincidence and synchrony, why not investigate dischrony, misunderstanding, general deafness, and local courage as well?"[20] Even Marxism has found itself transformed by this new sense of the openness of the course of history, as in the writings of Stuart Hall.[21] Newton sums up the construction of history that she finds prevalent across several new historicisms: "There is the notion that 'history' is best told as the story of power relations and struggle, a story that is contradictory, heterogeneous, fragmented."[22] Similarly Brenkman writes: "we recognize that a condition of modern culture is that indeed all effective heritages have to be constructed, and that the dialogues provoked by this necessity are not encompassed within any monological horizon."[23] By theorizing history as a fragmented realm of competing voices, rather than a predetermined and scientifically knowable course, critics enable themselves to insert their own voices into the conversation. But what is the nature of that voice? From where does it come?

The concept of the "subject," which used to be taken for granted, has become a crucial topic of debate, especially for the question of enabling change. Is there such a thing? Is it worth talking about? Are the writers, at one extreme, conscious, freely willing, individually purposive and responsible agents, or, at the other extreme, merely nodes in a network of larger active forces that write, as it were, through them the way our body might express its sweat through its pores? In the latter case, the authors may be not only unconscious of the meanings of their work but even irrelevant to its discussion, insofar as it expresses the larger purposes, aims, and fears of a whole social community (class, subclass, race, etc.) and an ideology to which the author, because of immersion in it, is necessarily blind.[24]

The definition of community, however, becomes as problematic as that of the individual, for its boundaries are never absolutely clear and distinct. On the one hand, one can deconstruct the subject as the incoherent effect of various social discourses. On the other hand, one can deconstruct various social groups (class, race, gender, profession, generation, etc.) as so many terms by which to describe the individual, categories no more real in themselves than the "persons" of whom they can be said. All these categories, including that of "individual," are what Kenneth Burke calls "terministic screens" that we select to use.[25] Texts are articulations that realize at once both the social codes in which one speaks and the particularity that no one else (including oneself later on) would have uttered in quite that way. To focus solely on the writer as an individual genius, as did critics at the turn of the century, or to say with Macherey that the individual is inherently uninteresting,[26] is to cut off the interplay between particular and general aspects of the text.

Marxist critics who devalorize or disable the individual subject nonetheless hope to write transformatively. Thus Eagleton can say on the one hand, "The languages and devices a writer finds to hand are already saturated with certain ideological modes of perception, certain codified ways of interpreting reality; and the extent to which he can modify or remake those languages depends on more than his personal genius. It depends on whether at that point in history, 'ideology' is such that they must and can be changed," while on the other hand ending his preface with, "such understanding contributes to our liberation. It is in that belief that I have written this book."[27] Thus too, Greenblatt and Jameson, while asserting "the collective production" of literature, go on to discuss individual writers.[28] Nor can Greenblatt's driving question about what makes Shakespeare's plays so powerful to us—the question with which he initiates the entire volume of *Shakespearean Negotiations* —be answered solely by reference to the contemporary relations among theatrical institutions, competing churches, and the state; otherwise, he would be asking equally about the continuing power of plays by Marston or Beaumont and Fletcher.

The issue can be seen as a question of where power resides, power to act and change things. It is akin to the older debates within history between the importance of individuals and of statistics, the opposing sides producing very different styles of narrative. In history, too, especially since the advent of computers has made statistical history easier, more productive, and more glamorous, the stories of individual choice and action have come to seem old-fashioned, although some historians are seeking to bring them back because their style is so much more appealing to the general reader. Perhaps that appeal has to do not only with hearing a good story but also with feeling empowered to act in a historically significant way. Where we used to hear right-wing attacks against "liberal humanism," the term *humanism* seems to have become associated now with the New Right of Bennet, Bloom, and Hirsch. Of course, the word has changeable, slippery meanings; nonetheless, it does seem that the Left has abandoned a notion of the conscious individual agent that used to provide the basis for liberal principles about human rights. Is this a self-undermining position? or have knowledge and understanding advanced to a point that leaves all notions of the individual subject to outmoded conservatives? Foucault suggests that we need not a return to old notions of the subject, but the formulation of a new subjectivity;[29] what that might look like, however, remains hard to perceive, at least in his writings, although there are some interesting attempts in that direction.[30] "It is indispensable to develop a theory of the subject as a decentered, detotalized agent, a subject constructed at the point of intersection of a multiplicity of subject-positions between which there exists no a priori or necessary relation and whose articulation is the result of hegemonic practices. Consequently, no identity is ever definitively established," suggests Mouffe.[31] We need to be aware of our own political positions, and of the implications of our views, that is, both where we are coming from and where we are heading. Anyone wanting to be politically responsible needs a theory that will not only provide an explanation of how identities become constructed in certain ways but will also allow one an active role—individually or collectively—in changing the way things are done or perceived.[32] This may look like framing the "truth" to fit one's desires, but the alternative is to live with contradictions between one's own theory and actions.

Some serious inquiry into the area between extremes is obviously needed. On one end of things, it is clear that individuals often do quite consciously and purposively write about what they perceive as historical reality, usually with a hope of altering it in specific ways and sometimes with influential success. Thus, for some recent thinkers, "the disappearance of historical teleology leads to a renewed interest in the role of individual human agents and their conscious intentions."[33] On the other end, it is equally clear that all writers are born into a culture that provides them—in its language and established phrases, genres, and conceptual categories—with the very medium of their thought and expression. To claim that writers are trapped inexorably by the values and views of their society or class is to make very difficult the explanation of cultural changes. But to limit one's understanding of a text to the consciously intended meanings of the author—even if one could determine what those are—is to deprive the work of a rich complexity that ultimately may tell us much more about our own conditions, including the things of which we try to remain blithely unconscious. Approaches that explore the give and take between conscious subjects and their unconsciousness entanglement in cultural values, the mutual construction of subject and society, seem to me the most fruitful to pursue.[34]

At stake is also the possibility of communication between persons not only across time and space but even within a given cultural moment. Marx yearned for a collective self-identity that would overcome the isolation of the individual; but although there are political or sexual occasions when one may glimpse what he was after, such moments are notably hard to sustain. The desire for union with the Other has been expressed by writers from Plato to Lacan, who both acknowledge its impossibility. Augustine suggests that no human can ever communicate effectively with another except through the mediation of God in whom all are united. Hence he addressed his *Confessions* not to us but to God, who is, for Augustine, both its author and its reader, writing through Augustine's mind and reading through ours.[35] For those who do not share in his beliefs, language—words instead of the Word—must serve as the secularized locus of our imperfect encounters. With language and identities both in flux, we must recognize each other as we do ourselves: as overlapping, dynamic and fluid rather than fixed and isolated situations.

There is a visual model for this in postmodern dance, such as that by the groups Momix or Pilobolus. The individual body is only one possible unit here; sometimes only part of the body can be seen, and sometimes the body is merged with another body or object to make a larger unit. But there is a fluidity among these various units, as the body emerges from and remerges with other bodies and objects. Sometimes we want to focus on the writer as an individual, and sometimes not. We need to remain aware while focusing that the individual has only provisionally emerged from some larger whole; and conversely, that the larger whole has been provisionally formed of individuals.

Experiments seeking to demonstrate the wavelike qualities of light and those seeking to demonstrate its particle-like qualities succeed equally. Some scientists therefore try to explain light as a wave packet that can act as a particle. Similarly one can think of the subject as simply a moment or node on a field, perhaps a moment of intersection of various fields (genetic, social, linguistic, etc.); or as a particular entity bouncing off others in a many-body interaction; or as a node or moment that can act as an entity.

Whatever analogy one seeks to understand its nature, a number of theorists have wanted recently to emphasize the "particularity" or "specificity" of the writing (and reading) subject to counterbalance the Foucaultian and (in some versions) Marxist sense of its absorption and dissolution into larger fields. Thus, for example, Raymond Williams criticizes those versions of Marxism in which "the 'social,' we might say, has been deformed to the 'collective,' . . . the living and reciprocal relationships of the individual and the social have been suppressed in the interest of an abstract model of determinate social structures and their 'carriers.' " "The theory that matters . . . is that realization of the socially constitutive which allows us to see specific authorship in its true range," where "as a social individual he is also specific."[36] Kristeva writes similarly: "Semiotics must not be allowed to be a mere application to signifying practices of the linguistic model—or any other model, for that matter. Its raison d'être, if it is to have one, must consist in its identifying the systematic constraint within each signifying practice . . . but above all in going beyond that to specify just what, within the practice, falls outside the system and characterizes the specificity of the practice as such."[37] Similarly, in his introduction to *Historical Studies and Literary Criticism,* Jerome McGann writes: "The historical particularity of a poem by Wordsworth or a novel by Austen have [*sic*] *to be clearly specified in the act of criticism if that act is to preceed* [*sic*] dialectically, i.e., if that act is not simply to project upon 'the work' its own conceptual interests."[38] Lauro Martines, who as a sociological historian explicitly privileges the communal, nonetheless remarks: "The root of my sameness with others is an individuality."[39] Whether that particularity comes from the body, or the consciousness, or rather (since both body and thought can be seen as open to, rather than closed off from, larger fields) from the particular intersection of general fields (these bits of the genetic pool intersecting with these years in this part of the world in this class or subculture, etc.), we continue to seek out the work of a favorite author as if that particularity mattered.

Fostering this attention to the particular, an emphasis on dialectics or dialogics has emerged separately in a number of theorists. By that I mean the notion that, since "history" or "the author" exists *for* someone, we are dealing not with things but with relationships. The author's words take on meaning in the reader's mind; thus the text becomes a locus for the overlapping identity of two voices. It is the reader who reconstructs from these words the implied authorial voice; but it is the author who put just these words and not others in just this order. Weimann speaks of the role of criticism in mapping out the confluences and divergences of past and present conscious subjects, the ways in which as reader I appropriate or alienate the meanings of the text, the ways in which its areas of strangeness both mark a difference and open a way from subject to otherness.[40] Lipking speaks of the reader bringing the author's voice to life like Odysseus giving the prophet's ghost a drink of fresh blood so that it can speak.[41] LaCapra writes of entering into dialogue with the voices of the past, recognizing how our criticism shares the same field of action with their own utterances, how we are trying to explain each other across time, like voices calling back and forth through the fog.[42] I call the implied author into being; but reading his or her discourse has contributed to making me who I am. I construct and am constructed simultaneously. Marx's notion of humans as conditioned creators of their conditions is foundational to this dialectic. Lacan's intersubjective formation of the subject is its psychoanalytic articulation, while his emphasis on language as the medium of this social construction of selves opens the possibility of an important role for literature and criticism alike.

Dialogics requires us to be aware—as aware as we can be—of our own historical situation and its effects on our perception of the text or past.[43] But it need not be thought of as a dialogue only between writer and critic. Any two texts can be made to speak to each other, and it is in this kind of dialogue that one recent answer has emerged to the following question: given the infinite multiplicity of histories and the ineluctable uncertainty of what we even mean by the term *history*, how—if at all—can we do a *historical* criticism? As Howard puts it: "if one accepts certain tendencies in poststructuralist thought, is the possibility of an historical criticism even conceivable?"[44] The practical answer that I see emerging, more or less explicitly, from critics such as Howard, Neely, Greenblatt, Montrose, and DeNeef, is precisely this kind of dialogical, intertextual reading. By setting two or more texts into relation—texts from the same period, according to Howard's suggestion, or from widely different moments according to DeNeef's—one derives from their convergences and divergences a history that one could not have assumed in advance. "I would argue," writes Howard, "that a new historical criticism attempting to talk about the ideological function of literature in a specific period can most usefully do so only by seeing a specific work relationally—that is, by seeing how its representations stand in regard to those of other specific works and discourses."[45] Neely calls this method "over-reading": "New ways must be found to surround, contextualize and over-read Shakespeare's texts and other canonical texts with new work by women's historians, social historians, and feminist critics . . . to over-read men's canonical texts, with women's uncanonical ones."[46] Rejecting a "delimited notion of history," and recognizing that "any and all history can only be the provisional effect of a certain arbitrary cut," DeNeef proposes: "only by a refusal to specify or concretize the historical conditions of my textual figures can I keep in question the nature and the pressures of history as such." "Rather than avoiding or foreclosing historical interrogation, such openness compels it by refusing to specify any particular objective context." Calling on Traherne, Heidegger, Lacan, and Derrida to participate in a conversation, DeNeef finds that "as they are made to say the same, the four authors continually speak difference and it is precisely in the gap between difference and sameness that the crucial question of the historical as such begins to be heard."[47] Waller's essay in this volume further exemplifies the possibilities of such an approach.

The presence of the critic at this conversation among texts, whether visible or invisible, cannot be forgotten.[48] In that sense, there is always more than one period involved unless one is working with contemporary writings. Moreover, the critic is not to be thought of as a scientist purveying knowledge about a literary object, but as a voice among voices, or text among texts, to be read in infinite further combinations. It is perhaps a Borgesian vision of historical criticism: one of his endless, labyrinthian, multiconnected libraries. Nevertheless, it implies, like Francis Bacon's proposals for science, that the time for grand, but suspect, generalizations is to give way to a new era of particular experiments.

If the number of such dialogues and of the local histories that emerge from them is infinite, the critic can nonetheless set up practicable projects while avoiding the problems of having to postulate "the Elizabethan period," to worry about the representativity of the texts selected, or to demarcate text from context. These are large and tempting benefits. The dangers also should be born in mind, however. One is that the fear of totalizing may lead to a loss of faith in the possibility of any large-scale connectedness, thus leaving us with fragmented studies that cannot be built up into the more macroscopic views required by some of our most urgent questions. A second danger is theoretical blindness to the necessary, but unstated, narratives or frameworks that, after all, enable one to select any particular set of texts to be read together. Perhaps the most workable solution is not to reject larger narratives altogether but rather to acknowledge them as both provisional and useful constructions.[49]

The essays in this volume are varied examples of current historical criticism embedded in self-reflexive theoretical commentary and responding in various ways to current theories. If the very notions of history and literature are in flux—not just in transition but in a permanent process of reconceptualization and reappropriation—then there is no point in seeking any fixed definitions of historical criticism. Theory, despite its desire for timeless laws, must accommodate itself to the historical nature even of "history." Therefore, this volume offers neither a definition of what is nor prophetic visions of the future,[50] but instead examples of what is being done and of the thinking that supports these practices.

These essays show a concern for the specificity of texts and writers and for literature as a kind of social action, while moving in different theoretical directions. I have arranged the essays in two groups according simply to the texts with which they deal: nineteenth- and twentieth-century novels, and poetry and drama of the Renaissance. The theoretical interconnections are multiple and complex. Many of these essays were originally part of a conference on "Historical Criticism in the Age of Deconstruction: A Comparative Perspective," sponsored by the Comparative Literature Program of the University of Illinois at Urbana-Champaign in October 1989. The inclusion of some of the discussion from the original conference enhances the interplay of concerns and perspectives.

Petrey, seeking to explain the possibility of a socially effective language, looks for a way to mediate the conflict between critical approaches to a Balzac narrative that emphasize, on one side, historical reference and realism, and on the other, a discourse of madness and "the absurdity of every attempt dependably to attach signs and referents." He argues that Balzac's story depicts a representation that, freed from the possibility of an existing referent, produces its own effective reality. "The real in realism is exactly this kind of social production, the fabrication of lived historical fact from language without factual content."

Like Petrey, Poovey highlights the mutual involvement of readers and of "texts," broadly defined as anything interpretable, in constructing "what counts as 'reality' now." She sees the recent appeal of historical criticism in the way it provides not an epistemological ground but rather "the specificity of particular social formations" and thus "something like a horizon for possible interpretations." Historical and literary narratives both share an unstable "network of connotations and associations" or "field of cultural meanings." In analyzing these shifting fields, the work of historian and historicizing literary scholar merge completely. Poovey's interest in the links of language across different areas of experience connects her work also with Martines's. Focusing on Dickens's *Our Mutual Friend,* she demonstrates the interconnected realignments of terms from various troubled areas: economic speculations, race and gender relations, and the relations of fiction to truth.

Ortega addresses the relation of Garcia Marquez's historical novel, *El general en su laberinto,* to deconstructive theories of history, suggesting that the novel, by blending history, myth, and fiction and by playing off its protagonist's perspective against our own modern view, opens up a new reality where intensely personal experiences can combine with larger shared historical ones.

Cohen surveys the reconceptualization of history by several postmodern French writers, indicating the disappearance of "history" as a legitimization of "various political realisms" and considering the possibilities of a nonnarrative historical theory.

Martines combines historical concern with a rhetorical analysis of gendered language. Because terms become metaphorically extended from one realm of discourse to another, poetry not ostensibly about politics at all can offer, through its uses of language, insights into political self-identifications and relations among men in the ruling classes of Italy. Sensitive to the small differences among conventional Petrarchan poems of the sixteenth century, he points out how those poems yield particular meanings and functions for writers in specific social situations.

While Martines focuses on the literate elite, Patterson seeks instead to recover the voice of the lower classes through traces recorded or represented in courtly Elizabethan texts. Her essay "takes as its question whether a historical criticism can now encounter a popular culture that was already in Shakespeare's time perceived by the educated as alien to themselves." Looking at texts that "ventriloquize" political protests of the common man, Patterson finds, in open argument with Greenblatt, that high culture is not necessarily synonymous with elitist social theory.

Weimann explores a sixteenth-century "crisis of authority" with its problems of "legitimating representations" in Reformation discourse. When "continuity in the representational use of signs is challenged by the self-authorized stance of an intense subjectivity in reading and interpretation," the debate over what authorizes meanings and representations openly links interpretive and political issues. Yet the Reformation crisis in authority appears not only to challenge but also to "broaden the function and structure of representational discourse, thereby transforming the very conditions upon which 'meaning' can be structured and signified." The connection between this sixteenth-century challenge of authority and the expansion of representational functions may give us pause to think about some widely held theoretical assumptions of our own day.

Waller tries to replace the stable relationship of present critic and past text with a more open intertextual reading that may "allow all the positions at play in our historical investigations mutually and continually to transform one another." To that end she analyzes the "rhetorical construction of the subject" in a Petrarch poem and in Wyatt's and Surrey's English versions of it, and in a passage from Derrida and Bass's translation; in so doing, she proposes to "create a 'historical' context that gives me a way of thinking about any number of issues ... without having to portray myself as a suprahistorical knower." Gender issues enter as well, for the kind of subject construction at work in the English poems and in Bass's translation "tacitly privileges and perpetuates, rather than locates, the universalizing, autonomous (male) subject." Like Cohen, Waller worries about the tendencies of narrativized history to present the historian as a stable identity and moral or political guide. Emphasizing "how Derrida's writing has infected my reading of Petrarch's, Wyatt's, and Surrey's poetry and, vice versa, how the poetry has motivated the readings and uses I have made of Derrida's writing, and how it has shaped my reading of Bass's translation," Waller argues that "such rhetorical readings can be more 'historical' (i.e., grounded in temporality) than an epistemologically double-binding historiography that implies and depends upon an illusory, atemporal, essential subject."

NOTES

I wish to thank the University of Illinois College of Liberal Arts and Sciences, the Comparative Literature Program, the Unit for Criticism and Interpretive Theory, and the departments of German, French, English, and Spanish, Italian, and Portuguese for their financial support of the initial conference, and also the colleagues and students whose interactions with me have helped me to think about a topic of concern to us all.

1. See Shoshona Felman, "Psychoanalysis and Education: Teaching Terminable and Interminable," in Barbara Johnson, ed., *The Pedagogical Imperative*, special issue of *French Yale Studies* 63 (1982): "Human knowledge is by definition that which is untotalizable, that which rules out any possibility of totalizing what it knows or of eradicating its own ignorance" (p. 29).

2. Terry Eagleton, *Literary Theory* (Minneapolis: University of Minnesota, 1983), writes: "You can say that perceiving eleven black marks as the word 'nightingale' is an interpretation, or that perceiving something as black or eleven or a word is an interpretation, and you would be right; but if in most circumstances you read those marks to mean 'nightgown' you would be wrong. An interpretation on which everyone is likely to agree is one way of defining a fact" (p. 86). Cf. Mark Cousins, "The Practice of Historical investigation," in ed. Derek Attridge et al., *Post-structuralism and the Question of History,* (Cambridge: Cambridge University Press, 1987): "But to reject any general foundation to historical truth or any general truth of History does itself not undermine a notion of historical truth as such. There is no need to enter a form of scepticism about statements about the past. It is enough to recognise that the justification for truth claims about the past are part of the particular practice of historical investigation. Historical facts are not illusions; we may well say they are true. But their truth is the finding of a particular mode of instantiation" (p. 134). Cf. also Catherine Belsey, "Towards Cultural History—in Theory and Practice," *Textual Practice* 3:2 (1989): "It is perfectly possible to recognize lies without entailing the possibility of telling the truth, least of all the whole truth" (p. 162).

I would add that while recognizing that our versions of truth are never either final or universal, we can nonetheless continue to posit some truer version toward which we collectively and perpetually grope. The alternative is to throw out rationality and any sense of limits to our interpretations. To eliminate any notion of objective truth (even one that is never reachable) on behalf of the truths constructed by power is to construct, in turn, a politics with which we may not really want to live, a politics of might is right. It replaces a loving desire to understand the other (text or person) and to place oneself in a relationship of mutual influence, with a philosophy of arrogant exploitation as politically dangerous as the ethnocentrisms from which critics have been slowly struggling away.

3. Quoted in Richard Kearney, ed., *Dialogues with Contemporary Thinkers* (Manchester: Manchester University Press, 1984), pp. 123–24. Cf. ibid.: "To deconstruct the subject does not mean to deny its existence. There are sub-

jects, 'operations' or 'effects' of subjectivity. This is an incontrovertible fact" (p. 125).

4. Frank Lentricchia, *After the New Criticism* (Chicago: University of Chicago Press, 1980), p. 171.

5. Jean Howard, "The New Historicism in Renaissance Studies," in *Renaissance Historicism*, ed. Arthur Kinney and Dan Collins (Amherst: University of Massachusetts Press, 1987), p. 31.

6. A. Leigh DeNeef, "Of Dialogues and Historicisms," *South Atlantic Quarterly* 86:4 (Fall 1987), p. 507.

7. Lentricchia, *After the New Criticism*, pp. xiii–xiv, criticizes "a history which would deny histories."

8. Stephen Greenblatt, *Shakespearean Negotiations* (Berkeley: University of California Press, 1988), pp. 2–3.

9. Hayden White, *Tropics of Discourse* (Baltimore: The Johns Hopkins University Press, 1987), "Interpretation in History," pp. 57–59 and 78n.; "The Historical Text as Literary Artifact," pp. 82–83, 88.

10. Dominick LaCapra, "Rethinking Intellectual History and Reading Texts," *Rethinking Intellectual History: Texts, Contexts, Language* (Ithaca: Cornell University Press, 1987), pp. 23–71, esp. 31–32.

11. Robert Darnton, *The Great Cat Massacre and Other Episodes in French Cultural History* (New York: Vintage Books, 1985).

12. Thus, for example, Lawrence Lipking, "Life, Death, and Other Theories," in *Historical Studies and Literary Criticism*, ed. Jerome McGann (Madison: University of Wisconsin, 1985): "revolutions in consciousness are less hazardous to join than barricades in the streets. But we had better beware of mistaking our theories of history for history itself" (p. 189). So too, J. Hillis Miller, "The Function of Literary Theory at the Present Time," in *The Future of Literary Theory*, ed. Ralph Cohen (New York: Routledge, 1989), mentions the basis of others' anti-Derridean attacks in "the nagging sense that reading may be cut off from the real obligations of life, the desire to make the study of literature somehow count, have effects of power in society and in history" (p. 104).

13. Alan Sinfield, "Give an Account of Shakespeare and Education, Showing Why You Think They Are Effective and What You Have Appreciated about Them. Support Your Comments with Precise References," in *Political Shakespeare*, ed. Jonathan Dollimore and Alan Sinfield (Ithaca: Cornell University Press, 1988), pp. 134–57, esp. 151. Cf. DeNeef, "Of Dialogues": "If all literature is historical and all history is literary, what privilege can the notion of history or historical have at all?" (p. 507).

14. Carolyn Porter, "Are We Being Historical Yet?" *South Atlantic Quarterly* 87:4 (Fall 1988), p. 782. Cf. John Brenkman, *Culture and Domination* (Ithaca: Cornell University Press, 1987): "Interpretation need not 'change into' critique. Rather, interpretations are socially critical or socially uncritical according to the commitments they develop with regard to the symbolic and social struggles between the legitimation and the contestation of domination" (p. 55). Thus for example, Sinfield, "Shakespeare and Education": "He has been appropriated for

certain practices and attitudes, and can be reappropriated for others" (pp. 137, 154).

15. Judith Newton, "History As Usual? Feminism and the New Historicism," *Cultural Critique* (Spring 1988): "My purpose has also been to suggest that a feminist and materialist literary/historical practice tends to produce 'history' in a way which allows us better to account for social change and human agency" (pp. 92, 103; cf. 117). Jean Howard, "The New Historicism": "the crux of any 'new' historical criticism, and that is to the issue of what one conceives history to be" (p. 13). Brenkman, *Culture and Domination:* "The heritage of modern culture has indeed to be actively constructed. As a consequence, we have not only conflicting interpretations and valuations of specific texts but also competing constructions of tradition" (p. viii). DeNeef, "Of Dialogues": "In short, history as such is the contested field" (p. 507). Newton suggests that this is one of the newly convergent assumptions of many recent historicizing critics, and articulates its political implications, especially with regard to feminism.

16. DeNeef, "Of Dialogues," p. 511.

17. LaCapra, "Rethinking," esp. pp. 30–32. Robert Weimann, *Structure and Society in Literary History* (Baltimore: The Johns Hopkins University Press, 1984): "it is surely no idealism to assume that the work of art is not merely a product, but a 'producer' of its age" (p. 48). Louis Montrose, "Renaissance Literary Studies and the Subject of History," *English Literary Renaissance* 16 (1986): "a new socio-historical criticism takes as its subject that interplay of culture-specific discursive *practices* in which versions of the Real are instantiated, deployed, reproduced—and also appropriated, contested, transformed" (p. 7).

18. Jonathan Dollimore, "Shakespeare, Cultural Materialism and the New Historicism," in *Political Shakespeare,* p. 9.

19. Maria Rosa Menocal's *Writing in Dante's Cult of Truth from Borges to Boccaccio* (Durham: Duke University Press, 1991) offers an excellent demonstration of how poets have repeatedly wrestled, in a constant struggle over literary values, with the narrative shape of literary history posited by other poets.

20. Thomas G. Pavel, "The Present Debate: News from France," *Diacritics* 19 (Spring 1989), pp. 26–27.

21. Stuart Hall, *The Hard Road to Renewal: Thatcherism and the Crisis of the Left* (London: Verso, 1988), warns against, as "fatal consolations," "the search for some philosophical guarantee that the law of history will, like Minerva's owl, take wing at five minutes to midnight, rescuing us from the vicissitudes of the present" (p. 4). Cf. Ibid.: "Gramsci is one of the first modern Marxists to recognize that interests are not given but always have to be politically and ideologically constructed." "There is no law of history which can predict what must inevitably be the outcome of a political struggle" (pp. 167, 169). For further discussion of the impact of deconstruction on Marxism, see a number of the essays in Derek Attridge et al., eds., *Post-structuralism and the Question of History* (Cambridge University Press, 1987) and Michael Ryan, "Political Criticism" in *Contemporary Literary Theory,* ed. G. Douglas Atkins and Laura Morrow (Amherst: University of Massachusetts Press, 1989), 200–213.

22. Newton, "History as Usual?" p. 89.

23. Brenkman, *Culture and Domination,* p. 55.

24. We could map out as follows the range of possible attitudes toward the author's conscious intentions: they are (a) *the* meaning that we seek (An example of this view is E. D. Hirsch, *Validity in Interpretation*); (b) one of the necessary objects of our inquiry; (c) one of the possible objects of our inquiry; and (d) an invalid and impossible object of inquiry. (See Michel Foucault's famous essay, "What is an author?" in Josué Harari, ed., *Textual Strategies* [Ithaca: Cornell University Press, 1979], pp. 141–60.)

25. Kenneth Burke, *Language as Symbolic Action* (Berkeley: University of California Press, 1966), pp. 44–62.

26. Pierre Macherey, *Pour une Théorie de la Production Littéraire* (Paris: Maspero, 1966), p. 85.

27. Terry Eagleton, *Marxism and Literary Criticism* (Berkeley: University of California Press, 1976), pp. 26–27, viii. Lee Patterson, *Negotiating the Past* (Madison: University of Wisconsin, 1987): "But a text is also a function of specific human intentions . . . and to empower our critical abilities by devaluing theirs is to initiate an exchange that will ultimately redound upon ourselves. To grant the social totality unfettered sway over the individual, who is then reduced to a helpless mediator of historical forces that can be fully understood only by the modern historian, is to invoke an 'absolute historicism,' in Gramsci's phrase, that entraps us all" (p. 26–27).

28. Greenblatt, *Shakespearean Negotiations,* pp. 4–5.

29. Michel Foucault, "The Subject and Power," *Critical Inquiry* 8 (Summer 1982), p. 785.

30. Various new formulations are suggested in Thomas Haller et al. eds., *Reconstructing Individualism* (Stanford: Stanford University Press, 1986); and in Eduardo Cadava et al. eds., *Who Comes After the Subject?* (New York: Routledge, 1991). Also relevant is the review essay by Rosemary J. Coombes, "Room for Manoeuver: Toward a Theory of Practice in Critical Legal Studies," *Law and Social Inquiry* 14 (1989), pp. 69–121.

31. Chantal Mouffe, "Radical Democracy: Modern or Postmodern?" *Universal Abandon: The Politics of Postmodernism,* ed. Andrew Ross (Minneapolis: University of Minnesota, 1988), p. 35.

32. Lee Patterson, *Negotiating the Past:* "to deprive human agency of any purchase upon the social whole is to signal the end of a politics we desperately need" (p. 72). Chris Weedon, *Feminist Practice and Poststructuralist Theory* (Oxford: Basil Blackwell, 1987) struggles with the issue of reconciling a poststructuralist notion of the subject with a political agenda: "We have to assume subjectivity in order to make sense of society and ourselves. The question is what modes of subjectivity are open to us and what they imply in political terms. Modes of subjectivity, like theories of society or versions of history, are temporary fixings in the on-going process in which any absolute meaning or truth is constantly deferred. The important point is to recognize the political implications of particular ways of fixing identity and meaning" (p.

173). Ibid.: "only a conscious awareness of the contradictory nature of subjectivity can introduce the possibility of political choice between modes of femininity in different situations" (p. 87).

33. Pavel, "The Present Debate," p. 22.

34. One example is the work of Louis Montrose, such as his essay "Renaissance Literary Studies and the Subject of History": "Instead, we might entertain the propositions that subject and structure, the processes of subjectification and structuration, are interdependent, and thus intrinsically social and historical; that social systems are produced and reproduced in the interactive social practices of individuals and groups; that collective structures may enable as well as constrain individual agency" (p. 10). Another example is Raymond Williams, *Marxism and Literature* (Oxford 1985): He says that the development of an author as seen through his collected works "can be grasped as a complex of active relations, within which the emergence of an individual project, and the real history of other contemporary projects and of developing forms and structures, are continuously and substantially interactive. This latter procedure is the most significant element in modern Marxist accounts of cultural creation, as distinct both from the better-known Marxist version in which an author is the 'representative' of a class or tendency or situation . . . and from bourgeois cultural history in which . . . every individual . . . creates quite separate work" (p. 196). John Brenkman, *Culture and Domination*, opposes "the notion that a psychology or a sociology can be founded on the naked relation of the individual to society, as though each is a simple entity" (p. 176). "Because the community itself is divided, the dialectic of subject and community does not take place between the poles of solitude and integration" (p. 174). Moreover, the self, according to Lacanian analysis, is equally divided; and the autonomy of the speaking subject "manifests itself not as self-sufficiency and completeness but as participation and interaction" (p. 158).

35. Augustine, *Confessions*, trans. Rex Warner (New York: New American Library, 1963). See esp. Book XIII, chaps. 31 and 38.

36. Williams, *Marxism and Literature*, pp. 193–94, 198.

37. Julia Kristeva, "The System and the Speaking Subject," *The Kristeva Reader*, ed. Toril Moi (New York: Columbia University Press, 1986), pp. 26–27.

38. Jerome McGann, *Historical Studies and Literary Criticism* (Madison: University of Wisconsin Press, 1985), p. 11.

39. Lauro Martines, *Society and History in English Renaissance Verse* (Oxford: Basil Blackwell, 1985), p. 17. Cf. also Mouffe's emphasis within "radical democracy" on "the importance it accords to the particular" ("Radical Democracy," p. 38).

40. Weimann, *Structure and Society*, pp. 271–74.

41. Lipking, "Life, Death, and Other Theories," pp. 195–96.

42. LaCapra, *Rethinking Intellectual History*, pp. 27–28, 31–32, 60–64.

43. Stanley Fish, "Being Interdisciplinary Is So Very Hard to Do," *Profession 89* (New York: Modern Language Association of America, 1989): "we will never achieve the full self-consciousness that would allow us at once to inhabit and survey reflectively our categories of thought" (p. 21).

44. Howard, "The New Historicism," p. 9.

45. Ibid., p. 19.

46. Carol Neely, "Constructing the Subject: Feminist Practice and the New Renaissance Discourses," *English Literary Renaissance* 18 (Winter 1988), pp. 16–17.

47. DeNeef, "Of Dialogues," pp. 511, 507, 513, 512. The recurring epithet "as such" seems meant as a prophylactic against the potential dangers of the word *history*—a reminder that the term remains in question.

48. Ibid., p. 512, includes this as an extra "level" of the dialogue.

49. Nancy Fraser and Linda Nicholson express a similar criticism against Lyotard's notion that the avoidance of universalization requires an avoidance of all large-scale analyses; they argue that such large-scale narratives are still possible—and politically necessary—without universalization. "Social Criticism without Philosophy: An Encounter between Feminism and Postmodernism," *Universal Abandon? The Politics of Postmodernism*, pp. 83–104.

50. See the ambitious titles of Ralph Cohen, ed., *The Future of Literary Theory* (New York: Routledge, 1989), and Joseph Natoli, ed., *Literary Theory's Future(s)* (Urbana: University of Illinois Press, 1989).

Part 1

Sandy Petrey

Balzac's Empire: History, Insanity, and the Realist Text

The obstacle facing those of us committed to studying history and literature together is that, however much we dislike it, history foregrounds the referent, literature the sign. The age of deconstruction has provided solid theoretical refutations of the binary logic manifest in the sign/referent opposition; it has been less productive with practical programs for articulating their overlap and interaction. We still have many more models for giving history and literature their due than for defining what about each is due to the other.

So overarching is the history/literature binary that it often assumes compelling form in the writings of those most committed to transcending it. Derrida's multiple explanations of what he really means when he says that there is nothing outside the text glaringly display the difficulty of taking history as one of the things inside the text.

Derrida, in the most recent contribution to his ongoing polemic with John Searle, writes: "Once again (and this probably makes a thousand times I have had to repeat this, but when will it finally be heard, and why this resistance?): as I understand it (and I have explained why), the text is not the book, it is not confined in a volume itself confined to the library. It does not suspend reference—to history, to the world, to reality, to being."[1] When a person with Derrida's aura repeats the same point a thousand times and still doesn't get through, you cannot help suspecting that the reason for what is here called "resistance" is something other than a broadly experienced, early childhood trauma. There can be reasons other than psychological for disagreeing with the position that there's nothing outside the text because everything is already inside it.

Later in the same essay, Derrida makes his point for the thousand

and first time. "What I call 'text' implies all the structures called 'real,' 'economic,' 'historical,' socio-institutional, in short: all possible referents. Another way of recalling once again that 'there is nothing outside the text.' "[2] In practical terms, how do you use a category including "all possible referents" when you want to construct a discourse relating one particular referent, a historical fact, to another, a literary work? Confined in a volume itself confined in a library, the text presents at least the virtue of being somewhere. If it is everywhere, we literary critics are hard pressed to justify spending so much time in libraries to study it.

The converse of deconstruction's perception of the world as text is a certain Marxism's commitment to seeing through the text to the world. Although their reasons couldn't be farther apart, both poststructuralists and historicists have expressed the conviction that their contact with literature is always also contact with the real, economic, historical and socioinstitutional determinants of collective existence. To illustrate, let me quote from Pierre Barbéris, a French Marxist whose monumental studies of Balzac consistently move back and forth between the library's contents and its exterior. "I insist. Universe of the signifier, universe of the symbolic: that's always a way not to be the universe of HISTORY."[3] Like Derrida, Barbéris looks at literature and sees all possible referents, here incorporated into the seven capital letters of the H word. In the starkest opposition to Derrida, he comes to see so much by excluding signifiers from his field of vision. Barbéris "insists" exactly what Derrida repeats a thousand times, that the study of literature and the study of history are not only compatible but inextricable. But each separate version of this common undertaking absolutely repudiates the other's theory and methodology.

Some years ago, the fact that history foregrounds the referent and literature the sign was most apparent in a broadly accepted demarcation of historical from literary works, of description of reality from construction of fiction. Although that division among the objects of scholarly inquiry has fallen by the wayside, the paradigms of scholarly inquiry have yet to be integrated.

In this essay, I want to suggest one possible form of integration while looking at the ways competing scholarly paradigms have been applied to a Balzac novella titled *Adieu*. Written in the first months of 1830, *Adieu* is one of the earliest works to be included in the inexhaustible storehouse for historians and literary critics called *The Human Comedy*. Since it is far from one of the best-known works in *The Human Comedy*, however, I give a plot summary. The novella is divided into three parts, the first of which introduces the protagonists and presents the mystery of their relationship. While hunting with a friend, Philippe de Sucy, a former officer in Napoleon's army, comes upon a secluded property where he sees a woman with all the appearances of raving insanity. Her hair and clothes are a mess; she jumps around in trees like a squirrel; she rolls in the grass like a colt; and her only use of human speech is to repeat the word *adieu* in a voice that reveals neither thought nor feeling. When she pushes her hair away from her face, Philippe falls in a dead faint, for he has recognized the disheveled maniac as the countess Stéphanie de Vandières, the only woman he has ever loved.

Philippe and Stéphanie had last seen each other seven years before, when, during the Napoleonic army's retreat from Moscow, Philippe was captured after helping Stéphanie and her wounded husband escape from the horrors of the French rout at the Berezina River. The second part of *Adieu* is a flashback that describes the ghastly events at the Berezina in vivid detail. This retrospective narrative concludes with Stéphanie floating away from Philippe on an overcrowded raft in the ice-choked river. Stéphanie's husband falls into the water and dies, but she can do nothing except shout a final "adieu" as Philippe collapses on the riverbank from cold, regret, and fatigue.

Balzac's third part returns to the present and describes Philippe's determination to cure Stéphanie's insanity and live happily ever after with her. He is undaunted when he learns that Stéphanie, her mind destroyed by the 1812 retreat, has spent the intervening seven years in so pathological a condition that she made herself sexually available to uncounted men of every class and even refused for a period to wear clothes altogether. Philippe is certain that, despite everything, he can triumph over the past and bring his beloved back to her senses. He holds her in the old way, speaks to her of their old love, cares for her with the old tenderness, but her only response is an occasional "adieu," still spoken in a voice expressing neither thought nor feeling, without "her soul communicating a single discernible inflection to this word" (200).[4]

At last, on the verge of suicidal despair, Philippe takes a desperate step. He leaves Stéphanie and constructs the setting for an elaborate psychodrama by converting a section of his property into a life-sized replica of the fatal countryside around the Berezina. A Griffith or von Stroheim *avant la lettre,* Philippe also enrolls vast numbers of people to fill his stage and takes attentive care that he and his supporting cast look exactly right. When all the preparations needed to reproduce the past are complete, Philippe brings in Stéphanie to relive the night she lost her mind. The hope is of course that what drove sanity away can restore it, but the plan is only partially successful. The light of reason does return to Stéphanie's eyes: she recognizes Philippe and says that she loves him, but she also utters a final "adieu" and falls dead. After a brief and heroic attempt to forget, Philippe joins his lover in death by shooting himself in the head.

Adieu was known to few people other than Balzac specialists before 1974, when it appeared in a paperback edition edited by Patrick Berthier with an introduction by Pierre Gascar. Gascar's introduction, which displays both deep concern for historical specificity and strong affinities for Balzac's prose, highlights the "most gripping realism" (17) characterizing *Adieu*'s representation of war. For Gascar, this story is among the very first texts in world literature to give verbal expression to the brutal truth of martial life. Balzac decisively broke with dominant literary conventions of military glory and produced something radically new. Thanks to the "realism, without precedent in the history of literature, with which war is here presented" (9), Balzac's battle scenes "suffice to give war its real face: that is, its contemporary face. . . . Balzac inaugurates the modern form of horror" (12).

In Gascar's vision, therefore, *Adieu* succeeds as a work of literature through its repudiation of reigning literary conventions, through its achievement of Ranke's goal of showing the past as it really was. In terms of Barbéris's opposition between signifiers and H–I–S–T–O–R–Y, Gascar's *Adieu* belongs squarely on history's side. In the place of signifiers imposed by a mendacious literary convention, it introduces language capable of effacing itself before the truth of its object.

The year after Gascar and Berthier's edition, Shoshana Felman put their reading through the wringer in an essay entitled "Women and Madness: The Critical Phallacy," which applies the categories and concerns of high deconstruction to the text where Gascar found the truth of history. Felman points out that Gascar's reading depends on ignoring two of the three parts of *Adieu*, those dealing with a woman and her madness, in order to focus solely on the middle section, which deals with men and their manly occupations. For Felman, it is not by accident that this act of repression is performed in the name of realism: the real and the manly are ideological constructs with reciprocally invigorating powers. "What, then, is this 'realism' the critic here ascribes to Balzac, if not the assumption, not shared by the text, that what happens to men is more important, and/or more 'real,' than what happens to women?"[5] Gascar negates the woman and validates the real because his emphasis and his neglect both help naturalize the male/female hierarchy.

To see here the great literary discovery of how to represent the reality of war is perverse: it ignores the text's lesson on the death blow feminine difference strikes against every reliable representation of the real. In the long futility of Philippe's desperate efforts to make Stéphanie stop saying "adieu" and speak his name, the text configures the absurdity of every attempt dependably to attach signs and referents. Philippe keeps begging Stéphanie to say who he is, Stéphanie keeps saying "adieu, adieu, adieu," and Felman reads this cataclysmic breakdown of the communicative circuit as eradicating all the tools realism needs. "To [Philippe's] demand for recognition and for the restoration of identity through language, through the authority of proper names, Stéphanie opposes, in the figure of her madness, the dislocation of any transitive, communicative language, of 'propriety' as such, of any correspondence or transparency joining 'names' to 'things,' the blind opacity of a lost signifier unmatched by any signified, the pure recurrent difference of a word detached from both its meaning and its context" (Felman p. 9). In the woman's refusal to name the man begging for recognition, Felman sees language's irremediable dissipation of the power on which realism depends absolutely. We confront here the hopeless impossibility of *"any* correspondence or transparency joining 'names' to 'things.' "

As a result, Felman's reading of *Adieu* is as indifferent to the work's second part as Gascar's to parts 1 and 3. The history/literature binary is immaculate. In the same seventy-page tale, the deconstructionist sees the "madness of the signifier" (Felman p. 10), and the historical critic sees the signifier finally coming to its senses and saying what war actually is. The deconstructionist sees the unmanageable metonymies of language's nightmarish *"lack of resemblance"* (Felman p. 8) to its referents; the historical critic sees language with so perfect a resemblance to its referent that the reader lives all the horrors let slip by the dogs of war.

Furthermore, these intellectually antagonistic readings, one set toward history, the other toward literature, produce strong personal antagonisms as well. Felman sees Gascar and Berthier as mired in a "naive, though by no means innocent, sexism" (Felman p. 6) that appears in their writings as a *"systematic* blindness to significant facts, [that] functions as a censorship mechanism, as a symbolic eradication of women from the world of literature" (Felman p. 6).

When his edition of *Adieu* was reissued in 1979, Patrick Berthier countered by deploring Felman's "spirit of intolerance" (308) and suggested that the best thing would be to "smile at those three pages" (308) containing Felman's critique. He coaxes smiles along by pointing out that Felman's insurrection against the authority of the proper name includes calling him Philippe Berthier when his name is Patrick. The history/literature opposition involves affect as well as methodology.

Besides seeing distinct texts, besides applying incompatible paradigms to the texts they see, each of these two instances of the history/literature binary confidently trashes the other.

Yet I like and admire both. I find Felman's reading of Balzac and his critics a brilliant statement of the violence to literature inseparable from readerly devotion to keeping signifiers in their place. At the same time, I think Berthier and Gascar are wholly correct to validate the historical density—the feel of sociopolitical reality—in the language representing Napoleonic militarism.

The discomfort induced by strongly positive responses to readings with strongly negative things to say about each other is, I believe, a common feeling among contemporary critics with historical concerns. Felman and Gascar's positions on *Adieu* are representative of many essays in their systematic invalidation of everything the other posits as important. Felman's denunciation of language's transitivity eliminates the foundational condition of possibility for an enterprise like Gascar's, namely the text's ability to locate its subject in time and space, to make a signifier like "1812" or "Russia" or "Grand Army" orient the reader's interpretation even while the signifier "adieu" is becoming a vertiginously disorienting announcement that interpretation is forever random.

So how do we bring disorientation and orientation together? The question put by *Adieu* and its readings is generalizable to the broad problematic of historical criticism in the age of deconstruction, to the need to locate signs in time and space while recognizing the dislocation inherent in their semiotic identity. I believe one way to address the problem is to look at how *Adieu* makes itself available for such incompatible critical operations. In the terms of my subtitle, this realist text's articulation with history is embedded in its assumption of insanity. If Balzac can integrate lunatic signifiers and world-historical events, maybe we can too.

One step toward integration is straightforward and easy. We can, even today, retain the historical specificity of Gascar's reading by simply substituting Balzac's intertexts for his referent, by comparing his army not to Napoleon's but to those in other literary depictions of war. Gascar in fact does just that, and we can share his admiration for Balzac's distance from his predecessors without agreeing that the distance is due to a perfect congruence of Balzacian language and objective reality. Even the most evangelical antirepresentationalists find some representations —of war, of gender, of race, of class, of Ronald Reagan and Daniel Ortega—more objectionable than others, and Balzac's stylistic novelties are a step away from the wrong direction despite the theoretical objections to calling them a step in the right direction. To make horror, in

Gascar's words the modern form of horror, integral to the experience of reading about soldiery is a semiotic achievement of no small historical substance.

If signs and history can coexist with Gascar's principal point, can they with Felman's as well? This problem's tougher, for Felman systematically repudiates historical location as the realist illusion. Her concern is less sexist practice in Western society than sexist epistemology in what she variously names "Western metaphysics," "Western thought" and "Western discourse" (Felman p. 3). Because all three have remained fundamentally the same from at least the age of Plato to at least yesterday afternoon, their differing manifestations in different social formations are of slight interest.

It is this commitment to the permanence of discursive and cognitive oppression across the ages that makes deconstruction resistant to historical applications. Nevertheless, if we admit that Western thought has consequences as well as patterns, there can be no principled objection to giving those consequences a social identity. As with his representation of war, the historical specificity of Balzac's representation of woman comes not from brute referentiality but from historical intertextuality. *Adieu* sets female madness in a society obsessed with writing up the rules for female identity.

And it takes care to give that society its name. Parts 1 and 3 of Balzac's text situate Stéphanie's annihilated subjectivity in the Bourbon Restoration as firmly as part 2 ascribes the origin of her madness to the Napoleonic adventure. Considered in relation to social history, this insistence on the stasis of a madwoman's condition across radical transformations of her nation is highly suggestive. Stéphanie insanely says the same word over and over while her countrymen are changing their government again and again. Between Stéphanie's first and last utterances of her meaningless "adieu," France went from the emperor to a king, came back to the emperor, then brought back the king and gave him a free hand to extirpate all memory of the empire and its acts.

Among the acts the king chose not to extirpate was the empire's violent relegation of woman to the endless status of man's ward. Whatever vestiges of female autonomy France possessed were eliminated when Napoleon's civil code gave husbands the same authority over their wives that fathers possessed over their underaged daughters, an authority that went so far as explicitly to require that mail addressed to a woman be on request delivered to the man responsible for her.

That article—by the way, it wasn't repealed until 1938; Simone de Beauvoir was thirty years old in 1938—is a fact from the historical past that resonates strongly with the deconstructionist present. Three of the most stimulating essays in contemporary criticism are Jacques Lacan's seminar on Poe's "Purloined Letter," Jacques Derrida's critique of the insufficient indeterminacy in Lacan's reading, and Barbara Johnson's critique of Derrida for making indeterminacy a predictable, even a determinate, lesson of writing. All three of these much-cited essays take letters and correspondence to figure the uncontrollable disengagement of all language from its origin. Because letters can be lost, or become dead letters, or end up in the wrong hands, letter writers are radically incapable of assuring that their words will either reach the intended destination or convey the intended message.

The Napoleonic Code's provisions concerning letters sent to women obviously depend on an analogous insight into the ability of correspondence to figure the power of what Derrida calls dissemination. In French law, as well as French theory, all transitive language and verbal propriety are irremediably dislocated; here too the authority of the proper name is dismantled, signs and referents disjoined. For over a century, to write a Frenchwoman's address on an envelope was to observe and experience the sign's own repudiation of its capacity to designate reliably.

Such historical acting out of deconstructionist principles means, I believe, that we can feel less uncomfortable about trying to combine historical concerns with a deconstructionist reading like Felman's interpretation of *Adieu*. Given the thoroughgoing denial of woman's subjecthood in the Napoleonic Code, given the determined commitment of the Bourbon Restoration to keeping this Napoleonic novelty in place, female madness could well result from a specific manifestation of phallocentric thought as well as from the hierarchical oppositions structuring phallocentrism for all time. To agree with Felman that "from the very beginning the woman in this text stands out as a problem" (Felman p. 6) doesn't forbid attending to the problem's temporal and spatial coordinates. There are sound historical grounds for female language's maniacal upsurge against the male desire for verbal recognition during the early post-Napoleonic era. Stéphanie refuses to give Philippe the same thing society refuses to give her. The seven years in which she mindlessly repeated the same detached signifier coincide with seven years in which almost nothing in French life stayed the same except for the legal, cultural, and political incrustation of woman's place on women's lives.

As a consequence, Stéphanie's antirepresentational language seems connected to the realist text's most celebrated representational tic, its indefatigable accumulation of the marks of historical situation. As part 2 of *Adieu* takes place in Russia in the winter of 1812, parts 1 and 3 take place in France between the summer of 1819 and the winter of 1820.

There is little purpose in assuming that these analogous notations have irreconcilable values simply because one identifies a historical event and the other disguises a fictional invention. Insofar as the realist text has any generic specificity whatsoever, it derives from history's presence throughout its narratives.

This interpenetration of history and fiction severely problematizes a certain understanding of realist prose, an understanding that paradoxically holds constant across both the critical movements with which Felman and Gascar's essays align themselves. Although the word *realism* is for Gascar a great compliment and for Felman a contemptuous slur, both authors take the word to denote an effort to put the actual world in the literary text. Yet either to admire the effort's success or to deplore its fatuousness requires ignoring the message of every imaginative fiction that it is, precisely, an imaginative fiction. Realist history seldom takes the form of straight description of facts; even at the Berezina, any resemblance between the characters and events depicted and actual persons living or dead is purely coincidental. Realism does indeed historicize its representations, but that's not the same thing as the unmediated representation of history.

Adieu urges us to meditate on the difference by making representation central to its content as well as its form. When Philippe sets out to reproduce the Berezina plain in his back yard, he makes laughably evident the impossibility of representation successfully incorporating its referent. When, as the text puts it, "he achieve[s] his goal" (210), he makes the distinction between successful representation and incorporating a referent equally obvious.

That distinction has critical generic implications. As Felman insists, there are striking resemblances between the way *Adieu* describes Philippe's undertaking and the way traditional criticism describes Balzac's. Philippe too "succeeded in copying" (209) the past in the present; he too created an all-encompassing representation of what actually was. "He ordered uniforms and faded clothing in order to costume several hundred peasants. He built huts, bivouacs and fortifications and burned them out. In the end he forgot nothing of what could reproduce the most horrible of all scenes, and he achieved his goal" (210). In style and content, Pierre Gascar's appreciation of what Balzac did in part 2 of *Adieu* is interchangeable with *Adieu*'s appreciation of what Philippe did in part 3.

It is therefore understandable that Felman sees Philippe's realist authorship the same way as Gascar's realist criticism. She reads the double death concluding *Adieu* as announcing that representation is always fatal to the humans and texts accepting it. "The tragic outcome of the story is inevitable, inscribed as it is from the outset in the very logic of representation. . . . Through this paradoxical and disconcerting ending, the text subverts and dislocates the logic of representation which it has dramatized through Philippe's endeavor and his failure. Literature thus breaks away from pure representation; when transparency and meaning, 'reason' and 'representation' are regained, when madness ends, so does the text itself. . . . Like madness and unlike representation, literature can signify but not *make sense*" (Felman pp. 9–10). In other terms, history *can* be represented, for Philippe does succeed in bringing 1812 back to life seven years later. But this success of historical representation kills the woman, her madness, and literature. The history/literature binary is so powerful the presence of one inevitably murders the other.

Once more, however, *Adieu* itself combines the two terms of the binary. Philippe's representation of the past is a textual presence before it becomes a textual scourge, a presence that moreover has extraordinary effects on woman and madness. Part 3 of *Adieu* is entitled "The Cure," and the word is not merely ironic. Balzac's prose is lyrically specific about representation's vivifying effects. When she enters Philippe's artificial world, Stéphanie sees, feels, and speaks once again. The language describing her rebirth, unrestrained and exuberant, joins italics and exclamation points to an insistently vitalistic lexicon. "She jerked her head toward Philippe and *saw him.* . . . Color feebly began to return to Stéphanie's beautiful face; then, finally, shade by shade, she recovered all the radiance of a young girl's gleaming freshness. . . . Life and happiness, animated by a burning intelligence, passed from part to part like a fire. . . . Stéphanie's eyes threw out a celestial ray, a vivid flame. She was living, she was thinking! . . . God Himself untied that dead tongue a second time and once more cast His fire into that extinguished soul. Human will came with its electric rush and vivified this body from which it had so long been absent" (213–14). The fire and light imagery is remarkable, as is its attribution to God Himself. This passage could stand as ekphrasis on the Sistine Chapel ceiling, except that God here conveys the spark of life to Eve instead of Adam.

When life culminates in speech, Stéphanie finally names Philippe and then, just before she dies, gives back meaning and reference to what she elsewhere makes a gapingly empty signifier, the word *Adieu.* "Oh, it's Philippe . . . Adieu, Philippe. I love you, adieu!" (214). Before it kills her, representation gives Stéphanie the warmth of life, the power of reason, and the control of language.

Let's defer the quandary of how this literal apotheosis of realism—its textual conversion into the God of Genesis making what it represents live, breathe, and move—can without transition develop into textual definition of realist representation as a death-dealing poison. For the present, I want to consider another riveting contrast, that between Philippe's power over Stéphanie here and his earlier helplessness before her. The page that describes Stéphanie's metamorphosis is stunning even in isolation. It becomes dumbfounding in the context of page after page that earlier presented the agent of her metamorphosis as comically ineffectual.

Moreover, the contrast between the man's success and failure in reaching the woman coincides exactly with the presence and absence of representation. As a character in a tableau, Philippe is omnipotent; as himself, he is abject. When he *represents* a lover, Philippe controls Stéphanie's vision, soul, voice, and mind. When he *is* a lover, he is wretchedly unable to elicit the slightest response.

Only after the repeatedly experienced futility of contact with Stéphanie in his own person does Philippe deck himself out as the person he no longer is. The woman to whom "life and happiness" return when she sees a disguised Philippe in an artificial landscape displays only stupor and unconcern when she sees and touches the real Philippe in a natural landscape. The text goes daringly far in specifying the titillating character of the touching that doesn't work. "She soon grew accustomed to sitting down on him, to wrapping her lean, agile arm around him. In this position, so dear to lovers, Philippe would slowly give sweets to the avid countess. . . . she let him run his hands through her hair, allowed him to take her in his arms, and received burning kisses without pleasure" (204).

To Philippe's ardor, Stéphanie responds with chilling indifference; to his stage set, her response involves every fiber of her being. If Philippe's reproduction of Russia in France figures realism's reproduction of the world in a book, then the demonstration in *Adieu* that realism works follows a prior demonstration that reality fails miserably. When Philippe takes Stéphanie on his lap and tells her what he feels and who he is, when referent and representation are in seamless conjunction, nothing happens. When Philippe brings Stéphanie to the space he has artistically transformed into an illusion, when referent and representation are a continent and a decade apart, everything happens. In this very early working-out of the literary forms that would impose Balzac's empire, the power of realism stands in point by point opposition to the impotence of reality.

So marked a contrast obviously raises serious objections to the realism-reality equation common to historicist and deconstructionist criticism. Here is Felman's expression of that equation: "Realism thus postulates a conception of 'nature' and of 'reality' which seeks to establish itself, tautologically, as 'natural' and as 'real'" (Felman p. 6). I see *Adieu* as rather a protracted disestablishment of nature and reality. The natural Philippe is not the man who makes Stéphanie say his name. It is precisely because reality does not work that realism comes to be.

On the other hand, Philippe's production of what the text self-reflectively calls his "fictive plain of the Berezina" (212) isn't the happy effect of a random conjunction of free-flying signs either. Philippe "succeeded in copying the riverbank in his park" (209) by adjusting his representational undertaking to a collective vision of what the river-bank was, that was shared by himself and those who were with him, including, he hopes, Stéphanie. In this sense representation can be historical without being reproductive; it articulates not what is but what is thought. The tonic shock of recognition comes from a stage set's conformity to the mental image Philippe holds in common with others: "he recognized the Berezina. This false Russia was of so frightful a truth that several of his companions in arms recognized the scene of their old sufferings" (210).

Louis Althusser and other theorists of ideology have insisted on the gap between authentic cognition and the deluded *re*cognition that constitutes a society's mythic understanding of itself. That gap is apparent here, in the double occurrence of the word *recognized* to designate Philippe and his comrades' vivid apperception of what they cannot perceive because it is not there. Like Althusser, however, Balzac's text is far from dismissing false recognition as inconsequential. It produces a world as well as conceals one, and the imagery of divine creation chosen to narrate Stéphanie's recognition of Philippe makes this productive power unmistakable.

In a deconstructive reading, the text would have to be deriding and undoing itself when it sets the word *recognized* in a context where recognition is objectively impossible. For historical criticism, the point is rather that objective facts are not pertinent to representational success in instilling recognition; we find reality where we put it. Look again at the language *Adieu* invokes to articulate its characters' perception of a presence in an absence. A "frightful truth" adheres to Philippe's "false Russia," as later an "awful truth" (211) will emerge from his false appearance. I take this commingling of truth and falsity as critical in the realist commitment to representing the truth society validates regard-less of falsity. Realism addresses what a collectivity accepts as real, and this early realist narrative makes that generic feature its lesson as well as its armature.

Deconstructionists' rush to repudiate realism has posited two kinds of language, one slavishly subordinated to extralinguistic facts, the other gloriously independent of everything except its own exhilarating playfulness. *Adieu* helps inaugurate the realist commitment to a third way, a form of representation that labors in the world even though it enjoys the same freedom from referentiality as the most effervescent postmodernisms. In the realism of *Adieu*, representation's falseness is irrelevant to its impact.

Realist depiction of that impact consequently does not contest but confirms the sign's untethering from all determinant origins, from every objective ground. The collaboration between semiosis and ideology would be impossible were signs in fact a nomenclature: language can produce what is lived in society solely because it cannot name what is in reality. Philippe's discovery is that theatrical performance is required because reality is not performing.

The specific achievement of Philippe's performance is to restore Stéphanie's womanhood as ideologically and socially constructed. One is hard-pressed to think of an early nineteenth-century text as concerned as *Adieu* with the distinction between gender, a social construct, and sex, a cluster of physiological features. Philippe can take possession of the insane Stéphanie's physiology for a few sweets, but he experiences only burning despair when he does so. He even defines womanhood as precisely what is lacking in the body on his lap. Because he knew Stéphanie "when," as he puts it, "she was a woman" (202), he finds nothing womanly in the hair between his fingers or the lips he covers with burning kisses while taking the "position so dear to lovers."

Social determination of Philippe's understanding of femininity is also apparent in the gestures that accompany his therapeutic representation of the Berezina plain. Throughout "The Cure," he is active, Stéphanie passive. As with Pygmalion, the man gives life, the woman accepts it, the man is the artist, the woman the work. The hierarchy is clear, and it comes as no surprise that Stéphanie's return to life is also her recovery of what social discourse says a woman ought to have, a beautiful face that glows for her lover with "all the radiance of a young girl's gleaming freshness." Moreover, she presumably dies because her seven years of nakedness and sexual license have made her what social discourse says a woman cannot be. When what Felman calls the sociosexual stereotype of femininity regains its sway, when she who was not a woman becomes one again, she suffocates under the stereotype's crushing weight. Reentry into representation fails to provide a life worth living. Realism and deconstruction agree on representation's deadly effects as well as on the vacuousness of its theoretical cause.

Yet realism alone recognizes that there is no life worth living outside of representation either. Within historical time, social constructs are the only sort we have. That which kills Stéphanie is the same thing that brings her back to life. Besides "feminine" attributes like a glowing complexion and a loving voice, she also regains "happiness and life," "human will," "burning intelligence." Stéphanie's passage from life to death is so sudden that the text invents a new word—*elle se cadavérisa,* "she corpsified herself" (214)—to specify it. Her passage from death to life is equally dramatic, and the same agency is responsible for both transformations. What representation takes away is no more than what it has just given.

During the time the insane Stéphanie was not a woman, neither was she a human being. Her maniacal "adieu" refuses human existence as well as repudiating orderly semiosis, and Felman is careful not to suggest that the pure iteration of a lost signifier gives Stéphanie the identity she eradicates in others. "Woman and Madness: The Critical Phallacy" approvingly quotes Phyllis Chesler's denial of every "intention to romanticize madness, or to confuse it with political or cultural revolution" (Felman p. 2). The resolute duality of representation in *Adieu* survives the text's self-deconstruction. Although death is within social discourse, outside it is nothingness.

The consequence seems clear. In order to produce a bearable existence, in order to make the political or cultural revolution that insanity is not, social discourse must be changed; repudiating it is not enough. The change will necessarily be a historical event, and the realist text scrupulously provides the historical coordinates of the representation it simultaneously denounces and reenacts. Stéphanie comes back to life in France of 1820, and the vision of femininity that destroys her has a precise socioinstitutional identity as well as a timeless logical structure. Her sexual adventures are when she awakens what they were when she passed out seven years before, an activity that cannot be tolerated in one sex however understandable it may be in the other. As one of the drafters of the Napoleonic Code maintained by the Bourbons put it, "the wife's unfaithfulness implies more corruption and has more dangerous effects than the husband's."[6] Stéphanie dies for the same reason the civil code punished female infidelity by prison and male infidelity by a fine, because social discourse was incapable of incorporating woman except through the forms satisfying to man.

Despite its shocking representational inadequacy, however, social discourse had the whole force of the most repressive state apparatus behind it. There are excellent historical reasons why Balzac's working title for *Adieu* was *A Woman's Duty.* The famous Article 213 of the Napoleonic Code reads: "The wife owes obedience to her husband"; exactly like the legislative pronouncement that a woman's unfaithfulness has more dangerous effects than a man's, that article doesn't prescribe, it merely states. In J. L. Austin's terminology, it is not performative but constative. It is, however, a patently false statement. We have to do less with a constative description than a constative failure, and Article 213 collaborates with Stéphanie's insane "adieu" in shattering language's claim to speak reality.

At the same time, such nonstatements of nonfacts also collaborate with the performative language through which a society polices and controls its members. Article 213 became a fearsome social truth in blithe unconcern for its objective falseness. It is directly comparable to more recent legislative efforts to combine the constative proposition that human life begins at conception with the performative apparatus needed to make that lie oppressively truthful as well. The real in realism is exactly this kind of social production, the fabrication of lived historical fact from language without factual content. Philippe's failure to get through when he is a man and his total communicative success when he is a realist character manifest a capital insight: language's expressive force always derives not from the nature of the world but from the will of a collectivity. Because representation works through the pressure exerted by those who accept it, denouncing its illusions while ignoring the forces mustered behind them misses the point altogether.

Realism takes that point as the core of its textual being, which is why the realist commitment to historical precision is more than an anachronistic survival of referential delusions. The realist message is that the death of the referent is the *precondition* for the life of social formations, that signs' availability for deconstructive play goes hand in hand with their contribution to historical work. Within a given collectivity, language's puckish dismissal of transparency is often inseparable from its regimentation among the forces that perpetuate a world by controlling how it is spoken, and realism knows this quite well.

Felman and Gascar have in common a single work furnishing grist for two very different mills. One finds in *Adieu* all the "faithfulness of the historian" (11); the other finds all the sense-destroying fission of "demented, dislocated language" (Felman p. 9). Both are right. The text that dislocates language from a referent also firmly locates it within a sociohistorical community, where it does things as well as undoes them.

Since the things it does include representing masculinity as well as femininity, there are tighter connections among the three parts of *Adieu* than might at first appear. One of the intertexts contested by Balzac's unprecedented representation of war was the *Bulletins of the Grand Army,* a multivolume chronicle of the Napoleonic epic as a vast theater for the courage, strength, and daring that make a man a man. Napoleon's personal influence was as important to the *Bulletins of the Grand Army* as to the civil code's provisions for making a woman a woman, a double authorial function that seems pertinent to the combination of women's and men's madness in Balzac's novella. During the two years before he wrote *Adieu,* Balzac was engaged in a long meditation on the civil code, especially on its representation of the sexes, and he consistently ascribed that representation to Napoleon himself.[7] The emperor who led Philippe and Stéphanie into Russia was for their creator the same man who imposed the statutes *enacting* their respective genders.

That bit of conventional literary history has an embarrassing sound in the age of deconstruction. I interject it with trepidation, but it does seem relevant to my contention that *Adieu*'s representation of representation is a unified whole. The single figure of Napoleon is intimately bound up with dominant ideologies of manhood and of womanhood, and the novella's separate sections combine in depicting those ideologies' uniformly disastrous effects. In part 2 as well as part 3 of *Adieu,* in war as well as in its theatrical reenactment, human beings live the consequences of invalid but hegemonic representation. In Russia as well as in France, among those consequences are intense suffering and sudden death. Stéphanie isn't the only character to be "corpsified" because representation produces a reality despite its glaring inability to reproduce one.

Where does this leave the history/literature and sign/referent binaries? In one sense, they're still very much in place; outside of literary works like *Adieu,* it remains the case that representations don't kill people, people kill people. Nevertheless, by making representation itself the murderer, *Adieu* reminds us that people don't kill people on a whim. They always shoot at a figuration as well as a body; whenever the shooting is more than pathological, this figuration is part of a historically specific social formation.

Part of a social formation; neither an adjunct to it nor an ideological distortion of it, nor the aleatory appearance in it of a timeless semiotic illogic. Whatever else they may be, societies are always also discursive processes that perform the reality they represent. The sociolinguistic fact of greatest historical moment is not joining words to things but doing things with words, making representation collectively real through an ongoing dialectic of articulation and enactment.

Societies couldn't enact and perform what they say if their language did in fact come attached to an unmistakable referent or an all-determining presence. If words are to *do* things, they can't *be* the passive label of things already done. I take Derrida's insistence on the nothingness outside the text as at least in part a statement that language's severance from all origins is what enables real, economic, historical, and socioinstitutional somethings to be in the text. Severance from the origin consequently creates language's capacity to perform historically as well as its tendency to disseminate deconstructively.

When language performs historically, however, the interesting thing is that it so often keeps its delight in dissemination concealed. To show that every such concealment is in fact a ruse may always be possible, but I find it worthwhile only when we've already looked at what language was doing *besides* pretending to be something it is not. As far as I am concerned, the fundamental opposition between deconstructionist and historical criticism comes not from defining what language is in and of itself but from evaluating what it does in and with a social formation. Representation is timely communal productivity as well as timeless philosophical delusion, and exploring how it can be both at once is a fitting task for historical criticism in the age of deconstruction.

NOTES

1. Jacques Derrida, *Limited Inc.* (Evanston: Northwestern University Press, 1988), p. 137.

2. Ibid., p. 148.

3. Pierre Barbéris, "Dialectique du prince et du marchand," in *Balzac: L'Invention du Roman,* ed. Jacques Neefs and Claude Duchet (Paris: Belfond, 1982), p. 183.

4. Page numbers in parentheses refer to Honoré de Balzac, *Le Colonel Chabert suivi de trois nouvelles,* edited by Patrick Berthier and with a preface by Pierre Gascar (Paris: Folio, 1974). All translations from Balzac, Berthier, and Gascar are my own.

5. Shoshana Felman, "Women and Madness: The Critical Phallacy," *Diacritics* (Winter 1975), p. 6. Future references to Felman's article are given in the text and identified by "Felman."

6. Quoted in Maïté Albistur and Daniel Armogathe, *Histoire du féminisme français* (Paris: des femmes, 1977), p. 362.

7. See Arlette Michel, "La Femme et le code civil dans la 'Physiologie du mariage' et les 'Scènes de la vie privée' de 1830." In *Le Réel et le texte,* ed. Claude Duchet, (Paris: Colin, 1974), pp. 135–45.

Mary Poovey

Reading History in Literature: Speculation and Virtue in *Our Mutual Friend*

In recent years, the neoformalism of deconstruction has finally encountered a powerful challenger. Whether in the guise of the New Historicism or of the return of literary history, this form of criticism has enabled many literary critics to articulate our conviction that literature and literary criticism do not exist in a formalist vacuum and, more specifically, that literature and literary criticism are inevitably concerned with politics.[1] I begin this essay by addressing the question of why history has recently begun to seem important (again) to many literary critics as a vehicle through which the politics of—as well as in—literary criticism can be addressed.[2] I then offer a model of deploying history that has affinities with, but also differs from, both the New Historicism and the old literary history. From this I move to a reading of Dickens's *Our Mutual Friend* to demonstrate the kinds of insights this new history can produce. I aim throughout to reconstitute what literary critics understand as "history" and, by so doing, to explore why this kind of analysis restores to visibility the political enterprise in which literature and literary criticism are inevitably engaged.

In a general way, the appeal of history for literary critics resides in the tendency of historical narratives to identify the specificity of particular social formations and events. In so doing, history provides something like a horizon for possible interpretations of "literary" texts.[3] I do not mean to suggest by this formulation that history provides a "ground" for interpretation in the sense of constituting a stable or unitary referent that contains the "real" meaning of the literary text. Instead, I want to highlight the extent to which the work involved in constructing a historical narrative can alert the reader to the network of connotations and associations to which the language of the literary text also belongs. In so doing, this work enables the reader to identify the ideological projects in which the text participated at its moment of production. This focus on history, then, partially shifts attention away from the (modern) reader and the play of textual meanings that this reader perceives and toward the object of analysis as it can now be seen to have participated in a field of cultural meanings. This shift foregrounds a kind of ideological work that is performed by language but that is not precisely equivalent to the production of indeterminate meanings, which is the focus of most formalist criticism. This work entails the symbolic management of contradictions that (also) reside in the social formation at the moment of the text's production.[4]

This shift away from the (modern) reader is only partial, of course, for reasons to which I will return, and it should be seen as a political intervention in the institutional practice of literary criticism rather than as a return to the "true" meaning of the text. One effect of this shift is to restore to visibility the social relations in which the literary text existed and in which the reader now operates, as well as to expose the dynamic role that texts (and literary critics) play in the constitution and destabilization of these social relations. Incidentally (but only incidentally), this shift in focus also gives some interpretations more "validity" than others.[5] I'll return at the end of this essay to the connection between this practice of reading and the politics of criticism, but first I need to address two prior questions, which are essential to this shift in focus. These questions are (1) what materials should be included in the kind of narrative history that literary critics read (and write)?[6] and (2) how does constructing this history in relation to the literary text alter the strategies of literary analysis, as it has recently been practiced?

One way of designating the materials appropriate to this kind of history is to limit them to a set of texts.[7] "History" would then be constructed from a parade of texts, chronologically arranged, whose subtle internal dynamics can be positioned in relation to previous and subsequent texts, which are distinguished by their own subtle internal dynamics. For a literary critic, the appeal of this approach is clear, for the feature that has most definitively characterized U.S. literary criticism since the 1940s is close textual analysis. This approach also has the advantage of preserving the materials of history from the reification, or false stabilization, that characterizes the work of some New Historicists.[8] But it has the distinct disadvantage of ignoring materials that were not originally textual (such as wars or childrearing practices)—of becoming, in other words, just a cleverer, more textually responsive version of intellectual history.

Another way to solve the problem of the material of history is to expand the field by construing everything—"events," like wars; continuing practices, like childrearing; and even social entities, like people—as "texts." This approach is based on the assumption that all of these "things" are internally organized signifying systems and, as such, "texts." It does not reduce physical relics, like buildings, to "mere" texts, but rather makes it clear that any human activity or artifact has meaning that can be "read" or interpreted. This approach also makes it clear that our only access to the past (as to all reality) is through representation. Events in the past undoubtedly "happened," but they are available to us only through the representational systems that also, and not incidentally, confer meaning.

The primary advantages to this approach are, first of all, that it gives us something more inclusive than written documents to "read" and, second, that it makes it clear that when we "do history," *we* are *reading*—that is, interpreting. In other words, textualizing the past or the world calls attention to the fact that actual events are accessible to us—in the sense of being meaningful—only insofar as they are produced (or read) *in relation to* the ideological problems of the present. This means both that the reader is inextricably implicated in the history she writes *and* that reading is a material practice that contributes substantively to the construction of what counts as "reality" now. This statement accounts for the partiality of the shift away from the modern reader that I described earlier; indeed, it makes it clear that the relationship between the reader and the past is one of mutual construction. When one reads the "past" so as to understand or write it, one is actually describing some of the conditions by which that reading has become possible. The reader does not confront the past as a veiled or partially obscured object but as that which can be seen through, and in the light of, the present precisely because, when read through the present, it can be seen to have made the present reading possible. Thus, this approach to history does not acknowledge the irreducible otherness of the past but insists upon its intertextual relation to the present that makes a reading of it possible. Postulating this mutually constitutive relationship between the contemporary reader and the past she reads generates a new object of analysis that enables literary interpretation and history writing to come together. Following Foucault, I call this object of analysis "the conditions of possibility for. . . . "[9]

Instead of the autonomous literary text celebrated by formalists or the monocausal narrative often constructed by historians, this object of analysis consists of the complex system of relations in which texts participated at their moment of production as well as the system of relations with the present that makes these past relations visible now. This object of analysis, then, is something extrapolated from all kinds of texts—and from social interactions, institutions, and practices, too— and reconstructed as the ideological conditions of possibility for those texts, interactions, and practices—conditions that are also, necessarily, related to the conditions that make these texts meaningful now.[10] In the most schematic sense, the "object" constructed through the interpretive relation is abstract or formal: it is a principle of organization or, better still, a characteristic system of relations that confers identity by inscribing differences. Inevitably, of course, this formal principle also has content, for it only exists in and through the representations that give it its historical specificity (and through the interpretations that bring it into visibility now). In the mid-Victorian period, for example, the most abstract conditions of possibility that determined, at the most basic level, what statements and actions would be considered comprehensible or "in the true" for the middle class consisted of a binary system of organization, which was articulated most "naturally," hence persuasively, upon the sexual difference. That is, the most characteristic feature of mid-Victorian, middle-class culture was the articulation of identity as a unitary characteristic, defined by its opposition to another unitary entity within a series of binary oppositions, the most fundamental of which—and here's the content—was the opposition male/female. Who one was, what counted as an action, the terms in which scientific principles and moral values could be understood—all of these were formulated in fundamentally individualistic terms, whose meanings were given by their implicit opposition to an "other" and in relation to gendered connotations apparently derived from anatomy. We can identify this characteristic system now because, given the persistence of individualism and binarism, we can recognize these as meaningful and, given the development of a theory of social construction, we can recognize them as constructs.

To describe this double object of analysis as a "set" of beliefs, a "system" of institutions and practices, or even a "characteristic relation" conveys the impression of something that is internally organized, coherent, complete, and (relatively) static. But there is another, equally important dimension to these systemic relations: they are uneven. In the most fundamental sense, this unevenness is a function of the constitutive instability of any system that attempts to stabilize identity within a field of differences. That is, within a field of differences, unitary identity can only be stabilized artificially, by repressing some differences (and similarities) and foregrounding others. The repressed differences, however, actually underwrite the identities from which they seem to be excluded in the sense that they constitute the material from which these identities—and the system as a whole—are constituted. In mid-Victorian England, this meant, in part, that what looked like a *binary* organization of difference always depended upon (and repressed) a *multiplicity* of differences (within every entity as well as in society as a whole) that could be stabilized into discrete, individualized entities only imperfectly. In part, it meant that the difference of *sex* was foregrounded in uneasy relation to other kinds of difference, among them the differences of race, class, ethnicity, and nationality. As we will see when we turn to *Our Mutual Friend,* the relation among these constituents of difference was itself uneven and variable across time. The visibility now of such tensions within what once looked to be stable units is a function of the relation between them and an interpretive schema that focuses on social construction, especially the social constructions of race, class, and gender.

The unevenness that can now be identified manifests itself in discrepancies within and between institutional practices, in the differential experiences of individuals positioned differently in society, and in contradictions within individual texts. This unevenness also characterizes the alterations of a social formation; that is, institutions change, but not in the same way or at the same rate. There is no strict parallelism, or homology, among the different parts of the social formation or among the patterns of change these parts undergo. This unevenness also helps account *for* change, because the fact that various parts of a culture are able to manage or symbolically resolve the constitutive instability to different degrees means that, occasionally and to some groups, the underlying contradictions and instabilities that inform the social formation become visible and available for analysis and resistance.

Depicting the social formation in this way dissolves the conventional opposition between texts and institutional practices or events because it casts all of these supposed entities as effects of—but also participants in—the culture's symbolic economy. It suggests that one kind of important historical work will concern itself with describing the *specificity* of a society's symbolic economy—its particular combination of coherence and incoherence, which underwrites the society's identity *and* its susceptibility to change. The privileged sites for this kind of analysis will be, on the one hand, the mechanisms that efface the constitutive instability of institutions and texts and, on the other hand, the contests in which the system's "other"—which points to the provisional nature of its stability—threatens to become visible. This model also suggests that one important literary-critical practice will abandon the pursuit of "complete" readings of discrete texts in favor of analyses that reconstruct the debates and practices in which texts initially participated as well as the contemporary interpretive practices that make these debates visible now. The privileged sites for this analysis will be textual details that (also) belong to (other) contemporary vocabularies and discussions, textual contradictions or symbolic solutions that reveal the presence of the text's "outside" in the fabric of textuality itself, and the features of the text that coincide with contemporary critical preoccupations. In practice, of course, such historical and interpretive analyses constitute two dimensions of the same enterprise, thus making clear the merely conventional nature of the opposition between "analyzing literature" and "doing history."

I won't deny for a moment the difficulty of the practice I'm outlining. It means supplementing the manageable Penguin paperback with all that archival *mess* with which traditional historians have always struggled. It means taking to unfamiliar and less self-consciously "literary" texts like Parliamentary debates or social behaviors or quantifications of slum housing the interpretive skills of a literary critic. It means maintaining a consistent level of self-consciousness about the critical enterprise in which one is currently engaged. This practice also implies material conditions that do not sit well with the four- (or five-) year graduate program, much less the six-year, two-book trajectory toward tenure, which somehow must also accommodate learning to teach, grading all those freshman essays, serving on committees, and starting a family or continuing a life. This practice can't be pursued at home or in your "spare" time. It requires access to some kind of research library or archives; it requires enormous amounts of time just to read, more time to understand what you've read, more time to write. Yet even given these difficulties, I want to argue that this is important work and that, if scholars work collectively, it is even possible work. While I can only begin to suggest here some of the challenges and rewards this kind of work entails, I can at least offer my contribution to this collective project. In this reading of *Our Mutual Friend*, I demonstrate how identifying the debate in which the novel participated enables the critic to describe the ideological work performed by Dickens's representations of the signifiers of difference whose relation to each other Victorian society both depended on and repressed: gender and race.

To reposition a literary text in the historically specific discussions in which it participated, one must first locate systems of textual details that also belong to other contemporary debates. This involves three related projects: using secondary histories to identify these debates, locating contemporary sources that participated in them, and reading the literary text for its treatment of the issues involved in the debate one chooses to analyze. Recovering the common problematic addressed by all these texts can then alert the critic both to the ideological conditions that informed the cultural debate and to the dynamics of coherence and incoherence that define the relative stability of this ideological configuration. Identifying the strategies by which all the texts attempt to resolve the contradictions inherent in the problematic, or to resolve symbolically the anxieties they generate, enables one to characterize the kind of ideological work the texts collectively perform, as well as to locate their distinctive characteristics. The process I am describing essentially involves working back and forth between the literary and the nonliterary texts, as one searches for the apparently coherent problematic that the texts share *and* the traces of incoherence that textual work reveals. What follows is the outcome of this investigative-interpretive work—my reconstruction and analysis of one of the most important problematics of the early 1860s.

One of the most volatile issues of the period in which *Our Mutual Friend* was written and published involved the complex of financial, ethical, and legal questions introduced by the apparently limitless opportunities provided by new forms of capital organization and investment. Patterns of capital holding and use acquired new forms during these years primarily because of the passage, between 1844 and 1862, of a series of legislative measures that culminated in the establishment of limited liability, a legal provision that permitted corporations to be established where only partnerships and unincorporated companies had previously been allowed.[11] Limited liability legislation enabled promoters to raise larger sums of capital for finance and investment than other kinds of business organizations because limited liability decreased the fiscal responsibility of each investor. Because a limited corporation had its own legal personality independent of its investors, each shareholder was liable only for the capital he had invested in the business, not for all of his—and his family's—holdings "to the last shilling and acre," as the law of partnership had mandated. Limited companies therefore could not only engage more investors than a partnership generally could; they also drew investors from a much wider pool than the family network, on which the partnership had often relied to guarantee fiscal responsibility. The Joint Stock Companies Act of 1856 and the more sweeping Companies Act of 1862 also helped facilitate company "flotations" by enabling as few as seven persons to incorporate a company merely by registering a memorandum of association; each shareholder, moreover, only had to subscribe to one share, with no minimum value and on which no money need have been paid.[12] As a consequence of this legislation, by 1862 England had the most permissive company law in the world. By the second half of the 1850s and early 1860s, England's joint-stock companies and corporations provided an extremely important source of monies for commercial expansion and capital improvements. At the same time, however, the permissiveness of this new legislation sparked fears about the abuses such a system could generate. Indeed, even after the Companies Act, resistance to limited liability continued, with opponents worrying that a corporation might constitute a "state within a state" and that fictitious companies could be floated by as few as seven unscrupulous men.[13]

The speculative boom of which these company flotations were a part was fueled by a number of factors in addition to limited liability. Among these were the abandonment of trade restrictions between 1842 and 1860, improved and expanded transport systems both at home and abroad, the increase in "invisible exports" facilitated by Britain's transportation superiority, and the influx of gold from California and Australia in the 1850s.[14] As confidence grew and knowledge about the financial possibilities available in various parts of the world became more sophisticated, both individuals and banks aggressively sought investment opportunities that could return quick profits and high yields. In London, it even became common practice for some businessmen to borrow money for their regular transactions in order to be able to invest their own resources in potentially lucrative joint-stock companies or foreign loans. A "general reluctance to keep even small tanks of capital stagnant" developed, in the words of one modern economic historian. "Everybody wanted [capital] to circulate and fructify the ground."[15]

Critical to the conditions that made such investment possible was the rapid expansion of banking and credit facilities.[16] Following the Joint Stock Bank Act (1844), the Bank Charter Act (1844), and the extension of limited liability to banks (1858), numerous joint-stock banks joined the central and still-dominant Bank of England. Equally important was the establishment of a bill-brokering business, much of which was consolidated in the London Discount Market, a series of houses and agents that allowed individuals and banks to raise capital quickly by "discounting" promissory notes at the cost of a proportionate service charge.[17] While this system of discounting bills was obviously essential to the liquidity and productivity of capital, it also contributed to the other side of the speculative boom—the increased opportunities for financial overextension and fraud. One factor that enhanced the likelihood of financial irresponsibility was the fact that discount houses could rely on the Bank of England to back up their loans. This guarantee encouraged discount houses to lend amounts far beyond the value of their own outstanding loans. The tendency of this unregulated system of discounting to generate a self-perpetuating cycle of borrowing and debt was further exacerbated in cases of overseas trade, for the sheer distances involved generated temporal gaps that could be turned to profit by wiley investors. As early as 1847, the India trade was being described as a prototype of the abuses generated in colonial investment.

> The India trade has been one huge system of credit. If goods were bought in Manchester, by a house in London, they were paid for by bills at six months' date; and, as soon as shipped, an advance was obtained again by a bill at six months for a large part of the first cost, by the consignee, who, again, in his turn, not infrequently drew upon the house in India, against the bills of lading when transmitted. The shipper and the consignee were thus both put in possession of funds, months before they actually paid for the goods; and, very commonly, these bills were renewed at maturity on pretence of affording time for the returns in a "long trade." Moreover, losses by such a trade, instead of leading to its contraction, led directly to its increase. The poorer men became, the greater need they had to purchase, in order to make up, by new advances, the capital they had lost on the past adventures. Purchases thus became, not a question of supply and demand, but the most important part of the finance operations of a firm labouring under difficulties.
>
> But this is only one side of the picture. What took place in reference to the export of goods at home, was taking place in the purchase and shipment of produce abroad. Houses in India, who had credit to pass their bills, were purchasers of sugar, indigo, silk, or cotton,—not because the prices advised from London by the last overland mail promised a profit on the prices current in India, but because former drafts upon the London house would soon fall due, and must be provided for. What way so simple as to purchase a cargo of sugar, pay for it in bills upon the London house at ten months' date, transmit the shipping documents by the overland mail; and, in less than two months, the goods on the high seas, or perhaps not yet passed the mouth of the Hoogly, were pawned in Lombard Street,—putting the London house in funds *eight* months before the drafts against those goods fell due.[18]

During the 1850s and 1860s, the relationship between the discount market and the banking system grew increasingly complex and strained, and the reckless borrowing that followed from the Bank's guarantee culminated in a general financial crisis in 1857.[19] In 1858, in response to this crisis, the Bank withdrew its guarantee of support and imposed restrictions on the discount houses' ability to rediscount their bills with the Bank. The Bank's rule did not really check the instabilities of the bill-brokering system, however, for simply the knowledge that the Bank was restricting its discounting services could generate a discount demand by scared investors that was all out of proportion to actual financial needs. This became clear in the spring of 1859, as fears that England would be drawn into the Franco-Austrian war led to a Stock Market crisis that spread throughout the economy, largely because of the Bank's rule.[20]

In April 1860, the tension between the Bank and the discount houses reached new heights when the most important discount house, Overend, Gurney, & Co., tested the Bank's rule by withdrawing £1,650,000 from the Bank on the day before it had to issue dividends. Despite this forcible attempt to make the Bank accept fiscal responsibility for the system of credit or for discriminating between bad bills and good, the Bank refused the role of moral guide and held fast to its noninterventionist position. As a result, the credit market remained extremely volatile and the fate of finance capital became increasingly sensitive to the vagaries of investor confidence and the influence of external factors, such as the stability of the foreign governments to whom many companies made loans.[21]

At the same time that the Bank was refusing to regulate or underwrite the credit market, some discount houses were expanding into the much more dubious field of general finance. While many of the "finance companies" that sprang up in imitation of the International Finance Society, Ltd. (May 1863) were both honest and solvent, others were willing to invest in high-yield, questionable securities. Others were increasingly willing to extend credit to all kinds of projects without much preliminary investigation, to ignore the principle of lending "long" only when one borrowed "long," or even to "accommodate" bills that were either purely fraudulent or drawn against anticipated, rather than secure, resources.

Taken together, then, the same conditions that linked capital investment and speculation to potentially enormous profits also made fraudulent enterprises not only possible but virtually irresistible. The mania for profit—combined with legal provisions that encouraged but did not oversee company formations and credit facilities that generated finance capital vastly in excess of gold reserves or even good debts—produced a concentration of financial abuses, which, for sheer recklessness and audacity, surpassed even the credit frauds of the 1840s.[22] Although the most egregious deceits only became public after the crash of 1866, signs that the elaborate system of speculation was built on a precarious foundation began to appear in 1863 and 1864. By 1864, Bank rates had reached the unprecedented figure of 7 percent and, even though a market collapse was narrowly averted, numerous businesses failed.[23]

Between the winter of 1863 and November 1865, while Dickens was composing *Our Mutual Friend,* the vicissitudes of the English economy inspired numerous books, pamphlets, and articles in all kinds of periodicals and quarterlies. Among these were the two long treatments of the speculation mania that appeared in Dickens's *All the Year Round* between March 1863 and August 1865—the three series by Malcolm Ronald Laing Meason on company flotations, the bill-brokering system, and international speculation, and Charles Reade's *Hard Cash.*[24] The first of these in particular deals with the moral ambiguities that were entwined with England's exhilarating new financial arrangements. Meason's series on company flotations, for example, sees the narrator first solicited for a contribution to a nonexistent company by one "A. L.," then, having learned from his mistakes, initiating his own speculative flotation.[25] From conjuring out of thin air a limited, joint-stock bank—the Bank of Patagonia—the narrator progresses to selling shares in his invention, then to circulating rumors about the bank's insolvency, then to overseeing—and selling the rights for litigating—its demise. At the end of the series, the narrator is content with the outcome of his "little speculation." "To get five thousand pounds for bringing a company into the world, and a year later netting a cool fifteen hundred for helping kill off the same concern, is what does not fall to the lot of every man," he coolly concludes.[26]

Meason's articles illustrate two aspects of the problematic inherent in the speculation mania. The first is the importance of international investments to the dynamic of speculation. While domestic investments continued to play an important role in the wealth of the nation and individuals, many company promoters tried to stress the superiority of overseas investments for those interested in high yields.[27] One form this argument took was developmental: England was adequate, the logic ran, for infant companies, because it provided a relatively protective environment where young companies could "cut their teeth," but, as a company matured, it needed room to grow.[28] Another form the argument took stressed the difference, or lack thereof, between the English investor and the English working-class market. The English working classes, after all, were different enough from the English middle classes to want what the latter had but not different enough to lack some of the services that yielded the greatest returns. Most obviously, the English working classes enjoyed the same banking facilities that all Englishmen used; in fact, favorable interest rates had been made available to the English working classes during the 1830s and 1840s in order to encourage saving and thrift.[29]

When company promoters celebrated overseas investment, they stressed two qualities of their enterprises, which positioned them in relation to the home market. On the one hand, they emphasized that the site of investment was sufficiently like the England with which investors were familiar to inspire confidence in the foreign country's political and economic stability.[30] On the other hand, they emphasized that the target country was sufficiently unlike England to want and need to emulate Britain's "success." At heart, these assumptions both projected and depended on an assumption about England's "natural" superiority. English investors, in other words, would most readily risk their money upon the assumptions that the peoples of their targeted markets both differed from and wanted to be like the "naturally" superior English man. The most salient mark of difference, in this regard, was nationality, and, more specifically, the "underdevelopment" that characterized colonial and other overseas countries. Hence, the current economic wisdom that a free market economy with high capital accumulation had to expand into foreign markets was built on assumptions about Englishmen at home as well as foreigners abroad.

The narrator of Meason's articles invokes these assumptions when he elaborates the fantasy that could be built on expectations about a foreign market. Here, the mirror that returns English investors' self-satisfied image is Patagonia—a real country nevertheless sufficiently far away and unfamiliar to provide no obstacle to this nationalist and capitalist fantasy. To the narrator, in fact, the name of the country where he will "locate" his fictitious bank is more important than anything else, for his aim is to conjure visions of untapped natural resources *and* the assumption that this country will be both like and unlike England.[31] Such visionary possibilities are ultimately more important than any realistic description of the actual country. What Patagonia is like, in other words, is not as important as the fact that Patagonia wants to (and can) become (more) like England. Thus the narrator launches his lucrative enterprise with a blatantly fictitious prospectus.

> To draw out a prospectus for our bank, it was necessary both to study the commercial statistics of Patagonia, and to quote largely from papers and other documents relating to its produce and trade, or else to trust to chance, and write, as it were, a pleasantly coloured picture respecting our prospects of banking in that country. The former I was afraid would take up too much time, and therefore I chose the latter. . . . I commenced the document by stating that "This company has been formed for the purpose of extending the advantages of banking to the country of Patagonia, which was well known to be overwhelmingly rich in all kinds of natural produce." I then took a philanthropic view of the subject, and endeavoured to prove, that, in order to make men happy and prosperous, a banking

establishment was of all things the most necessary in every country. After this I looked at the question from a missionary point of view, and showed that without banks there could be no Christian teaching. Lastly, I quoted extracts from letters—imaginary of course—written by Europeans resident in Patagonia, proving that with proper management a clear profit of not less than twenty per cent must be made out of any amount of capital employed in banking operations between London and that country. I then . . . ended by assuring the readers of the prospectus that we had promises of support from all the most influential native chiefs in the land, and that, in a word, our success and triumph in the matter was certain.[32]

Obviously, Meason's fictitious prospectus capitalizes on the various rationales by which Englishmen had authorized their presence in less economically developed countries throughout the nineteenth century. But it also brings the earliest rationales for colonization—philanthropy and missionary conversion—into alignment with the latest, most explicitly economic rationale: in his description, banking—and, by extension, the flow of English currency—becomes the vehicle by which (English) profits confer happiness, prosperity, and Christianity upon the "natives," thereby simultaneously acknowledging their difference from Englishmen and beginning to close the enormous gulf between the two peoples.

The second point that Meason's articles make about such speculations is that they call upon and presumably appeal to a complex nexus of assumptions about familial relationships. If the projected bank is represented as bearing a benevolently paternal relation to this immature economy, then bringing the scheme to a profitable end deploys familial images of another kind: the imaginative work behind the bank is represented as the labor of begetting, then destroying a child. Calling his speculation a "child that we expected would have grown into so very large a man," the narrator repeatedly refers to the problem of "kill[ing], as it were, my own offspring."[33] Far from being a problem, however, killing the child has become another opportunity for the exercise of the founding father's ingenious wit. According to this metaphor, infanticide has been rendered painless—and, more to the point, lucrative—by the limited liability acts, which not only limited the investors' fiscal liability, but also absolved investors' families, as well as the corporation's (noninvesting) directors, from all fiscal responsibility. Because the new companies were internally free of the constraints of the investors' literal families, investors were free to alter—if not dispense with—the metaphorical familial bonds that the conditions as well as the language of the partnership involved.[34] Company founders could therefore dispense with ideas of parental responsibility and control, even though they retained a metaphorics of family to describe their actions.[35] Investors could figuratively beget, give birth to, and destroy companies without regret, as Meason's investors do here.

By the same token, of course, as the image of infanticide suggests, this situation was also hedged round with dangers. The freedom from parental responsibility and control for some meant the susceptibility for others to a situation without protection against loss or fraud, with no guarantee of loyalty, honesty, or even shared interest. More specifically, and more ominously, it meant an economic situation in which women were erased—not only literally, as dependents whose support rested on cautious investment, but also figuratively, as the mothers whose maternal instinct would compensate for and offset the sterner ambitions of the father. In fact, far from guaranteeing fiscal responsibility, as dependent women might have done, women under the new laws could facilitate fiscal irresponsibility, for husbands could use them to "shelter" monies otherwise at risk in corporate investments. In Meason's essay, significantly, there are no images of childbirth and thus no feminine influence to protect the infant company from the ruthless calculations of masculine self-interest. As men usurp the mother's place, the myth of bonded brothers, reproducing and supporting themselves for the sake of women, gives way to a more exhilarating and terrifying image of a world without women or a feminine function, where men not only bond together to "beget" little enterprises but also turn against each other to "kill" their "offspring." This world without a feminine principle is the world made possible by the economic arrangements I have been discussing.

The issues of national (or "racial") otherness and gender anxiety that Meason discloses within the problematic of speculation also appear in *Our Mutual Friend*.[36] Dickens's explicit treatment of speculation seems to assuage some of the anxieties that Meason comically arouses, but at the same time, the novel also draws out the connection, which Meason does not make, between the issues of racial difference raised by Patagonia, and the threat to men implicit in the image of infanticide. To tease out the strands of this connection, it is necessary to see how *Our Mutual Friend* works through the problematics of the speculation theme.

In Dickens's treatment of Alfred Lammle in *Our Mutual Friend*, the fraud that accompanied the speculative boom of the late 1850s and early 1860s is explicitly addressed. Lammle, who has generated the appearance of a substantial income and the reality of influential connections by speculating in shares, provokes the narrator's most vitriolic criticism of the groundlessness and power of speculative wealth. "As is well known to the wise in their generation," the narrator bemoans,

> traffic in Shares is the one thing to have to do with in this world. Have no antecedents, no established character, no cultivation, no ideas, no manners; have Shares. Have Shares enough to be on Boards of Direction in capital letters, oscillate on mysterious business between London and Paris, and be great. Where does he come from? Shares. Where is he going to? Shares. Has he any principles? Shares. What squeezes him into Parliament? Shares. Perhaps he never of himself achieved success in anything, never originated anything, never produced anything? Sufficient answer to all; Shares. O mighty Shares! To set those blaring images so high, and to cause us smaller vermin, as under the influence of henbane or opium, to cry out, night and day, "Relieve us of our money, scatter it for us, buy us and sell us, ruin us, only we beseech ye take rank among the powers of the earth, and fatten on us"![38]

The specific nature of the threat Dickens targets with this diatribe becomes clearer in another authorial aside concerning another stock exchange. While the Exchange referred to here is metaphorical, the stakes are even higher than in the literal Stock Exchange, because the commodity on offer consists not of shares or political power, but a child. This "orphan market" springs into being from the Boffins' desire to locate a child to replace John Harmon, who is missing and presumed dead.

> The instant it became known that anybody wanted the orphan, up started some affectionate relative of the orphan who put a price upon the orphan's head. The suddenness of an orphan's rise in the market was not to be paralleled by the maddest records of the Stock Exchange. He would be at five thousand per cent discount out at nurse making a mud pie at nine in the morning, and (being inquired for) would go up to five thousand percent premium before noon. The market was "rigged" in various artful ways. Counterfeit stock got into circulation. Parents boldly represented themselves as dead, and brought their orphans with them. . . . Likewise, fluctuations of a wild and South-Sea nature were occasioned, by orphan-holders keeping back, and then rushing into the market a dozen together. But, the uniform principle at the root of all these various operations was bargain and sale; and that principle could not be recognized by Mr and Mrs Milvey. (244)

The target of Dickens's dark humor is obviously the infiltration of economic motives into the domestic sphere. In *Our Mutual Friend*, Dickens sets out to counteract the modern version of this tendency in the plot that inaugurates and vies to dominate the novel's action—the John Harmon deceit. This plot is specifically formulated as a "speculation" intended to convert Bella's lust for literal wealth into an appreciation of more emotionally substantive gratification, the "true golden gold" of domestic affection (843). Thus the John Harmon plot works to rewrite "value," to exchange the false currency of literal money for the "true," metaphorical coin of love. As an "acquisition to the Boffins" (361), Bella initially both wants money and stands for the commodification of human beings. At the beginning of his deceit, for example, Mr. Boffin tells Bella, "Value yourself.... These good looks of yours are worth money" (526). Bella's moral education essentially takes the form of her learning to prefer honesty and affection to the rewards money can buy. As Bella learns this, the weight of the figuration associated with her shifts. Whereas Bella was previously converted into a figure of commodification, now money becomes the figure for value. In the process, Bella becomes a metaphorical rather than a literal commodity: "she's the true golden gold at heart," Boffin exclaims of the reformed Bella (843).

Two critical moments in this process of conversion are the encounter between Lizzie and Bella in which Lizzie's statement that a woman does not seek to "gain" anything but belief through her love shames Bella into seeing her own aspirations as "mercenary" (590), and the confrontation between Boffin and John Harmon, in which the Dustman's accusation that Harmon has turned Bella into a "speculation" makes her see her own selfishness (654–61). In the picnic in the counting house where Bella, her father, and John Harmon celebrate the triumph of love over riches, Rumpty Wilfer explicitly points out the apparent paradox involved in this rhetorical conversion: Bella, he says, "brings you a good fortune when she brings you the poverty she has accepted for your sake and the honest truth's" (673). When Harmon, still disguised as Rokesmith, takes a job in the city, Dickens toasts another version of this conversion. Once more Bella is figured as a *commodity*, but now the metaphorical status of the term is clear and powerful enough to displace the literal commodities in which the stock market trades: "He cared, beyond all expression, for his wife, as a most precious and sweet commodity, that was always looking up, and that never was worth less than all the gold in the world" (750).

According to the logic of Dickens's plot, taking money literally, as a good and an end in itself, leads to the literal commodification of human beings. By contrast, recognizing the metaphorical nature of money facilitates exchanges that enhance domestic relations and bring out the humanity in people. Significantly, Dickens locates the action that effects this conversion in the domestic sphere, for there men are able to exercise precisely the kind of control that is not available in the unpredictable world of financial speculation. The John Harmon plot proves that in the domestic sphere, the return on a man's investment of intelligence and love satisfies all of his desires. Through his calculated deceit, Harmon turns Bella into the wife he wants, so that when he realizes her wishes at the end of the novel, he actually realizes his own.[39] In the long campaign of deceit that ultimately reforms Bella, John Harmon also transforms the iron yoke of his father's will into its opposite: far from limiting the son's opportunities to make decisions for himself, as it was intended to do, old Harmon's will becomes the occasion for the son to discover what he wants and calculate how to get it.

Converting the literalism of commodification into a metaphorics of worth and the tyranny of a parent's will into permission to have what one wants takes place not only in the domestic sphere but, more specifically, on the cultural terrain of gender, for these transformations entail—and depend on—two assumptions about women. The first is that the "true" woman desires only what the man who (legally) represents her desires, that the law of coverture does not so much bind the wife's desires to those of the husband as recognize a community of interests that really does exist. The second assumption is that women can themselves stand in for the inhumane systems that control men. Literal women, in other words, can function like metaphors, which represent and displace something they are not. Thus, substituting a woman for stocks, as in John Harmon's depiction of his work, seems to allay the man's anxiety through literal displacement—because the domestic sphere apparently offers him an antidote to the demands and deceits of the marketplace. Actually, of course, this comfort depends on another kind of displacement—it depends on men effacing any desires that real women have that do not coincide with men's. Because of the two assumptions I have just described, this double displacement works, at least symbolically: because men assume that a good woman wants only to make a man happy; and because women can stand in for other forces beyond men's control, the illusion can be produced that that which seems to be beyond man's control actually answers his deepest needs.

Through such logic, John Harmon's domestication of Bella can serve as a corrective substitution for the entire system of exploitation and fraud associated with speculation and debt. Yet in this novel, the domestic "solution" only works in what amounts to a narrative vacuum; by the end of Our Mutual Friend, the John Harmon story is almost completely cordoned off from the other plots, and the mutually gratifying partnership that Bella and John share cannot correct even the domestic imbalance that lies closest to Bella—the travesty of her parents' marriage—much less the economic system that has enabled the bill broker Fledgeby to profit while good men like Twemlow stay poor. If we turn for a moment to the subplot of Our Mutual Friend, in which money and domestic virtue seem *least* entwined, we can begin to see why what happens in John Harmon's home cannot lay to rest all of the anxieties associated with speculation and deceit.

In *Our Mutual Friend,* the clearest example of domestic virtue free of mercenary interests is provided by Lizzie Hexam, the waterman's daughter. Lizzie's immunity to self-interest is figured both in her domestic loyalty and in her generosity. Her love for her father Gaffer has made her sacrifice her own education, and she has devoted her scant savings to her brother's training. Her virtuous passion for Eugene Wrayburn, moreover, is proof against short-sighted ambition, and Dickens presents it as so compelling that it eventually inspires emulative self-sacrifice, first in Bella, then in Eugene. Yet at a deeper level, Lizzie's virtue can be seen to engender almost as many harmful effects as does the orphan market or the Lammles' plot to trade upon Georgiana Podsnap's loneliness. Not only is Lizzie implicitly responsible for the blame cast upon her father by Miss Abby Potterson; Lizzie also explicitly causes Eugene to feel like a criminal as he tracks Gaffer, to become a peeping-tom as he spies on Lizzie, and to consort with Mr. Dolls as he seeks to discover where she is hiding. Unintentionally, of course, Lizzie is also the first cause of the assault upon Eugene and of the duplicitous conspiracy that results in the drownings of Bradley Headstone and Rogue Riderhood. In the scene of his agonized proposal, Bradley Headstone insists that Lizzie incarnates this dangerous doubleness: she can effect either evil or good because she has the power to precipitate in the desiring man either baseness or virtue. "You draw me to you," Headstone raves.

> If I were shut up in a strong prison, you would draw me out. . . . If I were lying on a sick bed, you would draw me up—to stagger to your feet and fall there. . . . No man knows till the time comes, what depths are within him. . . . To me, you brought it; on me, you forced it; and the bottom of this raging sea . . . has been heaved up ever since. . . . I am under the influence of some tremendous attraction which I have resisted in vain, and which overmasters me. You could draw me to fire, you could draw me to any death, you could draw me to any exposure and disgrace. . . . But if you would return a favourable answer to my offer of myself in marriage, you could draw me to any good—every good—with equal force. (454–55)

The power Headstone attributes to Lizzie assigns her the responsibility not only for gratifying his desire, but, more importantly, for domesticating his passion, for making him desire the right thing. Yet the doubleness he identifies in her ("you could draw me to the gallows . . . you could draw me to . . . good") renders this power dangerous to

Headstone and all the other men who come under her influence. The precise nature of the danger Lizzie poses seems to reside in the fact that she is not only powerful but independent. Certainly, Dickens suggests that Lizzie's independence is dangerous when he repeatedly links it to sexual susceptibility, if not sexual agency. Not only does Lizzie betray a dangerously willful desire for Eugene (in explicit defiance of her brother's prohibition), but she also occupies both thematic and structural positions that imply a dangerous female autonomy: two of her occupations, that of seamstress and factory girl, epitomized female promiscuity for mid-century Victorians.[40] Her status as an unmarried lodger, first with Jenny Wren, then with Riah's friends, was also considered a state of "precocious independence" for a woman.[41] And her secret riverside meeting with Eugene follows directly upon Bella's euphemistic announcement that she is pregnant, thus acquiring from the legitimate relationship the connotations of sexual activity to which the pregnancy explicitly alludes.[42]

The "precocious independence" associated with female sexuality reappears in Lizzie's economic agency. From the opening chapters of the novel, Lizzie has money—not much money, of course, but enough to underwrite her brother's education and his employment as a pupil teacher (115, 117). After her father's death, Lizzie becomes a seamstress who "keeps the stockroom of a seaman's outfitter" (271); and after Wrayburn's and Headstone's unwanted advances drive her out of London, she becomes a factory girl in a paper mill. Even more ominously, Lizzie's agency is also figured in her physical strength. Lizzie literally saves Eugene not by her moral influence, but by the skills and strength she developed as a "female waterman," which enable her to pull his broken body into the boat.

The combination of Lizzie's ambiguous "purity" with such stereotypically "masculine" traits as economic autonomy and muscular strength suggests that Lizzie's dangerous power may not so much originate in her independence from men as it expresses her assimilation to men. That is, despite the fact that Lizzie is said to have the ability to reform both Eugene and Bradley because she is different from them, she is actually, in some very basic ways, a better man than either of her suitors. Lizzie's "masculinity" is most obviously attributable to her class position: as a working-class woman, Lizzie lacks both the leisure and the resources to enhance her "femininity." Yet Dickens specifically downplays her class origins: she never speaks as a working-class woman; she (correctly) imagines that Eugene will see her as his equal; she never wants for resources or protectors; and at the end of the novel Twemlow decisively declares that she is a "lady" (891). Moreover, that her suitors' competition for *her* is transformed into an obsession with each *other* suggests that Lizzie's class position is, in some important senses, subordinate to her role in bringing these two men into a cross-class, homosocial relationship.[43]

Lizzie's ambiguous status—as a working-class "lady" and a "masculine" woman—begins to explain why the Harmon marriage can provide neither the moral center nor the organizing principle for *Our Mutual Friend*, as David Copperfield's marriage to Agnes was able to do in Dickens's earlier novel. The key to this insufficiency lies in the peculiar nature of Lizzie's ambiguity: she does not become a literal lady or a literal man but demonstrates instead that she can metaphorically cross class and gender barriers—that, in other words, class and gender identities are, in some sense, at least, *only* metaphorical. Despite the fact, then, that Lizzie is Bella's opposite in being immune to the desire for money, she brings into the novel the same association between woman and figuration that is thematically associated with Bella. In Lizzie, moreover, we see that the cultural association between woman and figuration posed threats as well as alleviating anxieties. In *Our Mutual Friend*, these threats acquire their peculiar urgency from the developments that distinguished the early 1860s.

To appreciate this urgency, it is necessary to place the developments of the 1850s and 1860s in the context of the historical relation between woman and figuration. As Catherine Gallagher has demonstrated, the figure of "woman" in the early eighteenth century was conceptually positioned in relation to the construction or redefinition of a number of critical concepts, including "politics," "virtue," "the public," and "fiction."[44] In a process I can only summarize here, "woman" and "the feminine" were conceptually linked to the anxieties generated by the new market economy and to the symbolic solutions formulated to resolve these anxieties. Thus, for example, "femininity" was associated with the fantasies and appetites unleashed in men by new commercial opportunities at the same time that social interactions with real women were expected to enhance the refined and polite behaviors that could theoretically control these excesses.

The financial revolution of the 1690s also generated a new model of politics and, along with this, new anxieties about the nature of political discourse. This new politics was "public" in the senses that it involved more people and that it was increasingly conducted in the newly expanded medium of the press. At the same time, however, the nature of this public political participation was shaped by the libel law, which virtually mandated anonymity, pseudonymity, and the use of allegorical or coded modes of description and analysis. The libel law, in other words, encouraged the use of fiction as a vehicle for political discourse. This use of fiction aroused the same kind of anxieties also generated by the newly expanded press, for both fiction and the press called attention to the possibility of creating a world of words that had no connection to the world outside language. As Gallagher explains, invoking the concept of "feminine" writing—and female practitioners of this writing like Mary Delarivier Manley—constituted a basis for discriminating among kinds of writing and thus for alleviating anxiety about public writing per se. "Reputable" writing was considered legitimate, grounded, and constructive, while the "disreputable" writings of women like Manley were baseless scandals, which could discredit and even undermine the government.[45]

These anxieties about fiction and the press were exacerbated during this period by another set of worries, which also followed the financial revolution of the late seventeenth century. In making the English crown dependent on loans, this revolution bound the very formation of a national government to new forms of financial transaction, which, in turn, encouraged both speculative investment and new forms of paper property such as bills of exchange and stocks. Just as the combined effects of the libel law and the press threatened to convert politics into fiction, so these new forms of commerce threatened to turn property into sheer writing. Once more, the "feminine" genre of scandal—and scandalmongering women in particular—epitomized the danger inherent in this threat. As Gallagher writes: "The scandalmongering woman was . . . a creature displaying the dangers of the new marketplace in political literature with peculiar clarity. Her merchandise resembled an inflated paper currency, the crediting of which would lead to the discredit of those who held the public trust."[46]

By the early 1860s, the links welded in the eighteenth century between "woman," "fiction," "politics," and new forms of commercial transaction like speculation had undergone significant alteration. In the first place, partly because of a general cultural shift after the French Revolution toward the moralism associated with the emergent bourgeoisie and partly because of the material role women played in helping men establish their creditworthiness in the 1830s and 1840s,[47] "woman" increasingly came to be associated not with "politics" or "fiction" as "scandal" but with morality and even "truth," both of which were held to be "above" or "outside" politics. In his celebration of the "angel in the house," Coventry Patmore deified this cultural association in the mid-1850s, but it is also important to recognize that Victorians believed this idealization to have a biological basis. The moralization of woman, in other words, was also a moralization of the female body—a displacement of the seventeenth-century obsession with female sexuality by an increasingly biologized focus on "maternal" instincts and the certainty of a woman's parental relation to her child. For example, J. W. Kaye, reviewing one of Caroline Norton's political pamphlets in 1855, writes: "There is no confusion as regards the woman's knowledge of the true and false. Whether her offspring be legitimate or illegitimate, she knows it to be her own. But a man, in this the tenderest relation which humanity recognises, may be the prey of a miserable delusion all his life."[48] By the 1860s, then, woman was understood by middle-class Victorians literally to embody and thus metaphorically to guarantee truth and to stand as surety against both the economic vicissitudes of the market economy and the competitive drive of one man to deceive another even in the "tenderest" relation of all.

The second important change involved the relation between fiction and political discourse. On the one hand, the repeal of the libel law and various stamp acts had considerably loosened restrictions on public participation in politics, thus obviating the need for political discourse to disguise itself in fictions. On the other hand, of course, partly through the "feminizing" poetics of Romantic realists like Wordsworth, Scott, and Dickens, fiction had acquired a moral authority of its own, and authors could advance political positions through fictions, just as fictions were sometimes cited in Parliament to further political arguments. While the relationship between political discourse and fiction had not been severed, then, fiction, like woman, had undergone a process of moralization that helped cleanse it of connotations of excess and scandal.

Finally, the relationship between commerce and national stability had been radically transformed by the 1860s, partly through the financial vehicles I have already discussed. While diatribes against the national debt erupted periodically in the century after its institution, by the 1860s the English economy was indisputably a system of credit and debt, and commercial transactions by individuals formed the backbone of the fiscal well-being of the now relatively bureaucratized and consolidated state. For my purposes, one of the most significant aspects of this transformation was the proliferation after 1757 of England's formal and informal colonies, which constituted sources of raw materials, markets for finished goods, and opportunities for investments of finance capital. An inevitable effect of England's growing dominance in a world market was a revaluation of the meaning of credit and debt. Whereas the Crown's status as debtor in the late seventeenth century had meant dependence on potentially seditious aristocrats at home, England's position as a creditor nation in a world economy in the 1860s meant that much of the debt was international and only enhanced England's independence as a nation and its domination in the world. Thus the "fiction" inherent in credit, paper money, and speculation did not automatically arouse the same kind of anxieties that it had in the early eighteenth century.

Given the revaluation of "woman" and "fiction," the naturalization of womanly virtue, and the removal of many of the threatening connotations previously associated with credit, why might Dickens reanimate the old anxieties once generated by the link between women and figuration? For this is exactly what Dickens's portrayal of Lizzie Hexam does: it ties what most Victorians thought to be the natural capacity of women to incarnate morality and value to a series of threats posed to the male characters. These threats, moreover, are specifically associated with the traditional connection between the fictional or metaphorical dimension of "woman" and the capacity of speculation to conjure something out of nothing. I want to suggest that this set of ominous meanings was available again in the early 1860s because of the historical conjunction between the economic factors I have already discussed and the emergence of the first specific challenge to the naturalization of female virtue. This challenge was articulated in the 1850s in a self-consciously politicized feminist movement, which was itself a response to the increasing number of women entering the workforce.[49] One of the first campaigns of this movement was to rectify the law that prohibited married women from being economic agents, capable of owning their own property or keeping the wages they earned. Even though the 1857 Married Women's Property Bill did not become law, the controversy it aroused interjected the issues of women's rights, property, and work into parliamentary discussion, quarterly review articles, and popular novels as well.

Dickens's representation of Lizzie Hexam and Bella Wilfer must be read in the context of these developments. For the most part, Dickens's treatment of women is a conservative, even nostalgic, recuperation of the domesticated female in defiance of some contemporary feminists' claims that sexuality was not the determinate characteristic of women and therefore that woman's biology was not the natural ground of her character or of womanly truth. Like many of his conservative contemporaries, for example, Dickens consistently marginalizes and discredits Lizzie's waged work: either he idealizes and marginalizes this work, as in his depiction of her work in the paper mill;[50] or else he subordinates it to her domestic relationships, as he does with whatever labor generated the money that finances Charley's education. In keeping with this, Dickens represents Lizzie's education as a means of increasing her value as a wife or as the vehicle through which her suitors vie to establish their influence over her—not, as with Charley, as a means of making more money. Similarly, Dickens gives Lizzie's moral influence more narrative attention than any of her waged occupations, and he grants *it*—not her money—credit for making Charley aspire beyond a waterman's life. Finally, Lizzie's moral influence over Eugene is depicted as being more restorative than her brute strength (even though it wasn't working *before* she pulled him from the water), since, presumably, had Eugene not seen the error of his ways, he would have been morally better off dead than alive.

Despite these nostalgic recuperations, however, Dickens also, perhaps inadvertently, reveals the threat implicit in the challenge posed to the naturalization of womanly virtue by women working and demanding rights. That the form this threat takes reanimates the eighteenth-century link between woman and figuration poses a particular threat to Dickens's narrative project, for he finds himself trying to use a fiction about women to quiet old fears about the link between fiction and women. This threat is alluded to in Mortimer's defense of Lizzie Hexam. When, at the end of the novel, Mortimer is asked whether Lizzie has ever been "a female waterman," he answers firmly that she has not (889). Mortimer's answer is correct in the strictest sense, since "waterman" was a term specifically applied to ferrymen and not to all-purpose boatmen like Gaffer, but, while Mortimer's answer spares Lizzie the association with manual labor that his interlocutor is trying to insinuate, it misses the import of Lizzie's having assumed a metaphorical version of this role: Eugene is alive only because Lizzie *has* been a kind of "female waterman." Acknowledging the metaphorical nature of the term "waterman," however, mobilizes the ominous nature of Lizzie's link to figuration. If Eugene's life depends on Lizzie's capacity to be like a man, yet his moral salvation depends on her being (like) a woman, then what is she by nature? Or, phrased differently, if Lizzie can be like a man when Eugene needs to be pulled from the water and like a woman when he is ready for a wife, then is it possible that her character is *not* an expression of some underlying female nature but merely the effect of a man's needs?

The implications of this question were far-reaching in the 1860s—and not just for the moralizing project of fiction. If the virtue men assigned to female nature proved to be only a figment of men's desire, then it might be possible that the sexed body did not guarantee moral difference. And if moral difference (or virtue) was not guaranteed by the female body, then it was possible that there was no basis for virtue at all—apart, that is, from men's desire that virtue exist. This structure of wishful projection, of course, is exactly the same principle that informs speculation and makes it so volatile and so threatening. For, if nothing but (men's) desire underwrites value, then there will be nothing outside of (men's) desire to counteract the desirer's darker impulses. In *Our Mutual Friend,* Dickens explores the vertiginous possibilities this raises by creating, as Meason had also done, a brief fantasy of a world without women.

At the dark heart of this womanless world is the scene in which John Harmon, disguised as the sailor George Radfoot, is attacked just after his return to England. Everything about this episode signals ontological chaos. The assault itself is focused not just on Harmon, but on the other man who resembles him, and it quickly spreads to every man in the room. The attack is narrated as a distorted, almost hallucinatory memory; and its disclosure marks the moment of maximum narrative dislocation in the novel—the eight-page segment in which John Harmon wonders aloud whether to remain dead or to reclaim his life and name.[51] Part of Harmon's description follows: "I saw a figure like myself lying dressed in my clothes on a bed. What might have been, for anything I knew, a silence of days, weeks, months, years, was broken by a violent wrestling of men all over the room. The figure like myself was assailed, and my valise was in its hands. . . . I could not have said that my name was John Harmon. . . . I cannot possibly express it to myself without using the word I. But it was not I. There was no such thing as I, within my knowledge" (426).

In one sense, as Rogue Riderhood explains it, the confusion of identity that Harmon experiences here is nothing unusual for a sailor. "There's fifty such [sailors] ten times as long as [Radfoot]," Riderhood laughs, "through entering in different names, re-shipping when the out'ard voyage is made, and what not" (416). In another sense, it is only an extreme manifestation of the proclivity for disguise men exhibit repeatedly in the novel, whether it be John Harmon miming secretary, Boffin playing miser, Bradley Headstone pretending to be Riderhood, or Twemlow counterfeiting Sophronia's father. But the ontological instability these episodes figure is no laughing matter, as the assault and all its ramifications reveal. Such instability is both cause and effect of the violence that Harmon, Wrayburn, and Riderhood all suffer, because it is the characteristic feature of a world deprived of any reliable criterion of difference, without an external "other" to anchor appearances or adjudicate right and wrong. This instability follows from the same mental gesture by which Bella can be made to replace stocks. It follows, that is, from turning what had been the guarantor of difference into sheer metaphor, which reflects only male desire, not some nature beyond fantasy and language. As this scene and all the other masquerades in the novel suggest, the effect of this gesture is to locate difference inside of man, hence to imperil both the guarantee of virtue and the integrity of male identity itself.[52]

The threat posed to the natural guarantor of difference by the developments of the late 1850s momentarily exposed the possibility that difference resides not between men and women but within every individual man. Like, but also because of, its conjuncture with the passage of the limited liability laws, this exposure generated profoundly ambiguous effects. On the one hand, both limited liability and the obliteration of natural difference catapulted men into a giddy world beyond moral restraint, where nothing checked their ability to speculate and conceive (deceits, plots, disguises, money-making schemes). On the other hand, the two developments exposed each man to the rapacity of his brother's desire, mirror image of his own, and, in pitting one man against another for what they both desired, such developments created value out of nothing and violence from the general struggle for scarce resources. In *Our Mutual Friend,* the first of these two effects is figured in the general hysteria that characterizes the scene of John Harmon's assault and in the speculations that energize Alfred Lammle and Fascination Fledgby. Even these explosions of energy have sinister effects, of course, effects that are elaborated in the scenes where sameness generates masquerade and finally a fight to the death. When one man can be "taken" for another, as Radfoot is taken for John Harmon, then a man can be taken down with another like himself, as Headstone takes Riderhood into their mutual, watery grave.

Even in *Our Mutual Friend,* Dickens's representation of the possibility that difference might not be natural and of the link between woman, figuration, and a world without grounded meanings is intermittent. In part, of course, this theme is intermittent because its challenge was so potentially ruinous to the social and psychological well-being of men like Charles Dickens. In part, however, the threat posed by the possibility that difference might not be anchored in sexual nature could be symbolically managed even as it was exposed because another principle of differentiation had become available by the 1860s to compensate for—and complicate—the difference of sex. This difference was the difference of race, and its increasingly foundational status was shored up by both contemporary events and the institutionalization of anthropological discourses that represented the differences among peoples as immutable and decisive.[53] Dickens's textually marginal, but ideologically central, invocation of racial difference holds the key to his ability to recuperate the moralized image of woman. To race I therefore turn.

Dickens invokes racial difference three times in *Our Mutual Friend.*[54]

The first reference to a "coffee-coloured" man appears in Bella's fantasy about her own glamorous future. In one of the visions she conjures, Bella is married to "an Indian Prince, who was a Something-or-Other, who wore Cashmere shawls all over himself, and diamonds and emeralds blazing in his turban" (374). The second black man is real but even more uncanny than Bella's fantasy. Struggling to be "exact" about his assault, John Harmon isolates one detail: "there was a black man ... wearing a linen jacket, like a steward, who put the smoking coffee on the table in a tray and never looked at me" (425). The status of the third black man is even more indeterminant than the fantasy or the memory. This black man is supposedly a real king but he exists only in a book "of African travel." When Mr. Wilfer alludes to this figure in describing his daughter's generosity to John Harmon, his reference obliterates whatever real king the traveler might have met with Wilfer's demeaning cultural generalizations: black kings, Mr. Wilfer says, are "cheap" and "nasty"; they bear "whatever name the sailors might have happened to give [them]"; and they tend to wear only "one good article at a time" (437). "The king is generally dressed in a London hat only, or a Manchester pair of braces, or one epaulette, or an uniform coat with his legs in the sleeves, or something of that kind" (438).

Why do black men appear in these three passages—at the heart of Bella's materialistic fantasies, at the site of maximum stress on male identity, and in the comic figuration of Mr. Wilfer's sartorial embarrassment? The answer to this question is partially revealed by the content of the first reference. Bella's fantasy that she will marry an Indian prince is the last in a series of fantasies about her future. In this series, Bella first imaginatively brings John Harmon back to life and marries him, then she "consign[s Harmon] to his grave again" and marries "a merchant of immense wealth" who gradually metamorphoses into the Indian prince. Bella's fantastic marital odyssey concludes with the comment that her "coffee-coloured" prince is "excessively devoted; though a little too jealous" (374).

What this passage suggests is the power of language to conjure characters from sheer desire. Because of the coincidence between one of the figments of Bella's fantasy and Harmon, a character in this novel, this power refers to and comments upon Dickens's power to do the same thing, but it also links this power both to murder and to male jealousy. Bella's imaginative "murder" of Harmon repeats the "murder" with which the novel opens (the "murder" that frees Bella to dream and that Harmon tries to control with his deceit), and her reference to the prince's jealousy casts the shadow of male competition over the parade of husbands she entertains. Thus the "coffee-coloured" prince is linked to figuration, desire, and the knot of deceptions and acts of homosocial violence that the assault on John Harmon most problematically describes. In this sense, the "coffee-coloured" prince has something in common with women.

The second clue to the significance of the black men is provided by the relationship that the last two passages bear to each other. That is, the reference to black kings, which occurs in the chapter immediately following the narration of John Harmon's assault, is offered as an antidote to the black servant: even if a black man dispensed the deranging drug, this placement suggests, such blacks are our puppets: we (white men) give them their names, their orders, and their desires. Just as Mr. Wilfer's story about Bella's generosity ostensibly offsets the heartlessness she has just displayed to John Harmon, then, and just as Mortimer Lightwood's assertion that Lizzie has never been a "female waterman" supposedly neutralizes the fact that she *has* been, the story of the black kings reveals that the black servant is really a projection of a white man's needs. In all three cases, however, the retraction does not actually cancel the initial assertion but merely completes a determinate contradiction central to *Our Mutual Friend* and to the structure of wishful projection that it addresses. That is, the fact that the deranging drug is passed to John Harmon by someone *like* him (a man "like a steward," who is dressed as a white man dresses)—like the fact that Bella and Lizzie are, in critical ways and at critical moments, like men—is as important to the ideological work of *Our Mutual Friend* as is the fact that Harmon is drugged by someone *unlike* him (a black man)—or the fact that, for most of the novel, Bella and Lizzie are *not* like men.

This contradiction—the other is like me, the other is different—is essential to the economic and representational systems that *Our Mutual Friend* simultaneously participates in and resists. It is impossible to separate these two systems or to determine which had priority in the 1860s, for the social and economic developments of the mid-Victorian period brought the fantasies inherent in this system of representation home to Englishmen as never before, while the representational system of self and other gave a particular semantic cast to the activities in which the English were involved. The logic of this system is as follows: the power of English men (hence the "proof" of their "natural" superiority) rested upon their ability to make the world over in their own image. In the 1840s and early 1850s, this quest primarily took the form of religious conversion, as missionaries set about transforming "heathens" in India, South and Central America, and Africa into Christians with the carrot of philanthropy and the stick of brute force. Economic investment in these areas accelerated throughout this period, often, as Meason's depiction of his Bank of Patagonia suggests, by piggybacking on the missionary and philanthropic rhetorics that already defined relations with these countries.[55]

Events in the late 1850s and early 1860s, however, most notably the Indian Mutiny of 1857 and the Jamaica uprising of 1865, gave England's relationship to at least some of these countries a new cast. Reports in 1857 about the slaughter of women and children at the Well of Cawnpore stressed the inhumanity of the dark-skinned Indians and prompted Englishmen to speculate about the "savagery" of the "brutes." The fact that these reports did not mention British atrocities at Benares and Allahabad in June of 1857, for which Cawnpore might well have been a retaliation, suggests the extent to which the likeness between the English and the dark-skinned Indians was denied or repressed.[56] The "savagery" of dark-skinned peoples was proved once more—to some Englishmen at least—by the Jamaica uprising in early October 1865. This native rebellion and the brutal retaliation it occasioned from Governor Eyre caused the leading English men-of-letters to choose sides and publicly declare their positions on race.[57] To Dickens, who deplored what he saw as the inhumanity of "the black—or the Native or the Devil—afar off," this episode merely hardened the opinion he had expressed as early as 1853 in an essay satirically entitled "The Noble Savage": "cruel, false, thievish, murderous, addicted more or less to grease, entrails, and beastly customs, [the black man] is a wild animal with the questionable gift of boasting; a conceited, tiresome, bloodthirsty, monotonous humbug."[58]

By the early 1860s, then, even as the proliferating examples of speculative fraud and violent rhetorical and physical retaliations exposed rapacity in Englishmen, newly intensified meanings associated with the difference of race had become available to guarantee that the likeness between the "natives" and "us," which was so crucial to establishing English superiority, had its limit. Englishmen conquered the formal and informal colonies economically by creating in "natives" the desire to be like the English man; but they contained the threat implicit in that assertion of likeness by emphasizing the "natural" difference of race. The native in whose country English men invested was like the investor (in his desires) but unlike him (in being "nasty" because black).

Here ends the neat parallelism between women and the racial other. For the fact that a woman—Bella Wilfer—symbolically drives home the difference between black men and white by giving her father what even a black king cannot have—a complete new suit of clothes—suggests that Dickens was not so much shoring up or even supplementing the difference of sex by invoking a parallel difference of race as he was establishing a relationship of mutual dependence between the two. That is, the same act with which Bella proves that her father is different from (read, better than) a black king also proves her to be a good (read, virtuous) woman. Bella's femininity, in other words, is momentarily stabilized as "other" to masculine self-interestedness through her relation to the black man, for femininity can now acquire its definition not only through acts of generosity to men, but, more specifically, through charitable acts that also inscribe racial difference with moral meaning. The one troubling aspect to this symbolic solution, of course, remains Bella's fantasy of "killing" John Harmon and marrying the Indian prince. This trace of violence within the "woman" lingers as a reminder of the instability of the solution Dickens advances, for, as the site of overdetermined meanings, this fantasy concentrates the threats to difference posed by the artificiality upon which it is based: in one reading, this fantasy shows a woman wanting a man who is unlike John Harmon (in being black); in another, it shows a woman wanting (another) man who is like Harmon (in being jealous); in another, it shows the rapacity and violence within woman; in another, it shows that this violence is in everyone: the jealous black prince, the woman, and the man who imagines them both.

The complexity of my argument in this essay signals in part the density of the relationships among the various historical strands I have highlighted here. Contemporaries' anxieties that new economic arrangements would undermine the English economy with fraudulent speculations coincided with anxieties about the threats posed by organized feminism to another traditional guarantor of social stability and moral behavior, the "natural" virtue of women. At the same time, the new economic arrangements promised riches beyond what most men could imagine, as the superiority of the English economic infrastructure made the world Britain's oyster. The complex plots by which Dickens raises and symbolically addresses these fantasies and fears expose their interpenetration and the cultural and narratives systems that contain them all. At the same time, the failure of Dickens's narrative ingenuity to stabilize the cultural system that produces these fears reveals the constitutive instability of the latter and therefore its susceptibility to destabilization and change.

In part, the complexity of my argument articulates the effects upon literary criticism of the recent turn to history. Relating the dynamics of the text—its patterns of repetition and transformation—to narratives of historical change is obviously a complex process, for it involves simultaneously constructing both the textual analysis and the historical narratives *and* reading the complex play of their interpenetration. But if, as many critics have argued, imaginative texts perform ideological work, then such analyses are the only kinds of readings that can begin to reveal the dynamics of this work. Only such readings, I suggest, can display the inherent instability of and emergent challenges to what appear to be homogeneous, unassailable ideological formations. Only such readings, therefore, can begin to account for change.

To a certain extent—and in some important ways—this kind of reading also participates in changes that are now underway in the practice of literary criticism. The political component of these changes has been described in various ways and with varying degrees of anxiety or glee, but by now it is clear to almost everyone who has a stake in the institutional (re)production of culture in the U.S. that a challenge has been mounted to the "great books" tradition of knowledge. This political component exists because one can never read the past or literature disinterestedly or from an objective standpoint but only from one's own position in the culture that the past produced. My position as a white woman who came of intellectual age in the 1960s brings sex and race into a kind of visibility that it did not have in the 1860s and makes this reading of that time very much a product of my own. The kind of reading I offer here is a form of dialogue, for in writing about the past I also write about the present. In writing about the present as one outcome of this past, all of us who do this kind of criticism inevitably participate in changing the conditions that make such readings possible.

NOTES

1. A useful collection of essays exemplifying and commenting on the New Historicism is H. Aram Veeser, ed., *The New Historicism* (New York: Routledge, 1989); see also Alan Liu, "The Power of Formalism," *English Literary History* 56:4 (Winter 1989), pp. 721–71. Another useful volume of essays on literature and history is Ralph Cohen, ed., *The Future of Literary Theory* (New York: Routledge, 1989).

2. My parenthetical acknowledgment of the role history has always played for some literary critics is meant especially to recognize its role in American studies. The way literature is now being read in relation to history, however, is significantly different from earlier examples of this practice, even within American studies. This essay contributes to defining this difference.

3. Throughout this essay I will assume the historicity of the concept of "literature," but I do not want to litter my text with quotation marks to signify

this historicity. Even though I drop the quotation marks around "literature," I hope that they will remain operative in the reader's mind throughout the essay.

4. See Fredric Jameson, *The Political Unconscious: Narrative as a Socially Symbolic Act* (Ithaca: Cornell University Press, 1981), chap. 1.

5. I hope it will be clear to readers that I am not agreeing with the position of E. D. Hirsch, Jr., here. I explain my position more fully at the end of this essay. See Hirsch, *Validity in Interpretation* (New Haven: Yale University Press, 1967).

6. In this paper, I am not going to engage in the debate *about* narrative in history writing. For discussions of this topic, see Hayden White, *The Content of the Form: Narrative Discourse and Historical Representation* (Baltimore: The Johns Hopkins University Press, 1987).

7. Here, I have in mind the work of some of our most exemplary intellectual historians, including Dominick LaCapra and Joan W. Scott. For examples of their work, see LaCapra, *Rethinking Intellectual History: Texts, Contexts, Language* (Ithaca: Cornell University Press, 1983), and *History, Politics, and the Novel* (Ithaca: Cornell University Press, 1987); and Scott, *Gender and the Politics of History* (New York: Columbia University Press, 1988).

8. For two examples of New Historicists whose work exemplifies this tendency to stabilize history, see Stephen Greenblatt, *Shakespearean Negotiations* (Berkeley: University of California Press, 1988); and D. A. Miller, *The Novel and the Police* (Berkeley: University of California Press, 1988).

9. In addition to Foucault and Jameson, the influences upon what follows include such disparate figures as Freud, Lacan, Mouffe and Laclau, Spivak, and Derrida.

10. For further development of this point, see Mary Poovey, *Uneven Developments: The Ideological Work of Gender in Mid-Victorian England* (Chicago: University of Chicago Press, 1989), chap. 1.

11. The most important acts were the 1844 Registration Act, the Limited Liability Act of 1855, the Joint Stock Companies Act of 1856, and the 1862 consolidating act, the Companies Act. Helpful discussions of limited liability include H. A. Shannon, "The Coming of General Limited Liability," in *Economic History*, ed. J. M. Keynes and D. H. MacGregor (London: Macmillan and Co., Ltd. 1933): 2: 267–91; J. B. Jeffreys, "The Denomination and Character of Shares, 1855–1885," in *Essays in Economic History*, ed. E. M. Carus-Wilson, (London: Edward Arnold, Ltd., 1954), 1:344–57; S. G. Checkland, *The Rise of Industrial Society in England, 1815–1885* (London: Longmans, Green and Co., Ltd., 1964), pp. 39, 43, 104–7, 129–30; and W. T. C. King, *History of the London Discount Market* (London: George Routledge & Sons, Ltd., 1936), pp. 238–45. One nineteenth-century view of limited liability is provided by David Morrier Evans, *Speculative Notes and Notes on Speculation, Ideal and Real* (London: Groombridge and Sons, 1864), pp. 228–36.

A helpful discussion of the differences among partnerships, unincorporated companies, and corporations is provided by P. L. Cottrell. "The key legal difference was that a corporation had its own legal personality, which was independent of that of its shareholders. In the case of a partnership, its rights and liabilities were simply the sum of those who constituted it. The unincorporated company was in a 'grey' area of the law, a consequence of being in some ways the product of opportunism—attempts to establish as close an approximation to a corporation or rather some of the attributes of a corporation without being subject to the scrutiny of the state" (*Industrial Finance, 1830–1914: The Finance and Organization of English Manufacturing Industry* [London and New York: Methuen, 1980], p. 39). See also Leland Hamilton Jenks, *The Migration of British Capital to 1875* (New York: Alfred A. Knopf, 1927), pp. 233–62.

12. See Cottrell, *Industrial Finance*, p. 52. Unlike England, other countries, including France, Germany, Belgium, and Italy, imposed safeguards on company formations. These included a minimum of paid-up capital, the registration of the company's prospectus, and the oversight of a registrar.

13. For a discussion of the objections to limited liability, see Cottrell, *Industrial Finance*, p. 41.

14. A discussion of these factors can be found in Checkland, *Rise of Industrial Society*, pp. 22–26. "Invisible exports" in the 1850s and early 1860s largely consisted of services that produced income for English companies and investors. The largest source of service income was shipping, but monies were also generated by foreign trade, overseas banking, administrative service, and pensions charged to colonial governments (see Peter Methias, *The First Industrial Nation: An Economic History of Britain, 1700–1914* [New York: Charles Scribner's Sons, 1969], pp. 303–20). In 1864, David Morier Evans estimated that the gold from California and Australia was contributing £21,000,000 per year to the precious metal reserves of England (Evans, *Speculative Notes*, p. 46).

15. Sir John H. Clapham, *An Economic History of Modern Britain: Free Trade and Steel, 1850–1886* (Cambridge: Cambridge University Press, 1932), p. 371.

16. Here is Checkland on the effect of new forms of mobilizing capital: "The rise of banks and finance companies meant that the centripetal forces were much strengthened—bringing into the money market all kinds of savings scattered about the country and concentrating them for investment. But the newly created centrifugal forces generated by the new institutions were even stronger—seeking means of placing capital with increasing skill. The net effect was a closer mobilization of capital for the more hectic exploitation of a boom, both at home and abroad" (*Rise of Industrial Society*, pp. 50–51).

17. Evans noted in 1864 that the banking system was in "a transition stage" and he speculated that the private system would soon be replaced by a joint-stock system (*Speculative Notes*, p. 29). For a history of the bill-discounting system, see King, *History of the London Discount Market*.

18. Quoted in King, *History*, pp. 135–36.

19. In 1858, Sheffield Neave testified before the Select Committee on the Banks Acts that the system of "money at call" was responsible for the stress placed on the system, not to mention the creation of dubious paper. "I wished to state that the system of money at call necessarily compels the broker, as well as the banker who takes it, to make immediate use of it, because he could not

afford to allow interest if it was not employed at the same instant at a better rate of interest, for the sake of his profit; it therefore occasions the party who takes the money at call to look out for securities wherever he can find them; and not to be very chary in the selection of them, when there is no difficulty in getting them. It leads therefore to the encouragement of an inferior class of bills, and is in some degree instrumental in giving currency to bills that probably ought not to be discounted" (quoted in King, *History*, p. 188).

20. See King, *History*, pp. 206–7.

21. Ibid., pp. 207–16.

22. Ibid., p. 238.

23. Here is Evans's densely metaphorical depiction of the spirit of the times: "Gaunt panic, with uncertain gait and distorted visage, stalks hurriedly through the land. Like the leper of old, downcast in mien and paralyzed in limb, his presence is the signal for immediate apprehension, lest his contagious touch should strike with disease sound constitutions, and bleach white the bones of living men. The slightest blast from his lividly scorching breath remorselessly crumples up credit, and destroys, as by the fell wand of the necromancer, the good fame and fortune acquired by long years of toil and steady accumulation" (*Speculative Notes*, p. 36).

24. Meason's articles include one on speculation and joint-stock banks: "Promoters of Companies" (*All the Year Round* 11 [March 12, 1864]: 110–15), "How We 'Floated' the Bank" (*AYR* 12 [December 31, 1864]: 493–97) " 'The Bank of Patagonia' (Limited)" (*AYR* 13 [June 17, 1865]: 485–90), "How the Bank was Wound Up" (*AYR* 13 [April 15, 1865]: 276–82); one on bill brokering and accommodation: "Wanted to Borrow, One Hundred Pounds" (*AYR* 13 [March 11, 1865]: 164–68), "Accommodation" (*AYR* 13 [April 8, 1865]: 260–64), "How I Discounted My Bill" (*AYR* 13 [July 8, 1865]: 557–61); one on "Going into Business": "Part the First" (*AYR* 13 [May 13, 1865]: 378–82), "Part the Second" (*AYR* 13 [May 20, 1865]: 404–8), "Part the Third" (*AYR* 13 [May 27, 1865]: 428–32); and one on "Amateur Finance": "Part I" (*AYR* 14 [August 12, 1865] 57–60), "Part II" (*AYR* 14 [August 19, 1865]: 87–91), "Part III" (*AYR* 14 [August 26, 1865]: 110–15). Meason also contributed an article entitled "Insurance and Assurance" to *AYR* 13 (June 3, 1865): 437–40. Some of these articles were collected and published as *The Bubble of Finance: Joint-Stock Companies, Promoting Companies, Modern Commerce, Money Lending, and Life Insurance* (London: Sampson Low, Son, and Marston, 1865).

The first number of Charles Reade's *Hard Cash* (serialized as *Very Hard Cash*) appeared in *AYR* 9 (March 28, 1863). The last number appeared in *AYR* 10 (December 26, 1863).

25. This is the series on speculation and joint-stock banks, cited above.

26. " 'The Bank of Patagonia' (Limited)," p. 490.

27. Shannon, who analyzed the limited companies registered in London, estimates that 15.15 percent of all registered companies and 17.18 percent of all companies formed between 1856 and 1862 were overseas companies. See H. A. Shannon, "The First Five Thousand Limited Companies and their Duration,"

Economic History, ed. J. M. Keynes and D. H. MacGregor (London: Macmillan and Co., Ltd., 1933); 2: 396–24. See also P. L. Cottrell, *British Overseas Investment in the Nineteenth Century* (London: Macmillan Press, Ltd., 1975), p. 29; and Jenks, *Migration of British Capital,* p. 239.

The question of the relative importance of home and overseas markets has been extensively discussed in the literature. Neil McKendrick in particular stresses the importance of home demand, but his focus is primarily the early part of the Industrial Revolution. See "Home Demand and Economic Growth: A New View of the Role of Women and Children in the Industrial Revolution," *Historical Perspectives: Studies in English Thought and Society,* ed. Neil McKendrick, (London: Europa Press, 1974), pp. 152–210. Recent treatments of this subject include P. J. Cain, *Economic Foundations of British Overseas Expansion, 1815–1914* (Basingstoke: Macmillan Education, Ltd., 1980); Cottrell, *British Overseas Investment;* and Michael Edelstein, *Overseas Investment in the Age of High Imperialism: The United Kingdom, 1850–1914* (New York: Columbia University Press, 1982). Edelstein emphasizes England's superiority in relation to other European nations in its rate of net foreign loans, especially in the 1860s and 1870s (*Overseas Investment,* p. 3).

28. McKendrick, "Home Demand," p. 181.

29. See Barry Supple, "Legislation and Virtue: An Essay on Working-class Self-help and the State in the Early Nineteenth Century," in *Historical Perspectives: Studies in English Thought and Society,* ed. Neil McKendrick (London: Europa, 1974), pp. 211–54.

Some proponents of the limited liability acts argued specifically that the new laws would overcome what differences remained between owners and employees. The new corporations, they argued, by promoting workers' investments in the concerns in which they worked, "would prevent the recurrence of those differences which ending in strikes are a disgrace to our age and to our laws" (quoted in Cottrell, *British Overseas Investment,* p. 48).

30. Jenks points out that promoters of overseas companies organized their firms in forms that would be attractive to British investors partly because they could not be sure that indigenous investors could support them. Thus securities had to be in pounds sterling and headquarters had to be in Britain (*Migration of British Capital,* p. 239). Edelstein stresses the importance of British perceptions of law, order, and commercial regularity in the countries in which new firms were proposed (*Overseas Investment,* p. 39).

31. The critical point at which Argentina became sufficiently like England to inspire investor confidence was passed after the dictator, Juan Manuel de Rosas, was driven into exile in 1852 and the country was unified under an American-style constitution in 1862. During the remainder of the 1860s, the Indians in Argentina were suppressed. See Charles A. Jones, "Great Capitalists and the Direction of British Overseas Investment in the Late Nineteenth Century: The Case of Argentina," *Business History* 22 (1980), 153, 157.

32. " 'The Bank of Patagonia' (Limited)," p. 488.

33. " 'The Bank of Patagonia' (Limited)," pp. 485, 488. See also "How the Bank was Wound Up," p. 277.

34. For a discussion of the relationship between limited liability and the family, see Leonore Davidoff and Catherine Hall, *Family Fortunes: Men and Women of the English Middle Class, 1780–1850* (Chicago: University of Chicago Press, 1987), pp. 200–205.

35. The persistence of familial metaphors, especially those involving growth, also distinguishes modern discussions of company formation. Shannon, for example, writes of "abortive companies" ("The First Five Thousand," 401); Jenks describes the creation of a finance company from the "parent" International Land Company as a "birth," and when the two join as "incestuous nuptials" (*Migration of British Capital*, p. 250). Jenks also describes company formation as "company obstetrics" (p. 251).

36. The word *race* was used in various ways in mid-Victorian England. Ethnologists in the Prichardian school of thought used the word to refer to differences that could arise from educational, religious, or climatic factors. As early as 1850, the word was also used to designate physical traits that were hereditary. Dickens's and Meason's works embody this imprecision, for they show national differences bleeding into what we would now call racial differences. For Dickens, however, skin color receives more attention than it does in Meason's articles. See George W. Stocking, Jr., *Victorian Anthropology* (New York: Free Press, 1987), esp. pp. 64–65.

37. Other treatments of speculation in Victorian novels include N. N. Feltes, "Community and the Limits of Liability in Two Mid-Victorian Novels," *Victorian Studies* 17 (June 1974), 362–67; and Michael Cotsell, "The Book of Insolvent Facts: Financial Speculation in *Our Mutual Friend,"* *Dickens Studies Annual* 13 (1985), pp. 125–43.

Characters specifically associated with various kinds of metaphorical and literal speculation include Silas Wegg; that "happy pair of swindlers," the Lammles; Mr. Veneering, who invests £5000 in the initials "M. P."; and Fascination Fledgby and his parents.

38. Charles Dickens, *Our Mutual Friend*, ed. Stephen Gill (1864–65; Harmondsworth: Penguin Books, 1971), p. 160. All future reference are to this edition and will be cited in the text.

39. Laurie Langbauer gives this principle more ahistorical significance than I would want to do, but her description of its dynamics is shrewd. She argues that "our forms of representation attempt to order our existence in a way that will establish for the male subject a comfortable relation to what controls him." Langbauer's thesis is that a woman is typically assigned the role of representing —so as to displace—whatever controls the male subject. "Although he cannot ignore or escape it, the system offers him this consolation: it directly reflects his desires . . . and is always there to minister to his needs" ("Woman in White, Men in Feminism," *Yale Journal of Criticism* 2 [April 1989], pp. 230–31).

40. See Elizabeth K. Helsinger et al., eds., *The Woman Question: Social Issues, 1837–83* (New York: Garland Publishing Co., 1983), pp. 114–33; and Mary Poovey, "Speaking of the Body: Mid-Victorian Constructions of Female Desire," in ed. Mary Jacobus et al., *Body/Politics: Women and the Discourses of Science,* (New York: Routledge, 1990), pp. 29–46.

41. See Leonore Davidoff, "The Separation of Home and Work? Landladies and Lodgers in Nineteenth and Twentieth-Century England," in *Fit Work for Women*, ed. Sandra Burman, (London: Croom Helm, 1979), p. 74.

42. Lizzie shares the name of another fictional good girl, who does become pregnant out of wedlock, the title character of Elizabeth Gaskell's "Lizzie Leigh," which was published in Dickens's *Household Words* in 1850.

43. For a discussion of this dimension of *Our Mutual Friend* see Eve Kosofsky Sedgwick, *Between Men: English Literature and Male Homosocial Desire* (New York: Columbia University Press, 1985), pp. 161–79.

44. Gallagher, *British Women Writers and the Literary Marketplace* (unpublished manuscript, 1990), pp. 175–212.

45. According to Gallagher, "as the press became an increasingly important political forum, the correspondence between the words that poured out of it and their putative referents became a topic of concern. Had politics become 'mere' words? . . . Was political discourse 'fictional'? One strategy for answering these questions and containing their attendant anxiety was to divide political writings into the reputable and the disreputable. Foremost in the latter category were the excessively 'feminine' writings of Delarivier Manley, for these were worse than mere fictions with no relation to reality; they were scandals, *dis*creditings, that bore a potentially negative relationship to the polity" (*British Women Writers*, p. 176).

46. Gallagher, *British Women Writers*, p. 193.

47. See Davidoff and Hall, *Family Fortunes*, chap. 6.

48. J. W. Kaye, "The 'Non-Existence' of Women," *North British Review* 23 (August 1855), p. 295.

49. Useful recent works on the Victorian feminist movement include: Lee Holcombe, *Wives & Property: Reform of the Married Women's Property Law in Nineteenth-Century England* (Toronto: University of Toronto Press, 1983); Sheila R. Herstein, *A Mid-Victorian Feminist: Barbara Leigh Smith Bodichon* (New Haven: Yale University Press, 1985); Philippa Levine, *Victorian Feminism, 1850–1900* (Tallahassee: Florida State University Press, 1987); and Mary Lyndon Shanley, *Feminism, Marriage, and the Law in Victorian England, 1850–1895* (Princeton: Princeton University Press, 1989).

50. Dickens even has Lizzie say that this work has "softened" her hands (590–91). This is a particularly ostentatious dismissal of women's work because women's labor in paper mills was actually one of the hardest and most poorly paid of women's occupations. See Wanda Neff, *Victorian Working Women: An Historical and Literary Study of Women in British Industries and Professions, 1831–1850* (1929; New York: Humanities Press, 1966), p. 100.

51. In his introduction to the Penguin edition of *Our Mutual Friend*, Stephen Gill calls the Harmon plot "the albatross about Dickens's neck" and book 2, chapter 13—the scene of Harmon's deliberation—"a confession of [narrative] breakdown" (p. 22).

52. In addition to the psychological instability figured in John Harmon's

assault, obliterating difference also both creates and destroys any basis for value. This is clear in the inherent structure of speculation. Speculation works as a form of investment because every investor imagines all desire to be the same (other men will want what I want); this similarity of desire, and not intrinsic worth, therefore confers value upon the desired object at the same time that it sets up a competitive relationship among men. Just as value rises out of the sameness of desire, however, so, too, does worthlessness. As every speculator knew, one rumor of insolvancy could trigger a panic capable of breaking a bank; one lapse of faith could plummet the price of shares. The structure of speculation is mirrored in the relationship between men and women once difference has been erased. As projections of male desire, women are like stocks. Their "value" is sheerly the effect of male desire, and the more men's desires mirror each other, the greater the value of the woman who is desired. As with stocks again, the rise in a woman's value primarily intensifies the competitive relationships among men. As *Our Mutual Friend* suggests, such competition—whether for money or love—soon turns to violence and a fight to the death.

53. The Anthropological Society of London was established by James Hunt in 1863. Hunt's extreme racist views informed the Society and were articulated in papers such as "On the Negro's Place in Nature" (*Memoirs Read Before the Anthropological Society of London* 1 [1863]). The membership of the Society had expanded to five hundred by 1865. See Ronald Rainger, "Race, Politics, and Society: The Anthropological Society of London in the 1860s," *Victorian Studies* 22 (1978), pp. 51–70. On race and Victorian anthropology, see George W. Stocking, Jr., *Victorian Anthropology* (New York: Free Press, 1987), especially chaps. 2, 3, 6, and 7.

54. Angus Wilson makes the following comment on Dickens's attitude toward race: "gradually, and markedly after the Indian Mutiny in 1857, [Dickens] . . . had come to believe that the white man must dominate and order the world of the blacks and the browns" ("Introduction" to Charles Dickens, *The Mystery of Edwin Drood* [1870; Harmondsworth, England: Penguin Books, 1987], p. 25).

55. Useful works on Victorian imperialism include: Lance E. Davis and Robert A. Huttenback, *Mammon and the Pursuit of Empire: The Economics of British Imperialism* (Cambridge: Cambridge University Press, 1988), abridged ed.; and Patrick Brantlinger, *Rule of Darkness: British Literature and Imperialism, 1830–1914* (Ithaca: Cornell University Press, 1988).

56. See Brantlinger, *Rule of Darkness,* p. 201 and chap. 7 in general. There is a vast literature on the Indian Mutiny. Some helpful analyses include: Sashi Bhussan Chaudhuri, *Theories of the Indian Mutiny (1857–1959)* (Calcutta: World Press, 1968); Pratul Chandra Gupta, *Nana Sahib and the Rising at Cawnpore* (Oxford: Clarendon Press, 1963); Christopher Hibbert, *The Great Mutiny: India in 1857* (New York: Viking, 1978); Ramesh Chandra Majumdar, *The Sepoy Mutiny and the Revolt of 1857* (Calcutta: Firma K. L. Mukhopadhyay, 1963); Karl Marx and Frederick Engels, *The First Indian War of Independence, 1857–1859* (Moscow: Progress Publishers, 1959); Eric Stokes, *The Peasant Armed:*

The Indian Revolt of 1857 (Oxford: Clarendon Press, 1986); and Evelyn E. P. Tisdall, *Mrs. Duberly's Campaigns: An Englishwoman's Experiences in the Crimean War and Indian Mutiny* (London: Jarrod's, 1963).

Charles Dickens's opinion about the Indian Mutiny was unequivocal. In 1857, he wrote to Angela Burdett-Coutts that "I wish I were Commander in Chief in India. The first thing I would do to strike that Oriental race with amazement (not in the least regarding them as if they lived in the Strand, London, or at Camden Town) should be to proclaim to them in their language that I considered my holding that appointment by leave of God, to mean that I should do my utmost to exterminate the Race upon whom the stain of the late cruelties rested; and that I was there for that purpose and no other, and was now proceeding, with all convenient dispatch and merciful swiftness of execution, to blot it out of mankind and rase it off the face of the Earth" (*Letters,* ed. Walter Dexter [Bloomsbury: Nonesuch Press, 1937–38], 2:889; see also 2:894). See also William Oddie, "Dickens and the Indian Mutiny," *Dickensian* 68 (1972), pp. 3–15.

57. John Stuart Mill, Thomas Carlyle, and Charles Dickens were among those who engaged actively in the Governor Eyre controversy. For accounts of this incident and the controversy it provoked, see Gillian Workman, "Thomas Carlyle and the Governor Eyre Controversy," *Victorian Studies* 18 (1974), pp. 77–102; Don Robotham, *"The Notorious Riot": The Socio-economic and Political Bases of Paul Bogle's Revolt* (Kingston: Institute of Social and Economic Research), Working Paper #28; Bernard Semmel, *The Governor Eyre Controversy* (London: MacGibbon and Kee, 1962); and Lorna Simmonds, "Civil Disturbances in Western Jamaica 1838–1865," *Jamaica Historical Review* 14 (1984), pp. 1–17.

58. "The Noble Savage," *Household Words* 168 (June 11, 1853), p. 337. Essays about Dickens and race include Arthur A. Adrian, "Dickens on American Slavery: A Carlylean Slant," *Publications of the Modern Language Association* 67 (1952), p. 315–29; Charles Barker, "Muscular Christianity, Race, and *Edwin Drood,"* unpublished manuscript (The Johns Hopkins University, 1991); William Oddie, *Dickens and Carlyle* (London: Centenary Press, 1972), especially pp. 92–93, 135–42; Donald H. Simpson, "Charles Dickens and Empire," *Library Notes of the Royal Commonwealth Society,* n.s. 162 (June–July 1970), pp. 1–28; and John O. Waller, "Dickens and the American Civil War," *Studies in Philology* 57 (1960), p. 535–48.

Julio Ortega

The Reader in the Labyrinth

El general en su laberinto (1989), the brilliant elegy Gabriel García Márquez dedicates to Simón Bolívar, is a fabled and fabulous reconstruction of Bolívar's last days. While Bolívar travels on the Magdalena River, the novel retraces the flow of narrative history.[1] Since, in fact, there is insufficient historical documentation about the final days of the defeated hero, the novel provides its own version of that voyage but, above all, it rewrites the character's adventure within the balance of his own historicity. In this implicit and implicating manner, to read is to become engaged in the novel's lucid political demand: it turns us into witnesses of the failure of the republican foundation and confronts us not with Bolívar's fate, but with that of our own countries.

In the extensive acknowledgments, García Márquez is careful to point out the novel's historical basis. History is taken up by the author as a system of verification: thus, what is known about Bolívar, about his daily speech and his political ideas, serves as a point of departure for this novelistic account of what is, indeed, *not* known about his last days.

Upon that blank page of history, which no longer has the final say over past deeds, García Márquez constructs the other events, those that interpret history as moral fable. Even though he must start from the established rhetoric typical of the biographical novel, *El general en su laberinto* is much more than a mere political biography of probabilistic speculation. Rather, it is written on the very margins of the official, institutionalized, tamed overwriting of Bolívar's history as well as that of the origins of the American republics. Writing upon the blank page of the death of the founding father—and from within the written, registered, and debated tradition—the novel finds that this page cannot be filled. The untold story consists of the question, intense and desolate, which exposes Bolívar's agony, and of the answers that the book posits in reading within itself the political enigma it elaborates and hands over to us in the journey upon the river of discourse and history. In this way, the labyrinth is the unwritten, the textual limit where the novel falls silent and the reader speaks.

It is upon the very page left blank by history that this novel inscribes the unanswered questions of historicity. Historical knowledge thus becomes the present-day reading of its own reflection in the blank page of the past; that is to say, the past is not altogether concluded and the present is relativized in the face of that history that does not fulfill it (or that it does not fulfill). This is the political dimension of the novel: we read the present, the now, of Bolívar's failure and of his revolutionary utopia of a united Latin America from our own present of chronic crisis. The political agony of the beginning is imposed upon us in this book, from the agony of our present day catastrophe. In this parable, the novel retraces the primeval discourse of the origins from the counter-discourse of the end. The utopian promises of the independence period are rewritten from within the reactionary antiutopia that has disjointed our societies with primitive capitalism, financial exploitation, and structural violence. Because of this, the reading of *El general en su laberinto*—from our own labyrinth of misery and domination—amounts to the act of responding to our own cultural context from the position of the unfulfilled and the yet to be done; reading, thus, is to start anew.

Between an unwritten page of the past and a page yet to be written of the present, what is written is the intertext of two spaces abysmally separated by their historical penury, by their unfulfillment. Here, the present emerges with its urgent demands over and over again: when the narrator uses the pronoun "we" to mourn Colombian violence, when he quotes Bolívar explaining conflicts of interest between North and South America, when indebtedness comes to define us in the past and in the present. But this is not a mere exemplary biography nor a belated historical moralism, reaffirming what we already know. Rather, it deals with something more rigorous and dramatic: it is an attempt to articulate historicity, the speech of our own historical experience, with the voice of our present day crisis. The resultant text is the discursive confrontation between our cumulative, catastrophic present and the synopsis of the primeval catastrophe. Bolívar's death is the tragic emblem of the agony and death knell of our yearned for ideals of emancipation and democratization.

This is not an invitation to pessimism. Politically, pessimism is anachronistic: it confers the space of intellectual debate to the neoconservative forces that have reduced contemporary Latin America's choices by imposing as the only alternative their neocolonial project of collaboration with the international financial system and the new international division of labor, conflating democracy and free-market policies. On the other hand, the political dimension of this novel opens up where the emblem—the dead Bolívar—closes: here, Bolívar is a wasted carnivalesque body in the wanderings of history. But, more than a legendary, historical character, he is a floating narrative subject, a sign whose meaning we as readers ascribe to him as we read him. Even as he approaches death, he sinks in the bitterness of his failure and clings to the precarious dream of his dismembered utopia. He is a specific character, but he is also a product of the narrative discourse, a figure whose very name within the novel renders him generic, between myth and utopia, without a prefixed place, like an open-ended question. Dismounting him from statuary horses, the novel makes him suffer his own body, his mortality; yet his passion—a magnificent faith in freedom—exceeds his devastated body. Like another Quixote, this Bolívar travels the road of defeat expelled from his own discourse; and just like Quixote, who recovers his hopes when he proposes to Sancho that they become shepherds (that is to say, that they assume a new discourse), Bolívar recovers his strength when the promises of utopia, the chance to begin anew, allow him the illusion of recommencing. This final illusion is the interpolation of mythic time and historical time, here resolved as a political becoming.

In this way, García Márquez attains in this novel a synthesis of two main discursive models that he inherited from the Latin American literary tradition. The first model is the "discurso de abundancia"— discourse of abundance—which is evident in *Cien años de soledad*. It is based on a proliferate economy of signs, on a genetic historicity, on a circular temporality that defines representation as generative process. The second model is the "discurso de carencia"—discourse of scarcity— which is visible in *El coronel no tiene quien le escriba* from the very first phrase where the old Colonel, a sign that has lost its exchange value, digs for coffee in an empty pot. In this particular case, history is conceived critically as a time of decay, and representation becomes a closure.[2] In *El general en su laberinto* the discourse of abundance is that of history as myth: the romantic, revolutionary hero embodies the passion for freedom and turns history into a subproduct of prophecy. In this way, the period of the establishment of the nation does not conclude: it is a perpetual act, and its vision of the future is the model for Utopia. This discourse of abundance, which the reader recognizes as characteristic of Bolívar and his heroic, emancipatory deed, interacts with the discourse of scarcity, articulated by the hero's agony, his failure, his decrepitude, his bitterness as well as by the more generalized political failure: the disunion, the "caudallismo" and the return of the conservatives. This discourse traces the footsteps (the novel tells us he retraces his steps) of someone who advances toward his own death, leaving memories and hopes in his wake.

Instead of a "bio-grafía" of Bolívar, this novel is a "moris-grafía," a discourse of death. Biographies, the novel implies, give us a glorious but erstwhile Bolívar, whose life is condemned to marble and iconography; on the other hand, this dying Bolívar, whose diminished and corrupted body we see wasting away, is more alive in his own death. Since within the story the hero does not stop dying, he thus belongs to the present and is saved from the documental and monumental history of the past. We know for a fact that Bolívar proceeds toward his death, toward the last page, where we, the readers, shall close the book; but, the generic ending's own narrated agony, upon becoming specific, opens up like a lack, a historical void. Once again, that blank page is in our present. In this way, by means of an internal narrative symmetry, death is in our midst, and from death we retrace the discourse of the promise, its abundance.

The irony of the narrative in the face of history: Bolívar hands us, not his life, but his death, not his great deeds, but his magnificent failure. The novel seems to tell us that while his life has been overwritten, his death remains to be inscribed. Perhaps for this very reason, the novel never fully describes its protagonist's countenance: it mentions his eager eyes, his ashen, curly hair, his gaunt appearance, yet there is no portrait of him like those of his servant, José Palacios, and of his friend, Marshal Sucre, found in the first chapter. Instead, Bolívar's frightful and absurd body (in its historical via crucis), his personality traits, and his everyday language are faithfully described to us. Thus, the reader is the one to provide not only the hero's face but the hero's name as well, since Bolívar is very often referred to merely as el general. But above all, the reader brings to the text an array of meanings associated with Bolívar's historical figure.

Thus, it is upon the reader's prior knowledge of Bolívar that the novel untells its own narrative of particulars. Indeed, a tension exists between the particular and the generic, between the narrative and historical, between the rhetoric of the fable and that of the chronicle of verification. The written aspect of the novel shifts between several diverse discursive intonations: chronicle (documented verification), legend (the oral versions of the hero's deeds), and narration (reconstruction of the specific). The chronicle introduces the lineal historical time (distinctively marked by chronology); the legend sums up mythical time (which perpetuates the founding father dimension of the hero, the space of his public glory); the narration implants discontinuous time in the remains of the discourse of scarcity and in the recurrences of the discourse of abundance (by the same token, circular time relativizes the present with each contrasting turn).

Regarding the relations of the referent and the rhetoric of historiography, Albert Cook has commented that, in the presence of the documentary verification of the chronicle, rhetoric supposes an implicit interpretation in the course of the narrated details.[3] Precisely, *El general en su laberinto,* whose closest model seems to be baroque historiography (noted in the discontinuity of the scenery that includes the emblematic river, the inhospitable mountain, the tropical jungle, the recurrent downpours, and the promise of the sea), is a historiographic novel, that is, a discourse where the analysis and the narration of the story nourish each other. A baroque funeral that illustrates romantic heroism, this novel rewrites history as an imaginary document about the historicity of the promise and the decadence. As in Edward Gibbon's great model about the Roman empire, García Márquez dramatizes the narration of historical misguidance in civil wars and political disintegration. Rome as model had already served to explain to Inca Garcilaso that the political Arcadia (the neoplatonic community of the Incas) had not survived fratricidal disunion.

Michel de Certeau has observed that historiography (history and writing) implies two antinomic terms: fact and discourse.[4] For that very reason, in modern times we see history not only as interpretation but also as fabrication. Therefore, the examination of historiographical operations presents a political problem: the procedures of writing history suppose a method of making history. The fate of García Márquez's "historical" novel is not different; the opposition between the new and the past, this tension inherent to narrative discourse that longs to venture beyond the traditional illusion of life made history, is solved in the name of the present, of the immediacy with which the novel speaks to us. In this historiographic novel (which is different from the old historical novel), the present is the fictive part and comprises, at the same time, the way in which the past becomes valid not only as part of the present but also as fluid, available, uncertain. The question of the subject becomes fundamental because the events are not the logical articulation of the story. Instead, the subject is the open space that unties the codifications that have explained and made legible those events turned into documents, chronicles, referents, and thus objectivity. The subject here is a name: Bolívar; but this name does not belong to the open ambiguity of the novel but rather to the generality of the historic. In this historic monumentality of the written, Bolívar is not only condemned to the past, but also to the bureaucratic repetition of his name, which becomes another form of domestication.

This is one of the great ironies of the novel. As Carlos Fuentes has commented, the Latin American novel acquires its own specificity when other discourses assume their responsibility of giving accounts of different spheres of social experience. Then, this novel by García Márquez tells us that, saturated as we are with social discourse, it is once again time to break out of the narratives of history, sociology, and anthropology and to dispute their articulation of the social. In fact, *El general en su laberinto* shows that history (the historical narrative) cannot say everything about history (the factual events), and that the new historical novel, the historiographic novel, is a more vital restructuration of our historicity. That Carlos Fuentes is writing a novel about Zapata, another revolutionary founder, is not accidental. It is as historiographic novels that we must read *Noticias del imperio,* by Fernando del Paso, *La noche oscura del niño Avilés,* by Edgardo Rodríguez Juliá, and *Terra nostra,* by Fuentes.

García Márquez's novel assumes, thus, the inherent tensions of historiographic discourse. In the symmetries and exchanges established by its controlled discursivity, the novel works thoroughly to go beyond the density of the generic through the use of the tangible texture of the specific. "El general" replaces "Bolívar" in this manner. From the very first page the subject "was no longer of this world" ("ya no era de este mundo"). He now belongs to the realm of narrative discourse: not to the world of the documented historical referent, but to the undocumented universe of metonymic narration, to that space where the succession of phrases replaces history with discursive historicity. Ironically, the constantly repeated title of "el general" or "mi general" designates the subject with the name of generality as function. The generic, the historical genre, becomes specific in the labyrinth of discursivity. In this way, the novel passes its hardest, most difficult test: the weight of its protagonist's name. When, along the journey, they find a mangy dog which the general decides to adopt, we read the following:

> El general estaba tomando el fresco en la proa cuando José Palacios se lo llevo a rastras.
> "¿Qué nombre le ponemos?"
> El general no lo pensó siquiera.
> "Bolívar," dijo. (107)

> The General was taking the air in the stern when José Palacios pulled the dog over to him.

"What name shall we give him?" he asked.
The General did not even have to think about it.
"Bolívar," he said. (100)

This christening renames the subject in the exchange: in this way, the character recuperates his own name with the dramatic irony of the specific.

Already on the first page the subject is his own body (naked in the bathtub) and he will become his speech ("habla gruesa," "coarse speech" 273). The very enunciation marks the character with the temporal reverberation of the voice: that time of the present, a present regained for a name which had been, generally and literally, written in stone.

In light of the theories that view the novel as compensation for what has not been lived, as lie that passes for reality, and as imaginary substitution—theories that have been disseminated in recent years by the narrative of entertainment: an ingenuous writing that refuses to acknowledge not only its responsibility as social discourse but also its own historical and political identity—García Márquez's narrative can be reread, from this more recent novel, not only as an imaginative task of powerful persuasion but also as a reflection of Latin American historicity and its political meaning. This reflection is given not as an external debate but as a reelaboration and restructuration of the discourse with which we interpret our historical processes and our political identity: that is, the formations and elaborations of the politics of culture, on which the theory and practice of the models and projects are founded. The fact that the novel can, from within its own narrative nature, restate this formative conflict of our social and historical experience is one aspect of the relevance of García Márquez's writing. Reading the novel thus becomes a production of historicity, a historicity recovered from oblivion as well as from memory. This narrating and reading practice supposes a theory of the novel as a decentering dialogic discourse that functions as a hypothesis of reconstitution and of opening. Thus, the novel subverts the regulating codes, actualizing the dilemmas that define us, and opening up an alternate space to the established discourses; in this way, the text initiates a reading of our common experience in terms of its critical, political, and communal reelaboration.

But if all is about to be reelaborated, the subject, that mobile and agonizing space, is also defined by uncertainty. Not only because he can no longer control his body but because the facts, contradictory and unwieldy, escape him, negating the meaning of his work. That indetermination comes from the narration: the subject is liberated not to historical causality, but to the defining uncertainty of politics. The political is represented in the novel from its negativity: the arbitrary exercise of opinions. The subject and the events get lost in that exacerbated, hyperinterpretative information, which changes according to the interests at stake, and which manipulatively relativizes intentions and words. In the process, García Márquez has written one of the most incisive sanctions of the political life of Bogotá, which appears as a Latin American emblem of recalcitrant and unthreatened conservatism. The subject, in any case, is not only uncertain but also contradictory: revolutionary, liberal, dictator, conspirator, he appears as a political sign that cannot be fixed. Because of the constructive dimension of the radical utopia that consumes him, he is constantly displaced between the center and the margin of power in a deterritorialized politics. The contrast between the subject's limited strength and his immense ideals, as well as his profound disillusion with his condition as exile from everywhere, is what the forsaken pulse of this hero communicates of the Latin American human condition.

All of this occurs thanks to García Márquez's extraordinary capacity for the specific: a capacity not just for the historical precision that designates objects without recurring to anachronisms, but also for the details with which the historical scene assumes its own weight vis-à-vis the immediacy of our own reading. The rhetorical strategy is, in itself, impeccable. Since the illusion of a realistic discourse that represents the logic of the historical narrator would not be enough, what is needed is an intersection of discourses, tonalities, and registers—a technique of which García Márquez has shown himself to be a master since the very first pages of *Cien años de soledad*. This new novel needs to compose the delicate disequilibrium of one and another interpolation, the plot of the documentary and of the fictitious, the turns of phrase forged at once of certainty and of the irony and agility of its profound game of substitutions. If the imaginary is, in the end, the most demanding form of truth, it is because its versions elaborate a sharper, more lucid, more engaged manner of responding to the reality in which we must live.

The first phrases already situate us within the magnificent rhetoric of temporal perspectivism:

> José Palacios, su servidor más antiguo, lo encontró flotando en las aguas depurativas de la bañera, desnudo y con los ojos abiertos, y creyó que se había ahogado. Sabía que ése era uno de sus muchos modos de meditar, pero el estado de éxtasis en que yacía a la deriva parecía de alguien que ya no era de este mundo. No se atrevió a acercarse, sino que lo llamó con voz sorda de acuerdo con la orden de despertarlo antes de las cinco para viajar con las primeras luces. (11)

José Palacios, his oldest servant, found him floating naked with his eyes open in the purifying waters of his bath, and thought he had drowned. He knew this was one of the many ways the General meditated, but the ecstasy in which he lay drifting seemed that of a man no longer of this world. He did not dare come closer but called to him in a hushed voice, complying with the order to awaken him before five so they could leave at dawn. (3)

The concluded past situates us within the precise activity of the story: the events are completed in a definite manner, a profile of omen and annunciation, the first image already being one of death. The second sentence introduces the synecdoche: it designates a variation in the continuity of the habit. The tense is now the past imperfect: the duration of the story where there is no beginning or end, but rather the pure activity of the fable. Looking like and being a corpse, but yet "not of this world": the tableau becomes an emblem. In the third sentence, we return to the perfection of the consummated: the voice becomes mute to awaken a dead man to the hour of the living; it is there that the day, the voyage, and the novel itself begins. The final part of the sentence belongs to the future: the verb is intransitive—to travel—and the light is that which opens up like the promise of the text.

Thus, the novel awakens Bolívar through his servant's voice, as he will later write his letters through his nephew's hand and will quote and copy phrases, information, and his own ideas through other mediators, all of which turn Bolívar into a character composed by others, by the witnesses that suddenly peek into his room to find him vomiting (17) or lamenting his fate (18). Between the date announced by his servant, March 8, 1830, and December 17 of the same year, when he dies, Bolívar's final voyage is organized according to the form of the chronicle. The density of the quotidian is plotted in the repetition and the recurrence of the narrative, the legend is retold by means of associative interpolation, and his moral and political agony is defined by the disbelief that debases him and the dreams that stir within him the hopes of a new beginning. The narrative focalization, which demands a precise distance, allows the narration to occur from the present, as if it were occurring from the events themselves: while it is inevitable for the narrator to assume prior knowledge of death, it is also necessary for the narrator to select the events and the evocations, to silence judgments and global valuations, so that everyday occurrences can flow with the firm presence of their typifying and tropological recreation. In effect, Bolívar's tenuous (and firm) presence and the presence of the other characters slips into a type of funerary allegory.

The knight and his squire, the sick master and his faithful servant compose a resounding figure, at once specific and cliché. Bolívar and Manuela Sáenz (who, smoking tobacco, dressed like a man and on horseback, is almost a Brechtian figure, very different from the version inscribed by Ricardo Palma) compose the solidary couple. The characters that turn up, one after another—generals, women, doctors, soldiers, whether present or evoked from the past—are in the same way distinctive and yet slightly cliché, synecdochical functions, as if they were rehearsing a possible ironical allegory of the casual turned destiny.

The last two sentences, on the other hand, are those of the end: the past is hurled into the suspended present of his death where the truth is no longer history but, rather, the General's own vulnerable and unique individuality:

> Examinó el aposento con la clarividencia de sus vísperas, y por primera vez vio la verdad: la última cama prestada, el tocador de lástima cuyo turbio espejo de paciencia no lo volvería a repetir, el aguamanil de porcelana descarchada con el agua y la toalla y el jabón para otras manos, la prisa sin corazón del reloj octogenario desbocado hacia la cita eneluctable del 17 de diciembre a la una y siete minutos de su tarde final. Entonces cruzó los brazos contra el pecho y empezó a oir las voces radiantes de los esclavos cantando la salve de las seis en los trapiches, y vió por la ventana el diamante de Venus en el cielo que se iba para siempre, las nieves eternas, la enredadera nueva cuyas campánulas amarillas no vería florecer el sábado siguiente en la casa cerrada por el duelo, los últimos fulgores de la vida que nunca más, por los siglos de los siglos, volvería a repetirse. (269)

> He examined the room with the clairvoyance of his last days, and for the first time he saw the truth: the final borrowed bed, the pitiful dressing table whose clouded, patient mirror would not reflect his image again, the chipped porcelain washbasin with the water and towel and soap meant for other hands, the heartless speed of the octagonal clock racing toward the ineluctable appointment at seven minutes past one on his final afternoon of December 17. Then he crossed his arms across his chest and began to listen to the radiant voices of the slaves singing the six o'clock *Salve* in the mills, and through the window he saw the diamond of Venus in the sky that was dying forever, the eternal snows, the new vine whose yellow bellflowers he would not see bloom on the following Saturday in the house closed in mourning, the final brilliance of life that would never, through all eternity, be repeated again. (267–68)

Here the narration not only substitutes history, but, because of the intimacy gained by García Márquez's interpretation, the narration is capable of recovering Bolívar's death in a luminous elegy. Once again the temporality of the concluded past dominates the retelling, only that each act is now dramatized by its own definite character. Death no longer occurs on the romantic discursive stage but rather on the most sober and everyday level of things that have been humanized, as in a poem by César Vallejo, by their sheer everyday quality. The future occurs outside of his life, from his past; separated from time, that final flickering confirms his unique, irrepeatable character. Only the two phrases that are delayed in their retelling prolong his life, suspending it between seeing and hearing: the narration is that very suspension in the occurrence of the phrase, in a language that constitutes it as a subject nourished by the novel in the dispossession of history. In this way death is an indisputable event that the entire novel has been announcing, preparing, provoking, as if it were that very death that would finally constitute the true individuality of the character. Bolívar's death is what the book shelters within it, what is expropriated from the history of great events and situated in the story as imminence, intimation, and naked truth. The sober amazement of the last paragraph dramatizes the General's individuality, yet almost all of it comes from literary tradition. From García Márquez's own narrative because he refers us to the sequence of simultaneity that Colonel Aureliano Buendía witnesses at the moment of his death. But this sequence had already been referred to by Borges in the enumerative amazement of "The Aleph," where the fragment was a synecdoche of the simultaneous totality of the universe. Furthermore, the testimony of seeing, the retelling of the vision returns us to the apocalyptical discourse of Saint John. This lineage of the "discourse of the end" is revealingly useful in Borges as well as in García Márquez because it serves to sustain the limit experience of an unnameable totality where we discover our own vulnerability.[5] If in Borges the marvelous is an abyss that opens up beyond everyday reality, in García Márquez it serves to illuminate the amazement of that very reality. In this way, everyday reality becomes more astonishing than fantasy. And in Bolívar's life, which is rewritten with the ink of his early death, that amazement refutes, in its ironic interpretation, the failures and the bitterness of the founder expelled from his own foundation; and that amazement also ignites, with its intelligence and empathy, the vital adventure of a soldier of freedom that we still owe to ourselves. In this novel, the interpretation as well as the empathy, the ironic plot and the mnemonic retracing enacted by the traveler in his final voyage, all serve to open a meetingplace, an intersection of history and narration, a crossroads where the discourse of death might sustain, once again, the recommencement of reading from the space created by the use of current speech, where almost everything remains to be done.[6]

All of this is most clear in the phonic game in the last paragraph, which repeats the syllables "vi" (clarividencia, vísperas, vio, vida, turbio) and "ve" (vez, verdad, salve, Venus, vería). This firm and delicate sound articulates anagrammatically the action of "vi" (saw) past and "ve" (see) present. "Vivir" (to see twice) is inscribed associatively as in a polyphonic poem where the language would involve a primeval space of redefinitions. A space where the affirmation of the historical being within the narrative occurs, and where history and the novel are two affirmations of a shared discourse.

NOTES

The author wishes to thank Mary Beth Tierney-Tello and Ariadne Hernandez-Rivera for translating his essay.

1. Gabriel García Márquez, *El general en su laberinto* (Barcelona: Mondadori, 1989), p. 286; all parenthetical references in this essay refer to this text. A useful summary of the criticism on the author's narrative can be found in Peter Earle, ed., *Gabriel García Márquez* (Madrid: Taurus, 1981). For a reading of representation, intertextuality, and the economy of signs in García Márquez's novels, see J. Ortega, ed., *Gabriel García Márquez and the Powers of Fiction* (Austin: University of Texas Press, 1988). George R. McMurray, ed., *Critical Essays on Gabriel García Márquez* (Boston: G. K. Hall, 1987) is a wide-ranging compilation of recent criticism.

2. Javier García Méndez, in his essay "El coronel no tiene quien le escriba: Novela de la carencia," *Casa de las Américas* 170 (Sept.–Oct. 1988), p. 28–39, discusses the literal meaning and the social value of scarcity in this novel.

3. See the excellent article by Albert Cook, "Reference and Rhetoric in Historiography," in *Criticism, History and Intertextuality*, ed. Richard Fleming and Michael Payne (Lewisburg: Bucknell University Press, 1988), p. 159–82. On history and literature, see Robert H. Cannary and Henry Kozincki, eds., *The Writing of History, Literary Form and Historical Understanding* (Madison: University of Wisconsin Press, 1978).

4. Michel de Certeau, *La escritura de la historia* (México: Universidad Iberoamericana, 1985). By the same token, his collection of essays, *Heterologies, Discourse of the Other* (Minneapolis: University of Minnesota Press, 1986), is also important.

5. For further information regarding "El Aleph" in this context, consult my essay on this story in *Poetics of Change* (Austin: University of Texas Press, 1984).

6. Ironically, the polemical discussion among historians and journalists regarding the novel which has taken place in Colombia (in which the author is accused of being pro-Bolívar and anti-Santander, for example) reveals the critical currency of his historiographical interpretation: the polemicists revive the historical dilemmas (Bolívar versus Santander) as political debate. If the dilemma has not been settled it is because its options are defined politically. García Márquez, instead of merely taking the side of one or the other founder, has proceeded to actualize the paradigmatic value of a Bolívar/revolutionary as

opposed to a Santander/politician. But the rivalry that separates them does not privilege one over another; it shows, again, that the end begins in disunion. Thus, the novel writes history with the political demand of an unrealized utopia: the revolution, that is abundance, is revealed from its own lack. It is the historiographic dimension that implies the nonfulfillment in Latin America: the present. In relation to this aspect, it is worth noting this observation of Hayden White in " 'Figuring the Nature of the Times Deceased': Literary Theory and Historical Writing" in *The Future of Literary Theory*, ed. Ralph Cohen (New York: Routledge, 1989): "It is the fact that historical discourse is actualized in its culturally significant form as a specific kind of writing that licences us to consider the relevance of literary theory to both the theory and the practice of historiography" (pp. 19–43). On the interpretation that constructs historiographic knowledge from the present, consult Robert D'Amico, *Historicism and Knowledge* (New York: Routledge, 1989), where the following is read: "Historicism does treat the objectivity of knowledge as constituted and internally justified. The diverse historical schemes, however, can only be known partially and provisionally from the vantage point of the present. Historicism accepts the skeptical argument against certain knowledge of the past and turns to reconstructions or interpretations" (p. 143–44).

Sande Cohen

Toward Events without History

The topics I take up here concern the idea of a "disappearance of history," of its becoming conceptually void, unable to inform criticism with plausible versions of various political realisms. Since any consideration of the concept of "history" is necessarily multiple, because the concept is never encountered in any pure state, let me start with two examples of history's contemporary formations, both of which try to sustain its cultural use-value.

Polarities abound in this cultural area, since history is regularly associated with sides (left/right) trends (positive/negative), movements (from cult-size to macro group), directions (increase/decrease), a real hodgepodge of times and spaces that are invariably bits of speculation drawn from larger cultural fragments. On the one hand, Professor Fukuyama has proclaimed an "end point" to "history" where "liberal democracy" is taken as "the final form of human government." This asserts a (mythic) identity between capital and liberal democracy wherein this "end of history" is placed beyond analysis and thereby precludes liberal democracy from being treated as an ideological name. "Liberal democracy" is called "a system of law . . . man's universal right to freedom and democracy insofar as it exists only with the consent of the governed." Severed from actual socioeconomic deformations, history has an end in the globalization of a mythified Western form; excluded are thoughts that would question capital's historical legitimacy.[1] The projection of an *ideal reality,* law, is confused with the formation and development of an end—consumerism—determined by the "knowledge of shoppers." In such cultural metaphysics, it cannot be acknowledged that the situation of law is connected to violence (law as an aggressive weapon) and to a crushing economics (that it is plainly too expensive). Derealized and remetaphysicalized, history is defined by the purest of continuities, that of law and order, a reading of Hegelian texts that strips them of their revelry in violence and mastery as agencies of transformation.

On the other hand, Kruger and Mariani, representing an art-critical university group, declare that the (classical and modern) historian is a "ventriloquist," as well as "masculinist and Eurocentric" (evils, after all, are always found in multiples) and is in the process of being overthrown by the conjunction of feminism and "examinations of ideology construction" derived "from the perspective of race and experiences of exclusion." The victims of the dominant history wish to assert their claims. Here, the category history is threaded to narrative practices that should "amplify destabilizing counter-narratives."[2] This model of criticism lays out an "anti-imperialist strategy" in which a "new history" is associated with "not only the pain of the past" or the "struggles of the present," but (directly, immediately) with "inclusive definitions for democratic futures." If I read this correctly, it is the writing of counter-history that empowers one to engage making *present* definitions, an absolutist politics, the elevated power of historical consciousness running in the smooth groove of owning the future. The loaded weapon of "inclusive definitions" (those who "counter-historicize" decide for others who do not) seems to stand in for the less acceptable term of revenge or gaining power-over, which implies repetition of the same, perhaps masks of political expansionism (= devaluation of the nonpolitical).[3]

The happiness principle embodied in the Western shopper meets its twin, its familial relative, the denied rival for the center, self-enslaved by the rhetoric of opposition. Each locked into moves by which to articulate their respective cultural zones, ready for the combat and contest of capturing public opinion, of making cases by which to convince new players that there are preexistent sides and choices by which to realize the future because one has taken possession of a past. History authorizes all this because, as Spinoza put it, "these terms signify ideas in the highest degree confused ... those notions have arisen which are called universal ... images ... that exceed the power of the imagination, not entirely, but to such a degree that the mind has no power ... to imagine a determinate number.[4]

In what follows, I first sketch arguments that pertain to the difficulties as well as myths of conceiving a history that is supposed to give cultural criticism legitimacy. I then go on to examine arguments from two contemporary critics, Lyotard and Baudrillard, that play out, as it were, connections between ahistoricity (history drained of its conceptual value) and theories of criticism. Much of what I have to say is based on the arguments worked up by Lévi-Strauss on historical thought, when he linked the latter to the code of chronology and not to any other anchor within cultural reals. The plasticity of "before/after" accesses no "historical reason" that could be taken as the starting point for a foundational theorization of any cultural sector; not only are the historians placed in intellectual suspension, the form of narration is bypassed in favor of conceiving as best one can connections to thought (and which movements the latter then can make are also modified).

Another way to put this is to emphasize that history does not coincide with past or memory or totality or individuality except by means of extracoding procedures, the overcoding of *semanticized* history-effects. In addition, substantively, the category history has ceased to offer any reliable model for understanding *actual* social arrangements not as Gordon Wood claims, because of "epistemological quarrels" that have finally struck the historical profession, but on account of the profoundly antihistorical force of capital. My aim in correlating ahistoricity and events must obviously evade becoming a metaphysics of conformity/opposition that, so far as I can see, results in an Hegelianized treatment of history or its double: the new homework assignments of radical-chic epithets.

Suspending Narrative and Historicity

Arguments concerning a disappearance of history are really about the idea that certain actualities have rendered the concept of history unnecessary to descriptions of reality and to theories of possibility, including those of cultural transformation. But many believe that it is just impossible for descriptions not to conform to history, one way or another. Obviously language is filled with past-referring forms, notably those of tense and aspect, yet grammatical forms are not the same as invoking history as the referent in our referring to the past. Instead of assuming the category of history to be the final referent (Peirce), it is worth considering that the concept carries no use-value at all; in Bataille's terms, the association between *history* (the term) and the foundations of things (actualities) has "fallen into a bottomless void," where "the human being arrives at the threshold: there he must throw himself headlong into that which has no foundation and no head."[5]

Modern capital is antithetic to history. While individual free actions are subjected to "races, peoples, classes, Churches and States" (Nietzsche) engaged in institutionalizing their reactivity, cut off from joyous anonymities as well as from expressive intensities, systems of culture dependent on capital train subjectivity as domestication, even when it stands in opposition.[6] The argument here is that capital is at once determinative of virtually every significant social and cultural effect (i.e., economic overdetermination) and this, in and of itself, eliminates the requirement to grasp its functions and effects in a historical manner. The concept of history belongs to the end of a pre-capitalist West. There are no conclusive historical phenomena because, paradoxically, history is irreducibly a speculative genre of presentation, tied, as it were, to a denial of facticity. Phrases like "processes of capital" are oxymoronic while phrases suggesting "processes of history" are speculative and belong to the realm of the unreal. Equations between capital and history are mythic, whether they have stressed capital's inevitablity and necessity or its (narrative) destruction. The aggressions of capital are such that to grasp its historicity is to sometimes excuse and forgive its factuality, a common theme in those histories that describe transitions to industrialization, for example, that the factory was more social than agrarian society. These aggressions, the elimination of what is not exchangeable, in particular capitalism's intolerance toward argumentative discourse or eccentric modes of life, require an attitude of incessant deconceptualization so as to shatter the settling in of a narrative peace pact with capital.

In this concept-scape, before/after is not just the code of every historicism but is also the semantic pattern of an entire social order based on sign-exchange. The latter is the dominant setup of cultural linkage; the oxymoron "real abstraction" (as in GNP numbers or speeches of politicians) spreads across what gets exchanged. In this, meanings that are historically derived are to varying degrees reactive or passive, particularly when they exude a "conscious misery . . . set up as the perfection of the world's history" (Nietzsche), which is what happens when we are exhorted, for the millionth time, to "adopt an historical viewpoint and attempt to make sense of multiple perspectives."[7] Making a perspective is not reducible to "making sense": it sometimes seems as if historical thought went forward as cause. Subordination of the multiple to the one both states and displaces the mythos of a historical problem; the much used phrase "Age of Reagan" is a progressive's delusion that unwanted transformations are reducible to political defeat or victory. Such notions are perhaps signs of an (unavoidable?) excessive cultural integration. In sum, before/after is better thought of as an essential married couple of Western thought, a device or apparatus whose expenditure of force results in making language cool (and dull?); before/after could easily be theorized as immediate semantic violence against present speech, against speakers who remain unhistoricized.

The nonhistorical nature of capital is of especial interest. The asociality (profit is immune to space) and desocializing effects of capital and the attending political groups that maintain their niches in capitalized bodies, for example, parties, associations, trade groups, trace a near global zero-sum world ravaged by each "improvement" of capital; *processes of knowledge are outstripped by new ignorances and productions by waste.* Even as argued on a historical footing, that capital represents a *stage or moment or formation necessarily progressive,* the empirical evidence is shaky: the rise in life expectancy from thirty-five or so to seventy-five or so was achieved nearer to rather than further from a hundred years ago. Rather than rehistoricize capital, we might analyze its joining of labor and desire in what rhetorical theory calls *dissociation,* where desire addicts itself to monetarized integrations. In this perpetual destabilization by capital, Deleuze depicts what makes histories of capital naive:

> The only modern myth is the myth of zombies—mortified schizos, good for work, brought back to reason . . . abstract labor alienated in private property that reproduces the ever wider interior limits, and that of abstract desire alienated in the privatized family that displaces the ever narrowable internalized limits. The double alienation—labor/desire—is constantly increasing and deepening. . . . codes are undone, the death instinct lays hold of the repressive apparatus and begins to direct the circulation of the libido. . . . Death is not desired, but what is desired is dead, already dead, images. . . . In truth, capitalism has nothing to co-opt; or rather, its powers of co-option coexist more often than not with what is to be co-opted, and even anticipate it.[8]

The production of images requires ceaseless scanning of images forward and back, which always yields to a "timeless area . . . that will survive by deterrence . . . out of fear that something too significant could happen."[9] Again: one is constantly invited to join the battle against that history and for another, progressive one; what is arguably dubious is the attending projection that capitalism is reducible to a recognizable *contest* of forces.

Models of temporal processes such as Habermas's (optimistic) "cumulative learning-process" or Foucault's (pessimistic) "disciplining of the body" or titles such as an "Age of Anxiety" (concepts of process, function and segment) are demoted to reactive attempts at maintaining *understandable reductions,* for example, processes one can and has to offer submission to in the end, as in every crisis, which demands one leap onto the least negative side, instead of freely choosing between affirmative choices. Even the radical authors of *Anti-Oedipus* offer one of the satisfactions of history with their "universal history" of "deterritorialization" or the washing of everything human in the cynical fluids of capital.[10]

The stabilizing force of historical consciousness, where a before/after assigns experience to a series itself assigned relative value by conjunction with other series, pertains to Saint Augustine's famous "now-then-will be" model of temporality. Modernized, a present social agent is thought to synthesize a transcendental subject (given in narrative form) and reference(s) to (pasts). Each side of "history-now" (past/future) is other, but recognizable since each now becomes past as well as a disclosure that reveals the future. This conceptual stability built into before/after is identical to the form of Western secular mythology. We think of noncapital as a precapital that *had to become* capitalized; this retrospective objectivism thus projected into the subject-name or that which occupies the position of a subject can then be taken—imaged, thought—as an "all encompassing Being" (Deleuze). Such "fixed paths in well defined directions" of history are really categories of language misidentified as objectivist realities. Instead of expanding alternatives from unsynthesized present-futures that one could use as one pleases (who is watching?), we adhere to the spectacle of, say, the struggles of "Germans" (there's a name!) to "reconcile" themselves with their enactment of a Final Solution or the Aztec lore that forecast the White Devils who would devour them; all such immersion in a historical problem becomes culturally consuming, so much so that it led Nietzsche to his argument that historical thought culminates in selves who inhabit "not a real culture but a kind of knowledge about culture, a complex of various thoughts and feelings . . . from which no decision as to its direction can come. . . . And so the whole of modern culture is essentially internal; the bookbinder prints something like this on the cover: Manual of internal culture for external barbarians."[11] On *cultural grounds*, we should remind ourselves that the sarcastic tone of an analytic structuralism toward the Hegelianized field of discourse, so evident in Lévi-Strauss's stinging refutation of a historical reason in the *Savage Mind*, was a version of the idea that historical thought attaches us to nontransformation, particularly in comparison to the violence of economic transactions whose "success means saving time," while "history's success" lies in legitimizing this saving.[12]

The conceptual obstinence of "has happened," which marks a past-real in the permanence of meaning, a touchstone for factism, actually sets off the interminability of *revisionism:* postmortem, speculation, guesswork, regret, counterhypothesis and more surround the reception of major, official, narrative histories. Robert Fogel's recent, narratively presented, supposition that slavery was profitable is an idea that can be mined for generations. The historiography of the Holocaust, or Final Solution—the distinction is itself of inestimable exchange-value in the production of monographs—might serve as a model for the internal structure of contemporary "historical knowledge": the "violence and the divisions of time" (Certeau) are done away with by positing what Karl Bohrer has called "falsely objectified traditions," narrative results that will make language silent—the archaic belief in grasping the "thing-itself."[13]

Technical semiotics is of some interest here. Let us take as a type of canonical historical statement the phrase "Kissinger believed he was acting as any tenured professor might in ordering the bombing of Cambodia." It is widely accepted that such a phrase, once properly contextualized, is an utterance with double referentiality, one part belonging to the past ("ordering the bombing of Cambodia") and the other pertaining to what is presently believed, which could be para-phrased as "evidence today suggests that what 'Kissinger believed' is consonant with generalizations about how professors and statesmen interacted in 1970." Now, what is disturbing about such "historical sentences" is the extent to which they suppose unwarranted continuity between saying-now and happening-then: how can anyone establish the plausibility of the interpretant "believed" when it may also have been willed (with malice), particularly when no perfect evidential decision can be made? To challenge, phrase by phrase, such usages is to confront a text that actually operates as if it did not want to be read at all.[14] The narratives of historians all too often suppose readers who accept the semantic undergirding as uncontested categories—the centrality of a subject, its continuity of substance, and so on (e.g., the "American people"). In melodramatic staples such as the Left's "crisis of Capitalism" (coined in the 1850s!) or the "end of painting," one perceives the constancy of a "solidification of being" that is all too often the linguistic expression of a metaphysicalized semantics.

All of which is to say that on the semantic level, at the level of the encoding of ideation, there is no cognitive requirement for history: the phrase "late capitalism" adds nothing to anyone's understanding of junk bonds or a depressed labor market. Real capitalism, the one that buys the land your house is resting on or the one that invests in providing the loans or the one that . . . is not itself directional or narrative, but operational: the particles called "conclusion," "completion," or "end" belong to a naive discourse, one that maintains the illusion of the constancy of subjectification. There is every reason to believe that just as actual capitalism is anticonclusional (how does profit ever really conclude?), where the right to borrow or to *have no end with money* is in fact definitive of contemporary practices (brought out in Gayatri Spivak's admonition for a criticism stripped of origin and end),[15] culture is all the more pressed into the service of providing such conclusions. It can also be said, to quote Charles Levin, that the category of history, like the category culture, is today "an afterimage at play in the field of effects, attached to the more than problematized 'always already' a memory, a misremembering or what acidheads used to call a 'flashback.'"[16] I think it instructive to note that in a mixed-up world of historical comparables, a reservoir, as it were, of gratuitously compared names, there are extremes of historicist decisions, such that Ben Gurion could state that he would have chosen to save half the Jews of Europe for a Palestine destination rather than all the Jews for emigration to England: even no-history is preferred to a failed history in the strange culturescape of narrative choices.

With history variously deployed as a cultural form, everyone thus becomes a claimant: Fukuyama's "end" and Kruger's "contestation" are but instances in a rivalry over signs of the future of the past (what we choose to endow as belonging to us, the past "for us"). The exchange-value of the concept of history is released in these projections, based on the idea that periodization yields insights into moral and aesthetic choices, particularly those involving the sustaining of social memberships.[17] We see this rivalry bluntly and negatively directed at children whenever the equation is released that youth = inexperience or, symmetrically, that older age = inability. One can say that such designations (lethal classifications) have the effect of simply limiting the playing field, of restraining individuals and groups within some culturally defined narrative apriority (compare, for example, the difference between the delay-promise of scholarly work whose commitment to take time is matched, horribly, in the contemporary willingness to pay lawyers at the start of their careers sums that demand a rapid turnover of capital). Those in control of such classifications—the historian, the manager, the politician—are actants of reducing temporality to our social functions. History, perversely, is a movement against time.

Taken up from another perspective, one can say that within a technocratically determined system, driven by values such as efficiency (in production and distribution) or rationalization (of *inefficiencies*), historical consciousness becomes anachronistic. A globalizing of the management of displacement tends to occur. As Hannah Arendt noticed, so many processes have been started whose trajectory only furthers the proliferation of events with arational goals, that this *perplexity,* a term that typifies the labyrinth that replaces narration (there is no story to get straight), entails a "melancholy haphazardness" as the actual thought-form of modernity:

> the particular incident, the observable fact or single occurrence of nature, or the reported deed and event of history, have ceased to make sense without a universal process in which they are supposedly embedded; yet the moment man approaches this process in order to escape the haphazard character of the particular, in order to find meaning—order and necessity—his effort is rebutted by the answer from all sides: Any order, any necessity, any meaning you wish to impose will do.[18]

In this anti-context, terms such as *tradition* or *historical need* contain attractive evasions of the highest cultural powers: an institution that claims authority today on account of tradition claims an actuality made entirely outside the conditions of modernity/capital and so *promises* distance from and otherness to capital; specific socialist groups will trace their ancestry and lineage/precursor status to a pre-capitalist people. All such tracings are suspicious. In a negative judgment concerning processes like class conflict or individual versus the State, Arendt argued that history has given way to a "world-alienation" that is self-devouring and has rendered "meaningless the one over-all process which originally was conceived in order to give meaning . . . [now] neither history nor nature is at all conceivable."[19]

If one considers that it is possible for capital to be thought of as ahistorical; if recourse to history entails self-legitimation of existing political players (e.g., Fukuyama and Kruger, above); if such maneuvers in fact support the larger subordination of criticism to a One (even when accompanied by the tag of the "plural"); if before/after activates philosophical repetitions of Being; if models of temporal processes are reductions of an integrative order, since they must cut out what cannot be integrated; if "has happened" is completed by revisionisms that are little more than "falsely objectified traditions" (Bohrer); if, in sum, historical knowledge is a semantic *restraint system,* then, I submit, the concept of history falls under the general formation of cultural reactivity: it fails to empower or set off a movement that might be construed as untimely and so is incapable of serious consideration as a stimulating movement of thought and language. "Historical knowledge" cannot effectuate thought of discontinuity. Or a discontinuous thought. More: if contemporary Western society is less a society of history than it is a nonintersecting series of groups engaged in self-consummation, where rhetorical categories such as oxymoron more and more resemble social setups (or vice versa), does it not become wildly impractical and probably senseless to speak of history? Can the compulsion identified with historians—that everyone have a usable past and that marks one as a socially responsible decision maker—appear unnecessary? Can the ethics of responsibility for history be cancelled—is it possible to repudiate this debt?[20] No doubt in a society that believes in the reality of lack and absence history is considered a necessary presence. It may well be impossible to separate the concept of history from the concept of possession. But it must be said that there are no compelling narrative proofs—convincing stories—to restock the passive memory whose force directs the obligation of *recollection,* which Norman Brown called a "religion of immortality," the "historical sense" as a form in an acceptance of the fear of death.

Lyotard: Detemporalization, Superhistoricity

Lyotard's semantic recasting of Arendt's analysis of the nonfit between history and experience is rendered in this formula of a creative, but not necessarily successful, event: "The expectant wait of the *Is it happening?* as silence. Feelings as a phrase for what cannot now be phrased. The immediate incommensurability of desire, or the immediate incommunicability. . . . The suspense of the linking."[21] Something happens that no historian can recount: so many things have already happened whose recounting is not what happened. Where a phrase such as "to further progress" installed the exchange-value of the signifier history because it seemed to offer resistance to other terms—one thinks here of stagnation or decline mythically defeated by progress—the game of such comparisons is made irrelevant once incommensurability is construed as an actual part of thought and not an interpretation. This failing of value is part of the disappearance of history. Since no one can situate themselves in front of or before the face of history, what happens to adjacent notions such as nostalgia/utopia? Such schematic questions can be recast in terms drawn from Deleuze but consonant with Lyotard: is there engagement with subjectification that shifts away from the dyad of revolutionary (temporal beginning) versus hermeneutic (temporal continuity) models?:

> To think means to be embedded in the present time stratum that serves as a limit: what can I see and what can I say today? But this involves thinking of the past as it is condensed in the inside, in the relation to oneself (there is a Greek in me or a Christian and so on). We will then think the past against the present and resist the latter, not in favor of a return but "in favor, I hope, of a time to come" (Nietzsche), that is, by making the past active and present to the outside so that something new will finally come.[22]

As modern philosophy of history claimed to put forward the necessary past, a move that automatically legitimated reduction of the future to continuous lines with the present, Deleuze and Lyotard's notions here are connected to an altogether different arrangement. The programmatic way of putting this is to say that such critics are now interested in a making (texts, events, objects) that expands what cannot be easily appropriated in the present and that would make it more difficult for existing players to bring about a future continuous with the present.

Shifting now to a consideration of art-as-event relations, the first thing to be said is that every signification here is treacherous. The category "art" exited, or vacated, its classical semantic determinations; its moves have displaced integrative semantic terms, making inoperative any properly socioaesthetic consideration; the active and reactive series that coalesce here are already distillations of other processes and fusions (do economic power and aesthetic indetermination belong analytically together?).

What does seem impossible to sustain is the argument put forth by Benjamin Buchloh, for whom modern art involves such categories as a "historical loss" and "decline of legitimacy" wherein terms like *critical* and *aesthetic* are energized only in their becoming *historicized.* Buchloh argues, for example, that Rodchenko's "introduction of the monochrome" and his "abandonment of conventional attributions of the 'meaning' of color in favor of the pure *materiality* of color" were driven by

> the demystification of aesthetic production . . . the elimination of art's esoteric nature, the rationalistic transparence of its conception and construction supposedly inviting wider and different audiences. Rodchenko aims to lay the foundations for a new culture of the collective rather than continuing one for the specialized, bourgeois elite.[23]

In this it is Rodchenko's historicism or anticipatory consciousness of such a new culture that serves as the temporal before and that allows Buchloh to periodize the after, which in the mode of the "neo-avant-garde" of the 1950's (e.g., Yves Klein), was determined by its subservience to the commodification of art making and was thus a falling away of the "critical avant-garde . . . where the primary process [supposedly] maintained its supremacy—this realm was now in the process of being converted into an area of specialization for the production of luxurious perceptual fetishes for privileged audiences."[24] Klein's work (which I am neither defending nor attacking) is codified by its lack, its nonimmolation on the funeral pyre of historicity, and thus represents the "disavowal of the historical legacy of modernism itself." The formal and substantive statements by Buchloh come down to the affirmation of an assertion: that historical consciousness is the way in which critical awareness locates the present and in which artists place themselves in the position of studying the past; the major corollary, it seems to me, is that the only valuable pasts are those which intended us *to study them.* As another critic has put it, it is the intelligentsia's obligation to recuperate "buried and mutilated traditions."[25] Once more: history produces the *game of speculation* whereby what threatens to fragment cultural space in the present, the difficulty of making a *ranking of awareness,* is overcome by the adhesion of a continuous history that restores everything to us.

The term *postmodern* has become another identity tag sustaining narrativity as one (but only one) tie of the social bond. Its having become a generally accepted term of periodization is well represented by Jameson's suggestion that it refers to a "third-order" movement of capital (global) as well as in Kramer's bemoaning it as yet another return of some dreaded avant-garde. This symmetry, this unity of (putative) opposites indicates the normal course of rehistoricization: it is widely accepted that time is "slipping away," that we are on the edge of some great transition.

On the other hand, one of the most interesting senses of the term comes from Lyotard, where it is used to postpone any clear historical register, where it cannot be fully reduced to temporal semantics:

> The postmodern would be that which, in the modern, puts forward the unpresentable in presentation itself; that which denies itself the solace of good forms . . . [or] to share collectively the nostalgia for the unattainable; that which searches for new presentations, not in order to enjoy them, but in order to impart a stronger sense of the unpresentable. . . . A postmodern artist or writer . . . cannot be judged according to a determining judgment. . . . Those rules are what the work of art itself is looking for. . . . work and text have the character of an *event . . .* too late for their author . . . their realization . . . too soon.[26]

As I read this, the stress of postmodern is of a pluralization of times, in that there is a real opening of an objective affect onto a depositioning subject, although there is a clear internal component (rules get broken) and plenty of objective references. Things that no one may fully understand get created. Meaghan Morris writes that such designations are banal: they "restore us to the paradox of a history driven by the sole and *traditional* imperative to break with tradition," but this seems to me to miss the point of detemporalization.[27]

The concept of desire in particular is decentered as a controllable, understandable *object,* and this, Lyotard argues, makes impossible the return of the *symbolic* for cultural allocation. Lyotard's systematic argument is that in face of the virtually complete *exteriorization* of the modern threatening to unravel the value of subjectivity, a principle of (mythic) agreeability is projected as an objectivist alibi in order to legitimize both capital(ist) engendering and Social(ist) critique; existing players mostly then affirm their identity (or reconfirm it), that of an optimizing performativity, which perforce enlists sememes of past and future and perpetuates symbolic promises of one sort of historicism or another. For example, the discovery—naming—of neurotic interiority was immediately transformed into a plethora of representations enunciated by artists, the analyst, the scientist. Sentimentalism of the neurotic, production of the neurotic, recodification of the neurotic, detoxification of the neurotic, etc. were all, and still are, legitimized by the projected historicity of the unconscious. What is liberated—become described— expands nothing else so much as the control codes placed in this socialization by academic protocols of interpretation.[28]

Lyotard challenges the political-aesthetic escalation which makes objects reducible to verbalized codifications and in which "the unconscious" is believed to "express" itself, but which really effectuates the reduction of its effects to language. The art-event has been chained to shuttling symbolic relations between subjects who found themselves in some historical bind or other and subjects-now who are similarly working out their supposed historical possibilities. In all cases, subjects remain prisoners of this overall "truth-work."

The symbolic, as expressive, representative and symptomatic, gives a sense of fulfillment of desire; it produces an ecstatic expansion of meaning, all the better when negative. When Adorno sponsored the atonality of Schoenberg, it was to delight "in recognizing its wretchedness and finds all its beauty in forbidding itself the appearance of the beautiful."[29] Such symbolism is effected in discursive formations of the barely endurable in which one comes to value one's alienating martyrdom and in that reproduces a historicism of hope, a conceptual lingering on of what has not happened in the West, utopia.

Expansion of the strengths of the existing players is maintained by the dyad move/countermove, in which such groups recode the presupposition that concepts and objects support and interpret one another. In and out of power such groups share a distaste for spawning ideas in which there may or may not be any corresponding conceptual resolution; both avoid what Lyotard esteems as a Kantian, nonnostalgic sublime, the inhumanity of Ideas that are not reducible to our politically driven demand for sense. For Lyotard, standard aesthetics and politics share an inclination for cultural terrorism in declaring the adequacy of image (or word) and concept to one another, whether as the taste that desires the satisfactions of a melancholic sublime (Malevich) or as the concept of political power which uses aesthetic forms (Brecht).

Symbolic systems that promise an art that renders to its audience(s) an enabling "incitement premium," as in figures (and interpretations) that would transcend "barriers of repression," make the unreal real, exemplified in Freud's passive, awe-struck bumbling, which turns into a satisfying aggression when "decoding" Michelangelo's *Moses*. A possibly unnerving idea is reduced to another, untroubling and knowable one and thereby eliminates from cultural disturbance the force of ideation, severed from affectivity or other relations.

A nonteleological or ahistoricized art-event suspends, if it can, the socially a priori narrative of language to set off what Rey Chow has called a "trampoline effect," in which an image or sense ricochets like the "tightening of a spring . . . [whose] sudden release will launch infinite vaster spaces of the unseen."[30] The point is to support, even against ourselves, that something *is happening* that testifies to the extracultural and political inbreeding of cultural politics and political cultures. In this sense, the "disappearance of history" opens on to an opportunity for "testing," as it were, one's capacity for experiences in the desubjectification of every cultural identity.[31]

One can say that postmodern does not have to set up another model of before/after attached to the language games of (projective) speculative ethics and (projective) speculative cognition. Manfred Frank spoons postmodernist over those whom he charges with a "certain return to the vitalism of desire," a "Nietzscheist retrogression." He writes as if trying to find terms for contemporary descriptions concerning the field of desire cannot be separated from prior academic confinements, as if one were engaged in defiling culture by the mere attempt to circumvent professorial discourse.[32]

Lyotard sets out from the consideration that within the modern/contemporary, determined by the general form of exchange/capital, historicism is blocked by "mutations" of "considerable significance" in which indifference to the *transferential function* becomes active. Here it is "demands for the order of representation" that are alienated, since such demands are attached to the "methodological nihilism" in which "entities of language, painting or music" are made to "stand for something else" and are thereby reduced to "a surface to be penetrated [and where] one finds the same prejudice: the notion that works of art have a substitutive or vicarious function. They are there only in place of a missing object, as the accepted formula has it; and they are there only *because* the object is missing."[33] Representation displaces the derealization of the world, and the active indifference toward representation suggests a conflict between active and reactive, not history and loss of history. Outwitting the visible is more stimulating than taking the time to mourn the

> theatrical schema in Freud's unconscious epistemological assumptions ... if it is indeed true that the primary processes know no negation, then in the economy of drives there is not, nor can there ever be, an absence of *the* mother, or especially an absence of *mother* (as absent object); nor will there ever be a person to suffer from absence. Pleasure and pain, or enjoyment, must thus be conceived as purely affirmative; one can have no recourse to the easy epistemological solution of "the lack," which is a major concession to Judeo-Platonic theology.[34]

Just Gaming's treatment of these topics partially develops the thought-form of a temporality connected to speech-acts that neutralize Western historicity, a mode of power that measures with its image of progress or regression. This latter pair of terms performs the service of an essentially bureaucratizing exclusion, blocking nonlinear formations. Art and language presentations that are indifferent toward historical times desymbolize and depsychologize events and their supposedly pure contents in an active forgetting of "I mean" and "it means," since "forgetting" allows something to come forward: "a notforgetting of time as a beat in place ... what does not get forgotten is the temporal beat that does not stop sending the narratives to oblivion."[35] The artificial symbol and the pseudo-communication (narrative model) of politicized "public cultures" gives way to a *disseizure,* where the double subjectivity of narrated and narrator (or any other version of the communication model) is rendered inoperative by a strategy of dispossession. The latter can come into existence when it is sensed that an idea, relation or object is irreducible to the privilege of unreality (e.g., the Lacanian symptom, the Marxist diagnostic). Artists and writers have to maintain an active paranoia toward integration, readability.[36]

Lyotard's arguments for effacing history thus suspend any officiality of interpretation and culture; just as the public world mostly comes under the sway of the well-connected, where time is stitched to completions, even failure, dispossession and related notions open onto the affirmation that capital and time are profoundly antithetical—the former only knows a transaction that must close, while the latter is incomprehensible as such. In relation to capitalism, artists and critics would be better off finding ways to denarrate it—undercut its narrative resubjectification. That is why, as the quotation above partially registers, the beat matters in actual social relations (one actively remembers the way someone else in conversation makes us forget time, an event in which time cancels time). Anyone can attempt to dispossess themselves of history, because this means speaking of the past in ways no one may ever have; there are reasons but no rationality for the bonding of social obligation to the performance of narrative legitimation—the latter is generally one of an irrational circulation of lethal sentimentalisms. The idea is that the chances and opportunities of fashioning different socialities are both difficult yet omnipresent: everything is received but completely worked over already; everything remains to be done.

To summarize: *Postmodern* evokes a surplus of effects, forms, impossibles—metonyms of the sublime—and not "after." The term is doubtless now irretrievable from neohistoricist applications.[37] If there is a real cultural contest over some of the senses to the name, it is over this surplus of interminable affects and effects, of sounds and ideations, sensations and energies versus their control, management, articulation and curation by managers of culture. Does this mean a decisive break with the sciences and humanities of interpretation and codification —university culture? If social bonds, including those of academia, are argumentative and not historical, then arguments which rely on questions of authoritative precedence carry no more weight than their capacity for inducing plausability. It is an open question whether universities can, sadly, survive a reign of uncontrolled speech. Lyotardian notions take us to the extreme: just as, for example, within musical practices, postmodern evokes a liquifying of the "element that selects what is musical" and severs the built-in mythic form that makes subject/object *mirrors* of one another, and that is to listen for something on the way, a generalized defiguration is unwelcomed by most going players. These practices of the figural—especially concerning narrative form—are secondary by comparison to "ephemeral traces" that might manifest a "maximum of anxiety" so that codifications of narrative resolution or semantic definitions are shortcircuited. Answers dissolve in the emergence of a *pagus,* that "place of ceaseless negotiations and ruses."[38] What matters, finally, is to engage in making moves that *expand* some part of *das Unform* (which does not exist until created).

Such proposals sketch a virtually unrealizable program for criticism: how could such practices be tolerated by an academic culture overinvested in myths of scientificity or political correctness? Who is going to valorize the setting-off of potentially uncontrollable energies? Therein lies one measure of not yet confronted relations to "history."

Baudrillard's Challenge

The self-serving narcissism of the Los Angeles and New York art communities have transformed Baudrillard's essays, the form of which is a mockery of theoretical authority (it refuses the authority of providing answers), into citations in the making of objects; indeed, artists who cite and quote Baudrillard in becoming representable have reproduced the sign-value of prestige (theoretical art is one of its names). Using Baudrillard involves the risk of one's work becoming a confirmation of his hypothesis that prestige value drives the nonproductive culture—the latter becomes productive the more it gives in to becoming a sign.

I want to take up some of the issues so far discussed and relate them to the all too-frequent misreading of Baudrillard, whose texts are uncritically regarded as defeatist, pessimistic, and cynical. Fredric Jameson speaks for many academics and artists who project that without a clear sense of a Hegelianized philosophy of history we might "fall into a view of present history as sheer heterogeneity, random difference, a co-existence of a host of distinct forces whose effectivity is undecidable."[39] This demand for *objective references*—for what, in another context, Geoffrey Hartman has wittily called "tradition as error," this demand for a foundation for meaning by which to decide for others misses that Baudrillard's writings are not driven by the mythos of providing intellectual or theoretical *comfort*. The question of form is not a historical issue but a practical one: how to write in such a way that the writing itself brings about some aspects of the very things that one wishes to occur? Now in reading Baudrillard within the context of the implausibility of philosophy of history, we do not engage with an interest in contemporizing an "immaterial subliminality" à la Lyotard, but catch the almost gnomic dimension of inquiry when "theory becomes an event in and of itself." Baudrillard's texts make—and should make—us uncomfortable since they suppose that irreducible powers (reduction being one of them) have already won out as structure, that we just cannot "get back to history" at all. The very thing Hayden White identified as the "burden of history" now comes not as literature but as thoughtful intellectual analysis.

First of all, to say that history is disappearing as a significant cultural construct is to say that our increasingly nonnarrative social forms anticulminate in a paradoxical recounting. The integrative powers of the West no longer require linear notions for social cohesion. This can be—and may have to be—articulated in narrative form although its import is nonnarrative. Baudrillard's narrative trajectory begins with an inaugurating early modern era that established the ranking of iconic

signs over indexical ones and that allowed for the maintainence of an
analogical connection between different orders or series of Being. This
was an era subject to *obliged* signs, what Louis Marin, in his *Portrait of
the King,* calls the conjunction of power and representation, whose grid
was composed of the categories of reciprocity and difference. This was a
society rent by "ferocious hierarchy, since transparency and cruelty for
signs go together. . . . signs are limited in number . . . not widely diffused.
. . . each one functions with its full value as interdiction. . . . signs therefore are anything but arbitrary."[40] This natural theater of life gave way
to the modern era of industrialization and the mechanized operations
that pervaded every series; its human pole, its subjective referent, was
manifested in indices such as are given in the philosophic order
(Cartesianism), prosthetic order (e.g., eyeglasses), arithmetized (repeatable)
and standardized.

The first order of iconic signs were absorbed by what Marx renamed
the triumph of dead labor: raw materials of every conceivable sort,
including human labor power, were subsumed by regimes of production structured by equivalence and indifference between the various
series. The disastrous synthetic unity of this period culminates with the
wars of the first half of the twentieth century, a time of lesser scope by
comparison to the Renaissance's enjoyment of doubles, mirrors, masks,
theatres and even Jesuits with their elaborate games.[41]

This second era is also that of the integrative ideologies (nationalism)
and media (film, advertising), a playing field where monetary forms
and their attending logics (e.g., accumulation, the conspicuous consumption analyzed by Veblen) successfully absorb what had been thought
to be relevant contradictions. The latter become, at worst, minor levels
of noise within the system as a whole. The discourses of value are
dissolved in a third era where "production no longer has any sense,"
where "the simulacra win out over history," where movements and
relations between series (e.g., family, work) are determined by "models
from which proceed all forms according to the modulation of their
differences. Only affiliation to the model makes sense, and nothing
flows any longer according to its end, but proceeds from the model, the
'signifier of reference,' which is a kind of anterior finality and the only
resemblance there is. . . . Not quantitative equivalences, but distinctive
oppositions. No longer the law of Capital, but the structural law of
value."[42]

This era—ours—is thus more like an oxymoronic disstructuration of
experience than any sort of reconstitution of a collective narrative
subject. Characteristic of this era is the triumph of a debt economy
that is immediately destructive as well as inevitable, and who can deny

even the "pleasures" of this debt, since it promises future destructive nonliberation? The success of liberations (sexual, workplace) have succeeded in expanding conflicts over the allocations of the system. Servicing the latter means an increasingly larger "share of cultural production" and passes to those groups aggressive enough to assert their claims as representative of absent wholes—Left and Right go on a cultural binge precisely at the moment when culture as such cannot, structurally, play the role of transforming consciousness because the latter is neutralized. An integrated Left whose business is the futile reasoning with the larger infantilized culture means that, for example, Lacanian discourse manifests a perverse Hegelianism: the derealization of criticism. No icons here (for collective values) and an evisceration of indices (the stock market going down is not causally related to deflation but to the satisfaction of certain investors) accompanies the spread of antiicons (Pop art) in which the clever and well placed further increasingly asocial agendas. The now unlimited realm of culture absorbs the category of representations: a veritable surplus of imaginary signs aimed at any receptive surface catches, as it were, the energy of the world.

In Baudrillard's construction, the dominant modernisms of critical social thought are thus stuck in a dysfunctional relation to society. Marxism and Psychoanalysis are indices of a critical impasse whose deployment by a university culture can only try—a priori nostalgia (oxymoronic?)—to rekindle an increasingly irrelevant notion of enlightenment.

A Baudrillardian "fact": the Western history incarnated at the 14000-year-old Lascaux caves with their prehistoric drawings are endangered by the carbon dioxide of human visitors; so government officials decide that only scholars and state-driven needs merit access to these monuments. Five hundred yards away from the original site is built an "exact replica," which, according to Baudrillard, is a "duplication sufficient to render both artificial."[43] This "fact" of Western ethnology or this "fourth dimension of ethnology" (simulacra = reality?), suggests that cultural significance is already a subject of curatorialism as soon as it is ex-posed, that is, as soon as it passes through the codifications of value (coding, encoding, decoding, overcoding, etc.). Any object or event that desires to represent (to further the exchange of signs rather than challenging them) destroys its own force: the fusion of culture with acts of criticism signals a demonic capital characterized by the virtually breathless destructiveness of everything becoming cultural. A statue of Brigham Young proclaiming Salt Lake as "the place" becomes the structural equivalent of Pharaonic sites. There is, for Baudrillard, an "irreparable violence towards all secrets, the violence of a civilization without secrets. The hatred by an entire civilization for its own foundations."[44] Impassed, or forced to pass between "excrescence and inertia," culture as such begins to be possible only on the basis of its repudiation of nonrepresentation, only when we make the contract that nothing in life will overrule our decision that no "sovereign object" will recreate "within us the . . . disturbance and seek to surprise us."[45] The form of sociality becomes that of an "eternal substitution of homogeneous elements" that "alone remains" (the argument of 1970's *La Société de consommation*) in the blind will to produce. Change becomes unrepresentable in any of its traditional guises. The Philosophy of History implodes.

Now it was Hannah Arendt who argued, in the "Concept of History" (1957) that modern historians had finally used up their rhetorics (*pace* Hayden White); historians, anchoring their semantic adequacy in an objectivity derived from a scientific myth of noninterference and nondiscrimination with the facts, set up the Idea of History as an autonomous process, one that thus released them from having to preface every narrative with a defense of its subjectivity. Who the historian *is* or what the historian *performed* as a social agent need not be raised if arguments are confined to whether or not the historian has got the facts right. Disengaged from everyday life and embedded in a scientific knowledge that the scientists were about to dismiss as naive (history was given to its readers as distant yet intimate, a mixture of just the right dosages of art and science), the past was more and more exterminated as it was more and more narrated by a general history thought under the form of *irreversibility*. Arendt emphasized that so many past processes are *still going off*, as it were, that it had become cognitively impossible to sustain models of causality, consequence, precursor, future implications, etc. Vico's "cycles" or Fichte's "plan" or Marx's "teleology" merely delayed the consciousness of a melancholy haphazardness that follows from the cultural circulation of historical consciousness. The irreversibility of capital perversely dehistoricizes every cultural difference that interferes.

Now on these matters Baudrillard argues that it is possible to think of Western reason as at once integrative and terrorist. Cultural institutions deemed rational are so on the basis of their functionality, of their reliance on the circulation and consumption of sign-values—prestige is superior in the realm of culture to monetarized valuations since it is even more intolerant. This means that prestige as violence has been installed as something culturally dominant: an interminable war of interpretations ensures that those involved will sharpen the identity of their conflicts and their common difference from those who do not belong to the cults of hermeneutics. The category of the outside becomes equated with death. The supposedly universal desire that belongs to each subject (the Freudian theory of cathexis) has been severed from affirmative lines of continuity and instead attached to the death instinct—ours is an era where intimacy is overthrown by information (e.g., talk-shows) and the demonics of communication. One is deemed antisocial if one refuses the immediate forms of sociality, no matter how debased.

In a kind of epiphany history has been cancelled ("what are you doing after the orgy") by processes that, when articulated, show us their unravelling (to describe the Western family is to narrate its collapse). While a "diabolical conformity" of images confounds everything, each claimant for mediation is dissolved in what Baudrillard describes as the "extermination of interstitial space" where

> When I pick up my telephone the marginal network hooks me up and keeps harping at me with the unbearable good will of that which seeks to communicate . . . Ecstasy, fascination, obscenity . . . games of the cold and cool universe . . . extraversion of all interiority . . . forced introjection of all exteriority which is implied by the categorical imperative of communication.[46]

Herzog, in the *State of Things,* tries, I think, to show something of this cinematically, where the demarcations between filmmaking and life-making dissolve: the rendezvous between an on-the-lam film producer and the director of a film within the film occurs in a parking lot offered up as a social space, where each is living out incomprehensible events to the other's impossible interpretations. This is not a case of misunderstanding à la Hitchcock (e.g., in *Vertigo,* the misunderstanding of doubles) but the texture of *incommensurable contexts:* nothing is comparable to anything else because each context of events is loaded with incomparables; yet, at the same time, everything is comparable by reduction to the sign-value of reproduction, of having to maintain the playing-out of economic codes because what matters is loss of strategic sign-value. There is not enough time for history to happen—or is there not enough space for time to be spread out?

In this dishistoricization of context—variously termed by Baudrillard *hyper-realism,* simulation, the triumph of the death instinct, the normalcy of distortion—the *category* entitled "history" disappears on the blotter of the social, nullified through all the acts that set up what John Fekete has called the "equivalence of simulations," which is to say that the modern West has succeeded in ridding itself of the *general* capacity for critical self-reflection:

the exchange economy of values unanchored to the great classical referents of theology, morality, economy or polity, solidifying operations of essences, necessities or objectives, and of the *panic search* for the lost value horizons that once cemented a more stable world of subjects and objects . . . causes and effects are uncoupled. . . . The dominant result seems to be an alogical, unaffective parataxis of recycled value referents, abstracted from originating contexts and circulating *ad libitum* in a rapidly expanding value universe of tactile manipulation, infectious contact.[47]

Such descriptions make *strange* every model of history that would *familiarize* us to the contemporaneous: steps and phases of conflict, knowledge, of spiritual quest are instead more attached to an "Evil demon driven by a silent strategy," which is capital in its pristine asociality, rather than giving us recognizable villains for all that is felt to have gone wrong with modernity. There is no question for Baudrillard of knowing the face of history, for in an object world without singular direction, where fatal strategies hold sway, where art is held out as the last or penultimate territory of valuation (which is thus a model for the destruction of values), perhaps there is only the superior irony of joining the enigma of ahistoricity.

Now the historiographic import of all this is that it reduces the philosophy of history to essentially *curatorial,* commemorative functions. This is depressing, yet challenging. The philosophy of history becomes a cultural machine that does not work, since it cannot direct and lead consciousness onto and through the paths of necessity; time is not straightened by means of its discipline. Put somewhat cruelly, since many of us are invested in the identity of some version of historicity, the language of ends and finalities in terms of the past's continuities with the present signify so many fairy tales for a history that has not happened and a future that must fail to conform to our expectations. Baudrillard reminds us in evoking one's going to the side of the object that capital is more adept than we are at initiating change. Signifiers such as "breakthrough" and "new" and "beginning" dissolve in the face of the success of the objective irrationality of our "iron cage" (the term is Weber's). "Historical consciousness," rendered *inoperative* by "the black box of the code, the molecular emitter of signals from which we have been irradiated, crossed by answers/questions like signifying radiations, tested continuously," thus becomes explicit myth. What occurs with the Lascaux caves—the replacement of the real by the artificial—becomes generalized. Thought and ideation concerning change may thus be said to pertain to the *perplexity* of meaning, not to its historicity.

Concluding Remarks

The West has enacted rules that relegate criticism to epiphenome-
nal status; the place of this relegation is mainly the university, within
which models of history have been proffered as an active, if not dominant,
ingredient of social understanding and the right to make decisions that
affect public life. There the stewardship of the collective historical
endowment of the West is widely accepted to represent a pedagogic
benevolence—our operations are unthinkable without this projection of
temporal continuity and benevolence. The modern university, with its
offerings of courses and free concerts and public lectures, with its potent
economic clout (e.g., UCLA is an economic conduit of some four billion
dollars in the Los Angeles basin) is authorized to determine the rules of
discussability. It is widely held that one cannot criticize relations between
the university and such functions until one has historicized it. Now for
Baudrillard this has become cynical, for the university is also where
those socially dominant learn to reduce ambivalence to what counts as
acceptable rationality.[48]

Consider the example of Foucault as recounted by Baudrillard. A
writer of real force of contemporary criticism, Foucault's arguments
gave way to the core myth of historicism, this idea of irreversibility—all
"history" is the "history of" power. Foucault, in believing that "power . . . is
the last term, the irreducible web, the last tale that can be told" actually
gave up on inventing a counterseduction of power or that which might
corrode it by practices that enact reversibility.[49] The Baudrillardian
antisolution is to make for ourselves, in innumerable ways, theories
that render self-serving interpretations impossible to believe. Not to
expand speech as an end, but to expand every form of objectification
that adds a space to be occupied. *Become-Disappearance:* existential
oxymoronicity. This does not involve rejection of the past nor a repowering
of it, but rather, as Nietzsche pointed out in the *Advantage and Disadvantage of History,* affirming alienation from being reduced to a story.

Such is the countermodel of becoming "ob-scenic" to actual processes
of Western narrativity. This is obviously complementary with Lyotard's
notion of "saving the honor of the name" (the Lost Cause?). But just as
Lyotard's deployment of the term *postmodern* alienates its semantics
from our temporal conventions, the fatal strategies of Baudrillard casts
the most rigorous doubt on every scheme of interpretation and meaning
that would provide contemporary players with models of what we are
doing when we do criticism. To the concepts of production, integration,
and finality that delineate a culture bent on historicizing itself into
exchange from which there is truly "no exit," there is a "seduction"

from which "we hope for surprise."[50] In joining a superlative power by which to decelerate events there is an opportunity, a perhaps, a . . .

NOTES

1. F. Fukuyama, "The End of History?" in *The National Interest* (Summer 1989), pp. 4–5.

2. See the remarks by Paula Treichler in *Remaking History*, ed. Barbara Kruger and Phil Mariani (Seattle: Bay Press, 1989), p. 66.

3. Barbara Kruger and Phil Mariani, "Introduction," *Remaking History*, p. xi.

4. Benedictus De Spinoza, *Ethics* (New York: Hafner, 1954), pp. 111–12.

5. Georges Bataille, *Visions of Excess* (Minneapolis: University of Minnesota Press, 1980), p. 222.

6. See Gilles Deleuze, *Nietzsche and Philosophy* (New York: Columbia University, 1983), p. 133–39.

7. Howard Gardener, "The Academic Community Must Not Shun the Debate Over How to Set National Educational Goals," in *Chronicle of Higher Education* (Nov. 8, 1989), p. A52.

8. Gilles Deleuze and Felix Guattari, *Anti-Oedipus* (New York: Viking, 1977), pp. 335, 337–38.

9. This is Baudrillard's parodic argument that capitalism signifies a *challenge* to be taken up, not a "history" or narrative to contest in the arena of public images. Jean Baudrillard, Günter Gebauer, *et al. Looking Back on the End of the World* (New York: Semiotexte, 1989), p. 38.

10. See the remarks by Vincent Descombes in *Modern French Philosophy*, trans. L. Scott-Fox and J. M. Harding (Cambridge: Cambridge University Press, 1980), p. 182.

11. Friedrich Nietzsche, *The Use and Abuse of History* (New York: Bobbs Merrill, 1957), pp. 23–24.

12. Cf. J. F. Lyotard, "Universal History and Cultural Differences," in *The Lyotard Reader*, ed. A. Benjamin (Oxford: Blackwell, 1989), p. 322.

13. See the very interesting article by Karl Bohrer, "The Three Cultures," in *Observations on "The Spiritual Situation of the Age,"* ed. by Jurgen Habermas (Cambridge: MIT, 1985), p. 154.

14. I have argued this at length in my *Historical Culture* (Berkeley: University of California, 1986), intro. and chap. 2. Hayden White has criticized this recently by claiming that I assert that narrative is "inherently mythical," a position I have not taken. I have argued that "historical narrative" is a mode of narration that cannot be *read and thought* at the same time without something giving: historian's cannot interrupt all the devices of "telling" that ensure the protection of the narrated story without self-destruction, a linguistic fact that bars, in my estimation, "historical discourse" from being considered "critical." In other words, there is no such thing as a "critical historical narrative" with the possible exception of narratives directed against other narratives. Cf. Hayden

White, "Literary Theory and Historical Writing," in *The Future of Literary Theory*, ed. Ralph Cohen (London: Routledge, 1989), pp. 37–41.

15. Gayatri Chakravorty Spivak, "Political Commitment and the Postmodern Critic," in *The New Historicism*, ed. Harold Aram Veeser (New York: Routledge, 1989), p. 284.

16. Charles Levin, "Carnal Knowledge of Aesthetic States: The Infantile Body, the Sign, and the Postmortemist Condition," *Canadian Journal of Political and Social Theory* II:1–2 (1987), p. 94.

17. See Hayden White. "The Politics of Historical Interpretation," in *Critical Inquiry* 9:1 (Sept. 1982), pp. 130–37.

18. Hannah Arendt, *Between Past and Future* (New York: Viking, 1961), pp. 88–89.

19. Ibid., p. 87.

20. See the remarks by Deleuze, *Nietzsche and Philosophy*, 137.

21. Jean François Lyotard, *The Differend* (Minneapolis: University of Minnesota, 1988), 70.

22. Gilles Deleuze, *Foucault* (Minneapolis: University of Minnesota, 1989), p. 119.

23. Benjamin Buchloh, "The Primary Colors for the Second Time: A Paradigm Repetition of the Neo-Avant Garde," *October*, 37 (Summer 1986), pp. 44.

24. Ibid., 50.

25. Andreas Huyssen, *After the Great Divide* (Bloomington: Indiana University Press, 1986), p. 198, takes this position.

26. Jean François Lyotard, *The Postmodern Condition* (Minneapolis: University of Minnesota Press, 1985), 81.

27. Meaghan Morris, "Postmodernity and Lyotard's Sublime," *Art and Text* 16 (Summer 1984), p. 63.

28. I am thinking in particular of the cottage industry involved in the redescription of the Euro-American avant-garde as both deformed by commodification (the Marxist element) and yet, as in Dada, working this through in resistance to the emergence of Fascism, which involves making psychoanalysis the proper interpretant. Dada et al. are reduced to Lacanian Marxism. Marxism and Psychoanalysis are joined to produce a "politically correct history" which is intended to then provide something like "leadership" in the cultural wars over interpretation.

29. Jean François Lyotard, *Des Dispositifs pulsionnels* (Paris:10/18, 1973), pp. 115–16.

30. Rey Chow, "Rereading Mandarin Ducks and Butterflies: A Response to the 'Postmodern Condition,' " *Cultural Critique* 5 (1986–87), pp. 87–88.

31. This is *not*, I should note, to ask how it is possible to put ourselves "out-of-dominance" toward both art and society. Victor Burgin proposes to link the idea of "postmodernism" with the "condition" of "feminism, Marxism, psychoanalysis and semiotics" for "critical work" within academic institutions, since feminism *etc.* are in pursuit of "projects . . . *held in common* by a constituency which may be, or may not be, large," but which nonetheless share a

"post-Romantic aesthetics" ("Some Thoughts on Outsiderism and Postmodernism," *Block* 11, [1986]). What is your definition of Romanticism? "Post" here means "after Romanticism," but exactly how is this periodization arrived at? Nonetheless, it then functions uncritically to rationalize criticism insofar as the latter is "post-romantic" = non-romantic. The end of art = a fulfillment of the "historicization" of art, where terms such as *create* and *making* are consigned to a historical oblivion.

32. Manfred Frank, *What is Neostructuralism* (Minneapolis: University of Minnesota Press, 1988), pp. 84, 86.

33. Jean François Lyotard, *The Lyotard Reader,* ed. Andrew Benjamin (London: Blackwell, 1989), p. 158. See also Lyotard's *Des Dispositifs pulsionnels* (Paris: 10/18, 1973).

34. Lyotard, *Lyotard Reader,* p. 159.

35. Jean François Lyotard and Jean-Loup Thebaud, *Just Gaming* (Minneapolis: University of Minnesota Press, 1985), p. 34.

36. Lyotard, *Dispositifs,* p. 10.

37. R. Krauss asserts that Minimalism prepared the way for the aesthetico-cognitive triumph of the demand for euphoric art, i.e., Postmodernism *continues* the economic processes of, say, overcapitalization. "The Cultural Logic of the Late Capitalist Museum," in *October* 54 (Fall 1990), pp. 4–5.

38. Lyotard and Thebaud, *Just Gaming,* p. 43.

39. Fredric Jameson, "Postmodernism of the Cultural Logic of Late Capitalism," *New Left Review* 146 (July 1984), p. 57.

40. Jean Baudrillard, *Simulations* (New York: Semiotexte, 1983), p. 84.

41. See Ibid., p. 95.

42. Ibid., p. 101; cf. Jean Baudrillard, *The Mirror of Production* (St. Louis: Telos, 1975), p. 107.

43. Baudrillard, *Simulations,* p. 18.

44. Ibid., p. 21.

45. J. Baudrillard, *Selected Writings* (Stanford: Stanford University Press, 1988), p. 204.

46. Jean Baudrillard, *The Ecstasy of Communication* (New York: Semiotexte, 1988), pp. 25–26.

47. John Fekete, "Vampire Value, Infinitive Art, and Literary Theory: A Topographic Meditation," in *Life After Postmodernism,* ed. J. Fekete (New York: St. Martin's, 1987), pp. 71–72.

48. Baudrillard, *Selected Writings,* p. 92.

49. Jean Baudrillard, *Forget Foucault* (New York: Semiotexte, 1987), p. 40.

50. Baudrillard, *Selected Writings,* pp. 186, 204.

Discussion

WALTER MCATEE: I would like to make two observations and then draw a question from them. First, you spoke of a Baudrillardian grid or a Deleuzian grid, which would most generally be characterized by the disappearance of history, an arresting of social forces, a denouncing of organic unity, and so on. The second observation refers back to Sandy Petrey's quotation from Derrida: the one about "a thousand times." Derrida was saying that he does not confine the text to a book and more importantly that he does not suspend reference to history, to the world, to reality, to being. Those are the two observations. My question is: do you believe that there is a Derridian grid that is unlike the Baudrillardian grid? Do you see something different?

COHEN: I just see a difference in emphasis. There is nothing more corrosive in terms of literary theory than Derrida. Once you have read Derrida, then reread works of literature and especially literary theory: Derrida is quite corrosive of any sort of integrated recuperative reading. On the other hand, Derrida has backed away from an engagement with social forces by comparison to Baudrillard. Baudrillard has written by now twelve or thirteen volumes on the general transformation from first to second to third order or simulacra, systems of socialization in the West. I see Baudrillard as a sort of historian; to use his terms, he is an ethnographer of Western society. He is an anthropologist of Western academic tradition. I see that as quite different from Derrida's operation. Derrida, to me, is a much more conservative figure because he has backed away from explicit critiquing. What I think connects these writers is an obsession in French culture from the end of the nineteenth century, from Rousseau forward in fact, with integration. This has been turned in France, in the writings of these people, into a major preoccupation. I also see it as an implicit existentialism—existentialism beginning all over again in the thirties and forties before Sartre's linking of existentialism to Marxism.

PETREY: Every single person you pulled in is a white, male, bourgeois, postmenopausal citizen of France.

COHEN: What do you mean by "postmenopausal"? When Deleuze and Baudrillard began writing . . .

PETREY: Right now they are all postmenopausal, which means that their intelligence was formed during a certain time; that is what I want to get at. It is extremely striking that every person you quoted fits sociologically into a very small geographic, social, chronological category. Part of the reason, I would argue, that all these people who are seeing the end of history everywhere tend to be the same age, the same class, the same everything else, in the same country, is that they are citizens of a country that has not been a serious presence on the world scene since World War I and has not gotten used to it, absolutely cannot get used to it—a country that spends a larger portion of its national budget on spreading its culture and preserving its language than any other nation in the history of the world, a country that is literally obsessed with wanting the rest of the world to think Louis XIV is still there, even though he is not, and that is coming to grips with its loss of presence in world history by saying that nobody else is present in world history either.

COHEN: What these people are trying to argue is that you cannot move from your descriptive language, situational language, analytic language, evaluative language, and so on, to a full blown theory of social history, as you are trying to do. In other words, your vulgar sociology simply is not appropriate to the task that these writers have taken up over the past forty years. Deleuze has been working on these problems since the forties.

PETREY: I agree. All these people had their sensibilities formed after it took Germany exactly four weeks to beat France.

COHEN: If these people make identification collectively (I don't think they do), it is not to Louis XIV but to American beatniks. If you wanted to do a real sociology of modern French theory, then you would want to look at its American idealizations, Deleuze in particular.

PETREY: The major difference between them is that the American beat-niks say, "America is present on the world stage and we don't like that presence, and we're dropping out." What they are saying is that France is not present on the world stage, therefore there is no world stage.

COHEN: No, no. The real difference here is the reading of capitalism. Baudrillard has argued that the ultimate myth shared by both liberal-ism and Marxism is the idea of a conjunction of subjective experiences with objective processes. This will generate the possibility of revolution-ary situations, counterrevolutionary situations, and so on. Now in Baudrillard's terms, which would be Derrida's as well, this is nothing but a postponement and a deferral of immediate challenging to the system. Their reading of capitalism is not that it is a neutralizing if bothersome or irritating social force, but that it is itself directly, immedi-ately cynical. Capitalism is the deconstructive agent in the modern world. That is their sociological construction, and I take that quite seriously.

LAWRENCE LIPKING: It does seem to me that Derrida is quite different from this, and one quick way to talk about it would be to suggest that the criticism of history is a criticism of something in the name of nothing. I mean in the name of liberation, which always already starts assuming different kinds of historical models. If I start to think about what it would be like to embrace the joy of freedom from history, I start thinking of performance art, minimalist music. There is plenty of stuff I can think of; but already the reason that I start thinking of it is to set up a kind of historical scenario. Even in the scenario of performance art and minimalist music as the cutting edge of the new antihistorical embracing of timelessness, of presentness, there is already a helpless reversion to a category that is in one way or another historical. Nothing will not replace something, is all I have to say.

COHEN: The argument is that we are always going to take events and reinsert them in some narrative or other, even if it is an antinarrative. The question is, can artists make works that are interesting enough so that in and of themselves the works alienate that historical language from hooking onto it? That is what they are trying to work out. And here it really is a question of existentialism within artistic practice: because this then involves the idea that the artist has to be in some sense, in Nietzsche's language, superhistorical, has to anticipate in advance that the historical consciousness is going to recuperate and to build that in. That is why Lyotard constantly returns to Cézanne, whom he thinks is a model for this anticipation of historical recuperation and who resists it as much as possible. I agree with you that this is not going to become dominant. Didn't I begin by saying that the notions here are not dominant but represent in contemporary theory, as far as I can see, the major alienations from the standard historical alternatives of left, central, and right?

JOHN BRENKMAN: It seems to me that all these things, as you have laid them out, are instances of a hyperbolic interpretation of the end of the philosophy of history. What you are calling history and the disappearance of history is a particular conception of and a particular mode of historical thinking, namely that one can tell a great narrative of the history of Western civilization in which there is an interlinking of necessity, sequence, implacable movement through time, a coherent overall pattern even if it is only discoverable after the fact, and so on. To abandon that, first of all, is not such a very new impulse: you go back to Nietzsche as a precursor moment. But the reason I want to say it is a hyperbolic interpretation is that there are a series of claims that seem to be consistent with the recognition of the demise of the philosophy of history but have been extended into another kind of claim, and that is where everything gets fuzzy.

I want to propose another kind of question that is very important to investigate in historical terms. For example, I can think of at least three competing models of the historical interpretation of Fascism. One was that it was the last stage of capitalism; that was the orthodox Marxist interpretation of Fascism in the thirties and forties. Second was that it was a moment of regression in the history of Western civilization. Third would be that this is one of the possible political formations of modern society; nothing in the movement of time guarantees that it will happen or that it will not happen. Now I am very sympathetic to that third view. When you move over to that, ninety percent of what you have to do to fill it out requires what to me looks like historical thinking. But it does not imply this philosophy of history.

COHEN: The ambiguity is that all three of these people are talking about a process, a nonhistorical process, a process of forces. The dominant force is capital. It is nonhistorical in the sense that it does not give rise to any particular phasing or necessary direction. Lyotard in the *Differend* puts it this way: capitalism is an economic genre whose very operation is to eliminate all other genres. There is no time frame with that. Capitalism is to them a force; that means it is always active without being historical. Baudrillard calls it the challenge; capitalism is a challenge to me: how can I think today, what can I say today, what can I do today, in order to expand an existence or develop an existence? Now that is quite different from normal readings of capitalism that restrict it to certain activities. They are suggesting that we have to take up a much more activist view. I think the attitude that they are all supporting is localism, site-specific criticism. Deleuze says that we are finished with general recipes. Foucault puts this in the language of the local intellectual as opposed to the rational universal intellectual.

BRENKMAN: But their diagnosis is completely global. It is the most global account of events in our world that you could come from.

COHEN: Your point is well taken. I see that as a paradox that is itself a part of the playing field.

There are two extremes in historical representation I should specify here. One is normal academic research and is generally positivistic. It begins in the past and remains in the past. A historian takes a problem and handles it or treats it within the existing literature and establishes a certain correctness or a narrative. It starts in 1500 and ends in 1502, or whatever. There is another extreme to historical representation, another type of book altogether, which historians write all the time, which are called general histories as opposed to special histories. Now the critique here is directed primarily against general histories. Deleuze is in effect saying: let your ideas loose. You do not have to contain them by models of representation. There is a surplus here of the signified and also a surplus of the signifier. Really only by repression do we create representation.

MICHAEL PALENCIA-ROTH: Your notion of history seems to be limited first to Hegel and Marx in the nineteenth century and second to Western notions. I wonder about other cultures and other traditions which have concept of history—which have histories—that do not fit into these levels. I wonder about oral history, oral traditions, and not only among preliterate people but also among people who come into contact with literate society and continue to maintain the oral traditions together with a very profound history. And I wonder also about, say, the Indian concept of history. Your concept of history is very limited.

COHEN: I am only dealing with a particular Western problem.

PALENCIA-ROTH: But then you are not dealing with history.

COHEN: Of course not. Nobody can deal with History. Nobody can make a statement about History. That is impossible; it is a semantic impossibility. I am talking about the concept of history as it is articulated in Western political and academic language.

PALENCIA–ROTH: An Indian would look at this particular moment and say, "Oh, but this is just a speck on the eternity of history and its time."

COHEN: That's fine. Then I could argue with that person about what do they mean by, how do they use, the term *history?* What is embedded in it? What is implied by it? What does it connote, evoke, and so on? We can get into a discussion about it.

What I tried to do in my book is to separate the word *history* from other terms such as *past, context, situation.* I think that is exactly what blocks us from thinking specifically, in a precise way, about a particular situation and having a much more particular and specifiable language for talking about differences within pasts, noncomparable pasts, and so on. My opposition is to the language. Let us take Fredric Jameson again: he says that history as such is about the struggle of freedom and necessity. Now that is the kind of statement that makes me go berserk; because if that is so, all I can do before that idea is to say, "Oh my God, here is the power I'm obligated to pay attention to." He does not say history is about leisure; history is about escape from social traps; history is about freedom and necessity. To me it is just marching orders. He is just getting me to line up with the existing political players. What I am trying to say is that none of us is obligated to line up with the existing political players. What we are obligated to do is to think for ourselves and take the full consequences of that kind of thinking. That is why I am still concerned with Neitzscheist existentialism.

BRENKMAN: I do not think you can get enough justification and backing for the Lyotard, Deleuze, Baudrillard position by saying that this rescues us from statements like Jameson's. Lots of things rescue us from statements like Jameson's.

COHEN: Well, Jameson's argument is implicitly directed against any anti- or non- or post- or pre-historical attitude. To me it's a disaster that Marxism linked up with historicism. I have no problem with Marxism as social critique. The critique of commodification seems to me perfectly appropriate. Unpaid labor seems to me to be the consummate normalizing activity of capitalism. I just think that to associate that critique of capital with a theory or (as you put it quite well) philosophy of history is to eliminate the critical insight. Because if the critical insight means anything, it means that we have to be involved with an immediate criticism, immediate practices of resistance, not historical anticipations of what will be possible next week. It's that deferral to the future that never happens that disturbs me.

LAURO MARTINES: Would it be bad to summarize your statements thus: that all artistic and intellectual labor that is in any way institutional thereby collects about it a kind of officialese and is therefore, from your point of view, censurable and to be eliminated? And what we want to do always is to fight, to resist the institutionalization of all thought and of the artistic process? But may I add to this, however, that the institution, the academic institution, generated you. The system has released you to attack the system, to try to undermine it.

COHEN: My critique is of the academic mode of presentation. I don't have any problem with people studying and doing research; those seem to me perfectly valid activities. What I object to is the mode of presentation. I think it's a disaster for historians that they have resorted to the narrative mode. There are many interesting things that can be said about many pasts in a nonnarrative way. What has happened, however, is that from the nineteenth century forward, with the institutionalization of history writing in academia, the mode of writing has itself become a control mode. And I think this is something that the professors are going to have to answer for at some point. In fact, we are answering for it in terms of the literacy rates in the United States. It's no accident that in the last forty years, as there has been a proliferation of academic writing, fewer and fewer people can read what we write. The key fact here is this ambivalent relationship between academic productivity and social dysfunctionality.

Part 2

Lauro Martines

The Politics of Love Poetry
in Renaissance Italy

The cultivated love poetry of the Italian Renaissance was something of a public exercise, often the activity of important men, a forum for figuring themselves out or plotting their next moves, and not seldom a bitter meditation on the fruits and failures of worldly ambition. Heart and scheming head came together in the verse, mingling the desire for perfection in love with thinking about the prizes and labors of "this blind world"—a commonplace of the time. Here the question of sexual politics was not preeminent.

No Italian poet was likely to think about love without also contemplating larger or "higher" matters. In the elite love verse of the age—Petrarchan, courtly, elegant, elevated—poets reflected inevitably on *fortuna,* time, death, nature, morality, and their lot in life; but frequently their lot had a prominent political feature, as is evident, for example, in the lives of Saviozzo, Rosello Roselli, Lorenzo de' Medici, Niccolò da Correggio, Gaspare Visconti, and Pietro Bembo.

All the courtly love poetry of the age carried a political charge because it was a poetry of compliment. A continuous rainfall of high compliment for the beloved made it courtly, that is, of the court: a ritual mode of speech most appropriate to the courts of princes. Flattery, eulogy, and verbal tribute was the idiom of negotiation and transaction at court. Where kings had an ancient standing, compliment might be less lofty or less strained, unless there was a female monarch, as in the case of Queen Elizabeth. But in Italy's fifteenth-century courts, where most power had been grabbed or usurped in recent times, where that power was nervously absolute, and where touchy neighbors were likely to covet or resent it, compliment became the currency of everyday speech, common even between spouses. It looked to legitimating the holders of power; it placated them; and it acknowledged brute realities. Compliment, however, was also knowledge, a way of worldly wisdom; and it was the way to curry favor—to sue for pension, place, or sinecure. Letters to Italian Renaissance princes are unctuous with compliment.[1]

Introduce the love object, the lady of refined amatory verse, into this world, and she must at once attract all the metaphors and adjectives so readily applied to the prince and also—if with some shifts in accent—to God, saints, and angels. We have here entered into a semiotic field where the paramount terms or signifiers are limited. And light, the radiance of light, is the chief of these: the divine light, the light in the alleged wisdom or justice or generosity of the prince, and the light of my lady's eyes. The lady's light purifies and elevates the base, or kindles love, or rouses joy in all those around her, or brings—in its oxymoronic impact—both death and life to the lover.[2] In part, doubtless, this was all a game of words. Poetry can live off or be spun out on crazy signifiers. And in seeming to point to nothing in the "real" world, love poetry may strike us as the least referential of all literary forms. For so often the signified is the heart, itself a signifier, a fiction or metaphor, a mere principal sign in the sign system of amatory scripture.

Yet the heart of the Renaissance poet also held a place in the real world. It was himself. He invoked it constantly to sum himself up and to signify a social identity that was all caught up in city life, in court life, or in political intrigue, whether at the top level of government or in neighborhood and guild politics.[3]

I have said that all love verse of courtly stripe carried a political charge. If God, prince, and madonna (mea domina, "my lady") were tied to the same substantives and adjectives, and if those ties were all cast in metaphor along the same lines, then the lady was being endowed with divine virtues; but she also had something of the power, tyranny, stateliness, and opacity of the prince. Not surprisingly, therefore, poets speak of her lordship, tyranny, dominion, or sovereignty (signoria, tirannia, dominio, sovranità); they refer to her as "my lord" (mio signore); and they speak of themselves, the lovers, as subjects and servants (suggetti, servi) held in servitude or bondage (servitù) to her.[4] The equations were also reversible: in verse to or for the prince, he was assigned the qualities that made him worthy of love, along with a lashing of physical love, as when a servant said to his Lord: I belong to you body, soul, blood, and bone.[5] In the assumptions of the age, servants and subjects owed a kind of tangible love to their princes and lords.

On the evidence of Renaissance poetry, systems of literary signification cannot be hived off into zones divorced from the historical world. The hyperbolic compliments rained on madonna belonged, in the trans-actions of everyday life, to God and to the prince or powerful patron: to God in prayer and supplication,[6] and to the prince or patron in daily greetings, in casual comment, and in all suits for favor. Like it or not, behind the image of the beloved in poetry—the divine part of the equation to one side—there was always a hint or echo of the prince or of the organized power of the community. If love poetry was to have efficacious conventions and be persuasive, it had to enlist the most compelling signs in the linguistic system, and these were keyed to prayer and power, God and politics. They were compelling in their referentiality. Thus Francesco Accolti:

> The eyes borne by my lord on her face
> were the brightest stars in the middle of heaven.[7]

Niccolò da Correggio writes:

> The lofty qualities, the noble blood and polite ways
> that make you scatter fountains of grace
> would, I think, move mountains as they do me,
> and cause rivers to stop just to look upon thee.[8]

Rosello Roselli cannot speak from fear to "my dear lord," though "Love has led me [in audience] into your presence":

> my life is in your power (potenza).
> You are lovely, gracious, and lordly (signorile),
> and you see that I serve you with utmost faith.[9]

Francesco degli Alberti tells us that the paramount social qualities "convene" in his lady:

> loveliness, nobility, lofty ways,
> dignified movement, a lordly look,
> eyes lit by a heavenly light,
> and all her other actions charming and gentle.[10]

The language of these passages—idealized because it is compliment—endows the lady with power and compelling social presence. But the diction is also realistic and even practical, because compliment is courtesy; it is the way of the world at court and among the powerful in Italy's urban oligarchies. Light, the sun, the stars, courtly bearing, exceeding might, nobility: in supplications and letters, all these attributes are obsessively ascribed to God, saints, princes, and lords—but they are here given to the lady to make her seem powerful or even transcendent (thus elevating the poet-lover), or else the job of investing her with the needed penumbra and dignity could not be done. She must have the supreme terms of eulogy in the language, and these could only belong, in realistic terms, to God and the prince. The image of the lady is thus a treasury of political and supernal qualities. Without the actual practice, then, of politics and religion in the community, she could not have been as she is in the poetry.

Yet compliment is rendered by means of generalization, or it cannot transact its social message. It is a public mode, all the more so in the fifteenth and sixteenth centuries, when private and personal space was far more limited. Owing to its generalizing nature, compliment could suggest a diversity of specific contents and so lend itself to a variety of purposes. As generalized compliment, therefore, the highbrow code of amatory verse—that is light, sun, stars, lordship, transfixed heart, ice and fire, rivers of tears—successfully served different individual ends, and this in part is why it was so vital and dominant for so long. Codified in the early and mid-fourteenth century, and best exemplified in the ingenuity and high polish of Petrarch's *Canzoniere,* the code prevailed for more than two centuries. When they were moved to write verse, leading noblemen, Venetian aristocrats, republican oligarchs, secretaries to princes, judges and lawyers, and educated merchants and bankers all turned to the conventions of the high amatory code, in the effort to articulate the experience of love.

Here, however, the sameness stopped. They drew largely on the same idiom, but their experience or dream of love was different. How could this not be so, given their social and regional diversity? Evidently, they were using the idiom in different ways.

In the fifteenth century, lawyers at Bologna and Florence used it to mark themselves off from the plebeian crowd.[11] As commitment and vision, the idiom provided an ethicosocial identity and bonded them together in male friendships. Lorenzo de' Medici, the unofficial lord of republican Florence, used his love poetry to win acclaim, to extend his and Florence's cultural influence,[12] and to strike a polished artistic and intellectual stance, as if to suggest that the delicacies of the elite amatory idiom were his consuming passion, rather than his domineering control of the Florentine political scene. Pietro Bembo (1470–1547), a Venetian aristocrat and careerist who finished life as a cardinal, had recourse to the code of love to make his way at the courts of Ferrara, Urbino, and Rome, to cultivate friendships there, and even, in the second part of his *Rime* (his lyric sequence), to enact a public purging of his "sinful" amorous life.[13] Bembo's *Rime* were also a campaign in cultural politics, designed to exemplify the force and elegance of the highbrow code (Petrarch's language) as the ideal idiom for vernacular love poetry. In the late fifteenth century, Niccolò da Correggio and Gaspare Visconti were leading noblemen at the court of Milan, courtiers par excellence. Compliment and *cortesia* (polite or courtly ways) pervaded their way of life, and so the language of love poetry was for them a language of contemporary experience.[14] They worked the urgencies of ambition and daily court life into their sonnet sequences by means of epithet, simile, metaphor, and rumination. Theirs is a living, malleable, uneven idiom, unlike Lorenzo de' Medici's in his *Canzoniere,* which shuns daily life and distances the love experience by its excessive artistry. In the 1430s and 1440s, a failed Florentine banker, Francesco di Altobianco degli Alberti, used the elevated idiom of love as symbolic action: as an escape from, or a "campaign" against, the corrupt policies of a loathed and tricksy oligarchy.[15] Again, in the years around 1400, Saviozzo of Siena produced love poetry in the elite idiom on request or commission.[16] Secretary in the course of his life to several petty princes, he was occasionally invited to rhapsodize in verse over a girl, in action denoting one of the ways of cultivated, highborn men at arms. But high compliment in this milieu easily turned into a proud, predatory form. A glance at a few particulars here instantly reveals the political and social elasticities of the amatory code.

In Pisa one day in 1403, the commander of the occupying forces, the Roman nobleman, Gian Colonna, who was holding the city for the Visconti of Milan, caught sight of a good-looking, upper-class girl as she was standing on a bridge facing the sun. Manuscript notes claim that he fell in love with her then and there, whereupon he had his servitor, Saviozzo, pen a *canzone* celebrating her beauty in the elite idiom of love. Here she is identified with the sun, light, blessedness, noble blood, and an "immortal language." Her eyes hold "triumph and empire" (*triunfo e impero*), and "a look sweet and intent / enough to move stones and reverse the flow of waters."[17] If we are to believe manuscript captions, Colonna soon got his way with the girl. One of the most telling passages in the poem is a mixture of elite idiom and haughty politics, as it asks rhetorically:

> What power or art,
> in a city now so disagreeable and vile,
> deprived of all nobility,
> agreed to the birth of such beauty here?[18]

Pisa had once been a renowned and proud city.

We may now more fully appreciate the uses of the privileged love idiom. Men from different social and political backgrounds—generally from the upper ranks—used it for differing purposes; but the process of rhetorical enablement, the basic strategy, was much the same. Petrarchan and *stilnovista* in its lineaments, the idiom uplifted the entire subject (love, beloved, and lover) by calling in the semiotics of God and prince, of power both temporal and divine. This ennoblement or aggrandizement (*amplificatio*) was the trick that went to mark off love, beloved, and lover; the trick that accorded these a special moral and social prowess, setting them off from the rest of humanity and endowing them with a vision, a transcendent status, and even their own speech.[19] Subject and actors were thus catapulted above the ordinary rules of conduct, to have singular ties with *fortuna,* with the heavens, with death, suffering, beauty, nobility, speech, pity, and fidelity. The verse could, however, highlight any one of these. Like lawyers at Bologna, the Florentine attorney (*notaio*), Niccolò Tinucci (c. 1390–1444), held that his dedication to love was antiplebeian and a negation of the base greed for money:

> If in desiring I burn, blaze, or freeze,
> whether my thought be sweet or bitter,
> what is this to envious money-grubbers? . . .
>
> And if I cook or break and undo myself
> for the eyes I love so much and hold so dear,
> why yet does the common herd (*la plebe*) want me to learn
> to keep its empty and deceitful ties?[20]

Courtiers accented *fortuna,* suffering, fidelity, and frustration, thereby opening the idiom up to input and perception gleaned from quotidian experience. Bembo and Lorenzo de' Medici—looking to a whole cultural program—emphasized the elements of beauty, nobility, and speech, in addition to the pains of love; and as their *canzonieri* progressed, they introduced a strong moralistic note, to go with the sense of their own developing public images and responsibilities. Other poets, again, such as Francesco degli Alberti, could turn to the images of the idiom in all their ideal perfection, letting these serve as negations, however symbolic, of the hated political order around them.

The essential stance was elitist. Love was the kingdom (*regno,* their word) of the privileged. Lovers were a moral elite; but here was also a mystification, for the argument and devices that privileged them depended, as I said, on the semiotics of power. The noble language of lovers would have functioned as an antilanguage in the society of commoners,[21] among the *vulgo* or mass of people. *Vulgo* was one of the most recurrent and essential terms in the entire lexicon of the amatory code. The *vulgo* (the vulgar mass) represented the very opposite of the loved lady's exalted qualities, the opposite of all the virtues of devotion and high-mindedness in the lover. For the poet Gambino of Arezzo, writing about 1470, love is naturally associated with the virtuous young, the gentle, the gay, and the lordly or the aristocratic (*signorile*); whereas *la plebe* or plebeians serve as love's foil and opposite.[22] So in a world of courts and oligarchies, love, beloved, and lover belonged to the caste of the privileged; and if the powerful were stained by sin and corruption, this was no indictment of the utopian velleities of poets.

I have suggested that *fortuna* was a point of thematic concentration in the politics of love poetry.[23] Here was a bastard notion that could be claimed by any man in distress—beleaguered prince, foiled lover, failed courtier, bankrupt merchant, poor man or beggar. It was rarely claimed in triumph. The notion was ancient, protean, slippery, and likely to be used self-servingly. But beggars did not write about it and men who were well-off, or who had been well-off, did. In the sixteenth century, an age of shattering political catastrophe for Italy, Italian political thinking was rife with the notion of *fortuna*.[24] The upper-class male lover and the professional poet were also well served by it. For being dependent on patronage, the latter was subject to the whims and changing needs of court or wealthy patron, hence he might be readily drawn into wailing against his ill fortune. As an image or dramatic stroke, however, fortune was especially associated with courts, wealth, and high place, because the fall from loftiness, the fall of princes and mighty folk, furnished the most remarkable illustration of the workings of fortune and the great turning of its relentless wheel.[25] The upper-class lover easily invoked *fortuna*, because the attendant imagery raised his complaining lover's plight up to a setting in which his woes involved suprapersonal forces, such as nature and destiny. His loving, therefore, is always a matter of life and death, war and peace, or keen anxiety—an enterprise in which the wounds always verge on being mortal. St. Sebastian's punctured body, St. Paul's being struck down by the light, and even the betrayal of Christ may all serve to metaphorize the condition of the suffering lover at the mercy of Love, his lady, and *fortuna*.[26]

The dialogue with or meditation on *fortuna* is in the self-ennoblement mode. Despite all the woes involved, when in the ritual of tormented love, none but the worthy or privileged are picked by *fortuna* for the engagement with love. This leads our discussion to a view of amatory scripture as an exercise in self-defining. The idiom is of course self-promoting, but it is also a means of self-analysis and self-definition; and in this labor, as we shall see, the elite stereotypes of the age come into play.

The *my lady* of our scripture usually has two different phases or manifestations, which elicit either the lover's praise or lamentation. In one phase, she is the model of moral and social qualities; in the other, she is icy, cruel, or pitiless as a wild animal. Her lordly, political, and domineering features may belong to either incarnation. But in contemplating her—and this posture is often one of self observation and reflection—the lover is perpetually defining himself. In a sonnet by Gaspare Visconti, a *didascalia* or caption tells us that a lady had deemed herself offended for no reason at all by the man whom she affected to love. The young lover addresses her:

> Like one desiring confession,
> I have examined my conscience well
> And find I have committed no sin,
> Nothing to turn your heart in anger against me.
> From before the time I was set on fire, I knew
> That I was not much honored by my star,
> That you would have to condescend to welcome me,
> Heaven having strewen in you all virtues.[27]

The poet identifies the self-defining procedure: it is the mode of religious confession, through which the lover gains self-knowledge and then, in effect, measures himself up against madonna. This matchup or comparison is fundamental to the entire canon. No love poem—sonnet, octave, song, or other—is possible without it. But in the matchup, the lover begins to draw some of her attributes to himself by means of aspiration, contrast, and recognition; for in recognizing her, he is already of the party of the elect. Thus, according as he defines himself, he also constructs himself: there is little to choose between these. All the highbrow love poetry of the age keeps defining and redefining the lover by his relations and proximity to, or distance from, her. When Bembo says to his lady, "I go about dear to myself only because of you," or says of her, "I like this life for nothing other / Than for her and her mercy, / Through whom alone I distance myself from the ruck,"[28] he has hitched all he is to her, who both provokes and overcomes all his schisms and self hatreds.

Insofar as the lady's qualities are purely moral (and heavenly), she appears to transcend politics and social class; so too, therefore, does the lover. But she also has, as we have seen, the political attributes of lordship and *dominium*, as well as other properties of capital importance in the verse. In her manifestation as model, the lady's appearance and conduct are courtly or upper class. She continually attracts the signifiers for certain of the dominant stereotypes of the age: *gentilezza, cortesia, leggiadria, arte, bel parlare, altera, nobile, saggia, peregrina,* and a synecdoche like *bianca* or *delicata mano* (nobility, polite ways, grace, artfulness or know-how, beauty of speech, dignified or proud, noble, knowing, uncommon or elegant, and white or delicate hand). She is or has all of these attributes to a degree rarely, if ever, seen among mortals.[29] Even the favored terms for the lady's beauty, *beltà* and *bellezza,* are not socially neutral, because the canon uses them only of women of the upper classes. Clearly, therefore, in the compass of item-ized signification, the scripture of love posits its own social place in the worldly hierarchy, and it is with the beautiful, the powerful, the well-born, and the educated. Poets and lovers look down on the *vulgo* from their select position, even if they in turn must look up to my lady, who "deigns" or "condescends"—in one of the most important verbs of the code (*degnare* vs. *sdegnare*)—to look down upon them.

In Milan, reacting to criticism from one of the more vernacular poets, Gaspare Visconti does not deign to name him and lashes out instead against the *vulgo,* who are alleged to find his love poetry obscure.[30] Love poets claimed that the mass of men cannot understand the high office or vision of love, being too steeped in ignorance. Only half in jest, Niccolò da Correggio asks rhetorically: if, as Love desired, Jove himself was guilty of theft, rape, incest, and adultery,

> how does it happen,
> o ignorant ruck (*vulgo*), that you cry wrong
> if a man of flesh, young, and a lord,
> seems transformed by the effects [of love]?[31]

As we noted, the Bologna poets are most emphatic about having their devotion to the love code distinguish them from the ignorant multitude.

But the *vulgo* in our poetry do not function as an unresonant mass who put an end to discourse. They are most of the society, the opposi-tion that helps to highlight and define love. In the sweet harmony of her speech, in her gracious or elegant ways, in her natural pride and wisdom, and so in her negation of everything mean and common (*vile* and *vulgo*), the lady stands in for courtly civilization: the manners and mores of the urban upper classes. Thus one poet declares:

> Love makes a man go about more joyfully,
> frequenting people more noble than himself,
> shunning matters low and base (*cose vile*).[32]

And others write:

> how much this lady excels the font and river
> of grace and correct speech (*parlar corretto*).[33]

> In her are charm and polite ways (*cortesia*),
> grace, magnificence, and nobility.[34]

She is:

> knowing, courteous, honest, and well-mannered (*costumata*).[35]
> "Who knows not the world's great good,
> Look upon my lady and see
> Honor, excellence, beauty, and grace.[36]

In effect, she is the touchstone of civility, even indeed as a courtly nymph in a fantasy countryside.[37] And in the society of the verse, in city-state society, this denoted the politics of oligarchy or a princely court. That is to say, truly to understand my lady entailed a whole working assumption about power—namely, that in human communities power is best exercised by the one or the happy few. It cannot be an accident that all the leading love poets of the age were either political insiders or men of profoundly conservative views: for example, Bembo, Lorenzo de' Medici, Poliziano, Niccolò da Correggio, Gaspare Visconti, Leonardo Giustiniani,[38] Saviozzo, Francesco degli Alberti, and others.

The elite amatory code, as I have called it, was often obsessively dialogic in manner, and here again the interest in self-defining comes forth clearly. The lady is nearly always silent, of course; but the poet-lover customarily addresses her either directly or indirectly, as if in reasoned but determined argument. In this give-and-take (for her answers are shadowed in the manner and variations of his responses), the lover uses a select, polished, and in part ritual language. She may be the lofty paradigm, but he and the genre or mode make and unmake her. The ritual part of the dialogue obeys the expected conventions of the mode, without which there can be no school, tradition, or style of highbrow love verse. For the male to love rightly in upper-class circles, and to recognize that feeling as the real thing, certified as such by the society as well, was to love in accord with the standard *topoi* of the code. The verse dialogue, therefore, had to feature some of the following: the oxymorons of ice and fire or death and resurrection, the blazon of the lady's beauties, or her social, moral, and political insignias. Since the poet represented all these matters by means of language, *he* was defining things, setting the tone, assigning the attributes, and casting the metaphors—in short, he was vitalizing the imagery and the ideal. As a social vessel, accordingly, the highbrow amatory code is both an elaborate statement of social identity and a school or language. It is a statement of social identity because it enunciates a complete code of conduct not only in love but also, by extension, in the larger society, at court, and in personal relations. I refer to the code's emphasis on *cortesia, umanità, pietà,* or *mercede, fedeltà, servizio,* and *sdegno* (politeness, a gentle or courteous humanity, pity, loyalty, service, and scorn or disdain for everything base or socially demeaning); but all this, to be sure, in an affluent setting where compliment was fundamental. The code even teaches ways of introspection and reflection by linking the track of self-awareness to *fortuna,* pride, ambition, time, patience, the vanity of human affairs, and other such themes. But the means of confirming or acquiring the implied social identity resides in the language of the high scripture of love, an idiom that begins with the recognition of the status quo by its essential stress on compliment and flattery. It works by paying verbal tribute to the mighty. God gets His due, but so also do princes, noblemen, oligarchs, patrons, patron saints, and my lady. From this viewpoint, the privileged love poetry of the Italian Renaissance may rightly be seen as a program of social and political celebration or even propaganda—sly, seductive, and tenaciously long-lived.

The business of getting at the history *in* poetry calls for a tricky procedure, and no short paper can begin to reveal the required turns and detours. I shall close, therefore, by simply listing the essentials and touching on a cluster of problems.[39]

1. I take for granted that all writing, apart from the strictly imitative, is of its time and somehow expresses that time.
2. All historians deal with a vanished world, that is, a world that was; yet they purport in their labors to be getting at it, although—needless to say—it is a world that has to be reconstructed perpetually in the minds of historians and their readers.
3. *Quattrocento* Italy is a world in minds (and in books), but there is remarkable consensus as to what it is among those who know about it.
4. The way to relate *Quattrocento* poetic texts to their vanished world is to move from their language, rhetoric, and imagery over to other parts of that world. It is a cognitive movement from one semiotic system to another, or from one order of perception and cognition to another. The point is that such a movement, a labor of imaginative reconstruction, is characterized by fine and complex negotiations.

I have focused on the idealized image of the beloved in amatory verse in order to underline certain political and public features. But the moment we begin to examine the whole lamenting or complaining side of this verse, we encounter an adversarial stance, where the poet-lover obsessively marks the separation from my lady, above all in her refusal to show any pity or understanding for his alleged suffering of the woes of love. The ritual language of woe opens up the dialogue to a host of historical questions, such as that of the love code's relation to fifteenth-century marriage, to household organization, to adultery, homosexuality, misogyny, religious belief, and relations between the sexes—the arena of so-called sexual politics. Here, in complaint, the misogyny and posturing of the educated male is often much in evidence, in a plaint that brazenly turns the society's patriarchal structures upside down, to reveal a hapless, powerless, pitiable male lover. There was no such thing, for this was negated or made most improbable by all the lineaments of everyday life.[40] Now my lady is a *ladra*, a thief who has stolen away the lover's heart. He may lick his love wounds out in a wild and mountainous region, and such a venue then becomes a foil for the evil city or the corrupt princely court (yet another political statement).[41] But whatever the venue, whether far from friends or among them in the city, the self-division of the lover and his separation from the lady are a slanting, symbolic reenactment of the relations between men and women in the urban society of Renaissance Italy. At this point the political face of our love poetry, though from a different angle, comes back fully into view. For the lover's self-division, which is also indeed his separation from the lady, is the social story of male and female living together in a world where all the major decisions of daily life—the decisions concerning them in public as in private matters—belong to the prerogative of the male. Church and state both preach and legislate this. Consequently, the image of the lordly, domineering woman—a fiction of the male lover—turns out to be the roundabout, inverted picture of the dominant upper-class male in his presence as *paterfamilias* and as master in society and politics. In fashioning a formidable loved one—paradoxically a peer of sorts, although lady and lamenting male must seem unequal—the poet is driven to figure her as the light, as a tyrant, a powerful lord, or a haughty and glacial creature. In fact, *mutatis mutandis*, he can only fashion her after his own image. Then, owing to her supposed cruelty, indifference, or scorn, he passes gradually over to his songs of blame and rebuke. And having started by soliciting her pity, he ends either by condemning her or by a moralistic rejection of earthly love. The rejection of love is well illustrated in the *canzonieri* of Rosello Roselli, Lorenzo de' Medici, Gaspare Visconti, and Pietro Bembo. Condemning the lady may easily turn into bitterness and misogyny, as we see in Roselli's *ballata*, "o falsa, pien d'inganni e senz fede / femina maladetta" (o false, faithless and full of deceptions / woman cursed).[42] At least one bourgeois poet from Bologna, an attorney, sought to idealize his own wife as his lady: an egregious misuse of the highbrow amatory idiom.[43] In a tribal world of family-arranged marriages, treasured virginities, visceral family fidelities, costly dowries, and weighty property considerations, married couples were no company for the language of refined love, which was the negation or the discontented ghost of this tightly regulated ethnology. And in any case, exceptions apart, women's education had not generally prepared them fully to understand this language. Down to about the year 1500, this was a public idiom for the self-definition and self-realization of the educated upper-class male. In this sense too the idiom was profoundly political.

NOTES

1. See, for example, Giuseppe G. Ferrero, ed., *Lettere del Cinquecento* (Torino: UTET, 1948); and Kathleen Theresa Butler, ed., *"The Gentlest Art" in Renaissance Italy: An Anthology of Italian Letters, 1450–1600* (Cambridge: Cambridge University Press, 1954).

2. On the lady's light, see any *canzoniere* of the period, passim: for example by Buonaccorso da Montemagno, Rosello Roselli, Lorenzo de' Medici, Niccolò da Correggio, Gaspare Visconti, and Pietro Bembo, in the editions cited below.

3. See Lodovico Frati, ed., *Rimatori bolognesi del Quattrocento* (Bologna: Romagnoli dell'Acqua, 1908), p. 186, on the poet and attorney, Cesare di Matteo Nappi, directly implicated in the murder of a rival over a major controversy in Bologna's guild of notaries. Francesco di Altobianco degli Alberti was hounded for years by Florentine tax officials. For an example, see Elio Conti, *L'imposta diretta a Firenze nel quattrocento* (Florence: Instituto Storico Italiano per il Medio Evo, 1984), p. 312; and note 15.

4. Examples: Angelo Poliziano, *Le Stanze, l'Orfeo e le Rime*, ed. Giosue Carducci et al. (Bologna: Zanichelli, 1912), pp. 528, 550, 551, 627; Bernardo Giambullari, *Rime inedite e rare*, ed. Italiano Marchetti (Florence: Sansoni Antiquariato, 1955), p. 158; Antonio Cappelli, ed., *Poesie musicali dei secoli xiv, xv e xvi* (Bologna: Romagnoli, 1868), p. 41; Raffaele Spongano, ed., *Rispetti e Strambotti del Quattrocento* (Bologna: Tamari, 1971), p. 17 (#6, 7); Gaspare Visconti, *Rithimi* (Milan, 1493), sonnets 63, 64, 83 (unpaginated); Roselli, in Bruti, "Il Canzoniere" (see note 9), p. 147.

5. Cf. Refrigerio's ardent language of love for his lord, the *condottiere* Roberto Sanseverino, in Frati, *Rimatori*, pp. 113–38; and Michele del Giogante to Cosimo de' Medici in *Lirici toscani del Quattrocento*, ed. Antonio Lanza (2 vols.) (Rome: Bulzoni, 1973–75), 1:670. Baldassare Castiglione, *Il Libro del Cortegiano*, ed. Bruno Maier (Torino: UTET, 1955), held that courtiers should "love and almost adore" their princes (p. 216).

6. Evident not only in the prayer of the period but also in the religious verse of love poets themselves: for example, Niccolò da Correggio, *Opere: Cefalo, Psiche, Silva, Rime*, ed. Antonia Tissoni Benvenuti (Bari: Laterza, 1969), pp. 138–39, 172; and Nappi, in Frati, *Rimatori*, p. 204.

7. Michele Messina, "Le Rime di Francesco Accolti d'Arezzo: umanista e

giureconsulto del secolo xv," in *Giornale storico della letteratura italiana,* cxxxii (1955), pp 173–233: "Gli occhi che'l mio signore in testa porta / fur chiarissime stelle in mezzo'l cielo" (p. 218).

8. Correggio, *Opere,* p. 154.

9. Ezio Bruti, "Il Canzoniere di Rosello Roselli," in *Atti della Accademia Rovertana degli Agiati,* ser. iv, vii (1925), pp. 81–199, citation from p. 151.

10. Lanza, *Lirici:* "leggiadria, gentilezza, alto costume, / modesto incesso, aspetto signorile / ed occhi accesi di celeste lume / ed ogni altro atto suo vago e gentile" (1:137).

11. Frati, *Rimatori bolognesi,* pp. 36, 126, 379, 389–90, 391; and Accolti in Messina, "Le Rime," pp. 216, 219.

12. Lorenzo reworked his *Canzoniere* over a period of nearly twenty years and, as is well known, compiled with Poliziano a famous anthology of mainly Tuscan poetry (the *Raccolta aragonese*) for Frederick of Aragon, with an eye to promoting Florence's literary supremacy. See *Dizionario enciclopedico della letteratura italiana,* 6 vols. (Bari: Laterza, 1966–70), 4:492.

13. Bembo, *Rime,* ed. Anton-Federigo Seghezzi (Bergamo, 1753).

14. See Correggio, *Opere;* Visconti, *Rithimi;* and Visconti, *Rime,* ed. Alessandro Cutolo (Bologna: Antiquaria Palmaverde, 1952), the last having been poorly edited, on which see Franco Gaeta, "Per le *Rime* di Gaspare Visconti," *Studi di filologia italiana,* 13 (1955), pp. 229–57.

15. Established by relating the characteristic preoccupations of Alberti's verse, Lanza, *Lirici,* 1.56–149, to his confessional tax returns in the Archivio di Stato di Firenze, *Catasto,* 617, part 1, ff. 348r–353v (dated 31 August, 1442), as demonstrated in detail in one of my forthcoming studies.

16. Emilio Pasquini, ed., *Simone Serdini da Siena detto Il Saviozzo: Rime* (Bologna: Commissione per i testi di lingua, 1965), as the editor of this excellent edition shows on the basis of numerous manuscript notes.

17. Ibid., pp. 43–46, *Canzone* 14, provides all the attendant details: "di lingua immortale essemplo in terra," "dentro dagli occhi ov' e triunfo e impero," "un mirar dolce e fiso / da far movere i sassi e volger l'acque" (lines 3–8, 14–17, 39–40).

18. In Pasquini, *Simone Serdini:* "Qual potenza o qual arte / in citta tanto ingrata e tanto vile / consenti nascer simile bellezza? / priva di gentilezza" (pp. 3–8, lines 20–33).

19. On the theme of "beautiful" and "harmonious" speech (*parlar*), see Saviozzo, in Pasquini, *Simone Serdini,* p. 232; Visconti, *Rime,* p. 50; Correggio, *Opere,* pp. 195–96.

20. Tinucci, *Rime,* ed. Clemente Mazzotta (Bologna: Commissione per i testi di lingua, 1974): "S'io ardo o avvampo o disiando agghiaccio, / s'e mie pensier son dolci o sono amari, / che n'hanno a far gl'invidiosi avari? /.... / E s'io mi cuoco o s'io mi struggo e sfaccio / per gli occhi ch'io tant'amo ed ho si cari, / perche vuol pur la plebe ch'io impari / seguire il suo bugiardo e falso laccio?" (p. 50, lines 1–8). For another example of the commitment to my lady as being antiplebeian, see Gherardi's sonnet 18 in Lanza, *Lirici toscani,* 1:647.

21. On this notion, see Michael Alexander Kirkwood Halliday, *Language as Social Semiotic: The Social Interpretation of Language and Meaning* (Baltimore: University Park Press, 1979), pp. 164–82; and Lauro Martines, *Society and History in English Renaissance Verse* (Oxford: Basil Blackwell, 1985), p. 113.

22. Gambino, *Versi,* ed. Oreste Gamurrini (Bologna: Romagnoli, 1878), pp. 12–14. Visconti, *Rithimi,* sonnet 33 (unpaginated), has his lady being unnoticed by "il vulgo obtenebrato."

23. Correggio, *Opere,* sonnets 1, 83, 348; Visconti, *Rithimi,* nos. 47, 49, 52, 53, 67; Lorenzo de' Medici, *Canzoniere,* ed. Paolo Orvieto (Milan: Mursia, 1984), nos. 8, 9, 20, 23, 24, 25, 27.

24. Lauro Martines, *Power and Imagination: City-States in Renaissance Italy* (New York: Alfred A. Knopf, 1979), pp. 310ff.; and Mario Santoro, *Fortuna, ragione e prudenza nella civiltà letteraria del Cinquecento,* 2d ed. (Naples: Liguori, 1978).

25. Imagery most abundantly found in Antonio Medin and Lodovico Frati, eds., *Lamenti storici dei secoli xiv, xv e xvi,* 3 vols. (Bologna: Commissione per i testi di lingua, 1887–90), passim.

26. Visconti, *Rime,* pp. 68, 107; Correggio, *Opere,* p. 241.

27. Visconti, *Rime,* p. 63.

28. Bembo, *Rime,* pp. 20, 23–24, sonnet 24 and *canzone* 8.

29. Tinucci, *Rime,* p. 15; Correggio, *Opere,* pp. 149, 176–77; Poliziano, *Le Stanze,* pp. 569–70.

30. Visconti, *Rime,* p. 34.

31. Correggio, *Opere,* pp. 184–85.

32. Laura Bellucci, ed., *Le Rime di Maestro Antonio da Ferrara* (Bologna: R. Patron, 1972): "Amor fa l'omo andar tutto giolivo, / usa con zente piu de lui zentile, / fugge le cose vile" (p. 116).

33. Benedetto Biffoli, in Lanza, *Lirici toscani,* 1:288.

34. Francesco degli Alberti, in Ibid., 1:69.

35. Ibid., 1:83.

36. Visconti, *Rithimi,* no. 69.

37. Particularly striking in Poliziano, *Le Stanze,* when Julio's hind turns into a beautiful nymph, pp. 274–88.

38. Although Giustiniani turned the refined code of love into a more vernacular idiom in his songs, these then became so popular that they betoken general utopian velleities. See his *Poesie edite ed inedite,* ed. Berthold Wiese (Bologna: Romagnoli, 1883); and Manlio Dazzi, *Leonardo Giustinian: poeta popolare d'amore* (Bari: Laterza, 1934).

39. For a fuller discussion, see my *Society and History in English Renaissance Verse.*

40. Actually, the society scorned men who revealed themselves docile with their wives or other women. See, for example, the ballad, "La donna mia vuol esser el messere," in *Poesie musicali del Trecento,* ed. Giuseppe Corsi (Bologna: Commissione per i testi di lingua, 1970), pp. 106–8.

41. As in, for example, Correggio, *Opere,* pp. 114–15 (#16), 142–43 (#72), 156 (#98), 205–6 (#198), 238 (#264), 257–58 (#302).

42. In Bruti, "Il Canzoniere," the ballad continues, "bene e pazo chi aspetta / poter trovare in te, crudel, merzede" (pp. 173–74). Jacopo Sanguinacci's famous *canzone*, "Non perche io sia bastante a dichiararte," in Carlo Oliva, ed., *Poesia italiana del Quattrocento* (Milan: Garzanti, 1978), pp. 261–65, for and against love, highlights the hidden misogynist strains in the love theme. See also Spongano, *Rispetti*, p. 33, octave beginning "Miser chi spera, per fedel servire."

43. Sebastiano Aldrovandi, in Frati, *Rimatori bolognesi*, pp. 386ff.

Annabel Patterson

"They Say" or We Say:
Popular Protest and Ventriloquism
in Early Modern England

I begin with a quotation from Shakespeare: "The toe of the peasant comes so near the heel of the courtier, he galls his kibe," (*Hamlet,* 5:1:117–18). In this disgruntled admission by Hamlet that the grave-digger's wit challenges his own and so brings to his attention the threat of social mobility, Shakespeare marked a turning point in his play, a turning away by Hamlet from the popular culture that had in earlier scenes saturated his own alienated discourse. As Robert Weimann demonstrated, Hamlet became, by adopting the stance of a social critic, both a spokesman for and a memorial repository of Elizabethan popular speech.[1] This appropriation had, however, its limits. Hamlet's proverbs, artisanal metaphors—the famous hawk and handsaw—and his lament for ancient festive practices ("O, O, the hobby horse is forgot") give place, in the last resort, in the graveyard, to an instinctive elitism that redefines the gravedigger as a threat to social hierarchy.

This essay takes as its question whether a historical criticism can now encounter a popular culture that was already in Shakespeare's time perceived by the educated as alien to themselves. Though perhaps not really as much an endangered species as Hamlet's hobbyhorse, Elizabethan popular culture has been notoriously difficult to recuperate; and some of its subsequent appropriations have also been shaped, like Hamlet's, by complex social attitudes whose presence is not admitted. Yet we are now, perhaps, at a peculiarly promising juncture. In the wake of deconstruction, historical criticism is enjoying the prestige of being at least temporarily the beseiger, rather than the beseiged. We can now return, and even without a propitiatory gesture toward the "textuality" of "history," to considering what the loosely packaged objects we call "literature" were doing in the worlds from which they came and to which they spoke. We can also now, in the service of historical inquiry, engage in what might be called deconstructive strategies of reading (though others might recognize these same strategies as having an older lineage) without buying into the philosophical premises, at once anti-idealist and antirealist, of Derridean deconstruction.

Further, we can engage a sceptical or suspicious hermeneutics in reading the texts not only of philosophy but also of literary criticism, history, and the social sciences, which perhaps more effectively than philosophy shape contemporary thought. In particular, and thanks to the infusion of another brand of suspicion derived from Marxist criticism, we can now recognize that the claim of disinterestedness in these disciplines must necessarily compete with the deep structure of the writer's beliefs—especially (and most relevant to theories of popular culture and social protest) political beliefs and social attitudes.

It is often assumed that the return to prestige of historical criticism has been thanks to the verve of the so-called New Historicism, named and most clearly represented by Stephen Greenblatt, and most strongly in evidence in Renaissance studies. But it has gradually become clear that this version of historical criticism has certain blind spots of its own that render its distance from the old, unfashionable historicism smaller than has been claimed. New Historicism has distinguished itself by calling attention to the wishful or willful structure of the criticism it would replace; it has also sent out frequent calls for self-consciousness on the part of its practioners as to where they stand, so to speak, before they begin to historicize.[2] But New Historicism has not, apparently, been able to identify fully its own inherited beliefs— those that determine both the object and the premises of inquiry. The object of study remains the canonical texts of the canonical writers— Shakespeare, Spenser, Sidney, Jonson—and they are still perceived in the canonical way, as courtly writers, monarchists, conservatives.[3] Tillyard's contention that Elizabethan writers did not only promote but incorporated a World Picture of ideal order and hierarchy[4] has certainly been replaced by more sophisticated models; yet the story remains that of an elite and self-satisfied culture, only momentarily disturbed by darker insights.

It may be that this *is* the only story that can be told. But there is very little evidence to show that New Historicism has as yet forcefully asked itself the following questions:

1. Can an earlier culture be known (adequately represented) by the texts (voices) of the dominant social group (elites)? If not, how do we go about recovering the voices of subordinate groups, the texts of popular culture? 2. To what extent is high culture, and especially the canonical texts that exert such centripetal power in our criticism, necessarily synonymous with elitist social theory?

In this essay, I shall address both questions simultaneously. In response to the first question, I shall show how a literature-based historical criticism can do better in recovering the voices of subordinate groups, better than it has done so far, better even than has been done by social historians, by looking or listening for those voices as ventriloquized by the dominant culture, in the texts of canonical writers. In response to the second, I shall show (unsurprisingly) that the social attitudes of Elizabethan writers are revealed precisely at the point where they themselves record the sound of the popular voice, especially that voice when raised in protest; or, to change the metaphor back to where we began, when they register, like Hamlet, the pressure of the peasant's toe against the courtier's heel. The surprise comes in showing that they do not all necessarily respond like Hamlet, who does not necessarily respond like Shakespeare.

As Sir Thomas Smith's *De Republica Anglorum* defined the English sociopolitical system in 1583, at its bottom was a "fourth sort of men" who "have no voice nor authoritie in our common wealth, and no account is made of them but onelie to be ruled." This group included, as well as "day labourers," "copiholders" " and "poore husbandmen," that is, the Elizabethan equivalent of the feudal peasantry, the urban underclasses: "marchantes or retailers which have no free lande . . . and all artificers, as Taylers, Shoomakers, Carpenters, Brickemakers, Brick-layers, Masons, &c."[5] If the total population of England at the turn of the century was approximately four million, roughly 95 percent of that total was accounted for by the "fourth sort of men" who, as Smith recognizes in a telling phrase, had "no voice" in the political or legislative structure.

That it could not receive formal political expression does not, however, require us to believe that the popular voice was completely silenced. And here we encounter the methodological problem of defining what should be included in the history of popular culture. It might look at first sight as if Peter Burke had expanded the "little" tradition of the folk by arguing for its interpenetration by the "great" tradition of the educated, and by avoiding the simple polarization of Robert Redfield's earlier model. Burke insists that the two-way traffic between high and low culture not only enriched and diversified both but also complicates the task of the social historian in receiving social messages from the past: "Whether one is considering songs or stories, images or rituals, it may be useful to ask: 'who is saying what, to whom, for what purpose and with what effect'? However, in asking this question we must not let ourselves assume that the message transmitted was necessarily the message received."[6] Yet the increase in subtlety has resulted, perhaps, in a decrease in sociopolitical focus; and in Burke's work the "little" culture still tends to be perceived as what remains when the "great" tradition is accounted for: "folksongs and folktales; devotional images and decorated marriage-chests; mystery plays and farces; broadsides and chapbooks; and, above all, festivals";[7] that is to say, what remains is primarily recreational, or at most at the convergence of recreation and religion.

At least one form of popular culture, though not entirely separable from festive practices, had manifestly nonrecreational functions. Even Burke alludes briefly to "riots and . . . organized non-violent happenings which it is convenient, if technically anachronistic, to call 'demonstrations.' "[8] But his cautious language here bespeaks an ideological issue, an extensive debate developed in this decade primarily between social historians of different political bias, as to whether such "happenings" were prepolitical and subrational, or whether they exhibited a political consciousness. It has now become evident that Elizabethan England was not the scene of national unity and social harmony presupposed by the traditional accounts of Elizabethan literature—those that were required to support and in turn supported a supposedly seamless philosophical account of an ordered world. Historians have always been less sanguine than literary critics about the managerial problems the queen and her ministers faced when aristocratic ambitions and religious controversy threatened the premise, necessarily unstable, of a single monarchical authority. And from the increasingly dominant perspective of social history, we have come to see that the spectacle of social *disorder* was in fairly frequent contest with an ideology that claimed disorder's nonexistence. As Roger Manning puts it with statistical clarity: "Between 1581 and 1602, [London] was disturbed by no fewer than 35 outbreaks of disorder. Since there were at least 96 insurrections, riots and unlawful assemblies in London between 1517 and 1640, this means that more than one-third of the instances of popular disorder during that century-and-a-quarter were concentrated within a 20-year period."[9]

To recover the social history of disorder does not, however, mean that we have disposed of the wish that the evidence were not there; and contemporary social history is full of struggles with this evidence. At the heart of the struggle is precisely the question of whether popular *unrest* can be taken as evidence of the popular voice raised in rational *protest;* and, as I have argued elsewhere, the majority of historians have been unwilling to entertain such a hypothesis. The cruder forms of the argument that the many-headed multitude could have no *mind* of its own have only been replaced by the belief that popular protest, while it might occasionally be rational, was always conservative, incapable of conceiving radical social change.[10] It is worth quoting the opening premises of Michael Mullett's recent study of popular protest in early modern Europe, which summarizes much of what has been written on this topic in the preceding decade:

> there was not a revolutionary, but only a reformist mentality underlying the lower-class protests of our period. Our lower orders ... often reacted forcibly, but pragmatically, to deteriorations in their living standards which they could blame on human agencies; they did not generally have alternative social structures to propose. It is true that there were movements like that of the Drummer of Niklashausen in Germany in 1476 which called for the complete equalization of society. Such movements tended to be heavily influenced, or indeed created, by the ideas of religious visionaries and unofficial charismatics. . . . Some of the most serious movements we shall consider, however, either harnessed some social radicalism with political deference towards kingship, as did the English Peasant Revolt of 1381, or combined both social and political conservativism in programmes that aimed not to have existing society swept away but rather controlled by moral, and specifically Christian, values.[11]

Such generalizations are possible if the popular voice is assumed to have gone mostly unrecorded. Mullett writes of "a popular culture of great richness whose main medium was speech," consisting of "proverbs, those conserved droplets of ancestral sagacity," stories, "their chief recreation and cultural activity," and only at moments of social crisis, political thought as expressed in written demands and manifestos. These, it is admitted, imply a certain degree of literacy: "verbal and argumentative aptitude, familiarity with custom, attention to details and knowledge of rights. . . . Those manifestos also show the limitations of the peasant outlook—the intense localism, the concern with minutiae that could become trivial" (p. 73). Given this restriction of the field of study, we could indeed continue to argue indefinitely as to what particular clauses in a "bill of rights" implied, as to which occasion of protest was the exception and which the rule.

Unless, that is, we expand the object of study to include the texts of the dominant culture at the moments where they engage, through a process of ventriloquism, with the sound and statements of the popular voice. In *Shakespeare and the Popular Voice* I developed an argument for sociological ventriloquism as a phenomenon of early modern writing to which a New Historical criticism ought to pay minute attention.[12] I deployed a theory adduced by Pierre Macherey to account for certain features of Balzac's *Les Paysans*, in which Balzac's unquestioned hostility to the French peasant nevertheless produced persuasive accounts of peasant grievances, in the very different context of early modern social polemic. As Macherey wrote of *Les Paysans*, "If one is going to speak against the people, effectively, one must speak of the people: they must be seen, given form, *allowed to speak.*"[13] And in sixteenth-century England, this dilemma often takes the rhetorical form of reported speech—what I called the "They say" formula—but it also poses a dilemma for the modern critic. How can we determine in any given instance whether the early modern writer who cites, by ventriloquism, the popular voice intends, like Balzac, to speak against them, or whether he intends, conceivably, to become thereby a spokesman of and for popular concerns and grievances?

In *Shakespeare and the Popular Voice*, I argued the latter position on behalf of Shakespeare—in the grave-digger scene in *Hamlet*, in *King Lear*, in whose topsy-turvy world the king himself becomes the spokesmen for the extremely underprivileged, and even in his treatment of Jack Cade's rebellion in *Henry VI, Part 2*, which might be taken as the strongest counterexample. Here, in accordance with my opening critique of New Historicist assumptions, I wish to engage not Elizabethan theater, which might be supposed to have had some strong interest in the demotic sector of its own audiences, but in "courtly" literature: perhaps an even tougher challenge. I have been fortified, in the interim, by discovering how easy it is to determine, when an "official" speaker is using the ventriloquist strategy, what are his objectives.

To cite but one example here: bishop Richard Bancroft, who would eventually, under James, become archbishop of Canterbury, was one of those who contributed to the official campaign, primarily by churchmen in high office, in the late 1580s and 1590s to discredit the Puritan campaign for greater ecclesiastical and liturgical reform, and especially the Martin Marprelate pamphlets, currently enjoying a succès de scandale. Bancroft assumed that there was a direct line of influence from the European advocates for a limited monarchy, Hotman, Buchanan and the anonymous author of the *Vindiciae contra Tyrannos*, to the authors of the first and second *Admonition to Parliament*. In his notorious sermon preached to coincide with the opening of the 1588 session of Parliament, Bancroft performed a double act of ventriloquism, not speaking the sayings of popular protest directly, but pretending to be what he would have called a demagogue, a spokesman for a popular movement that was conflating religious protest with socioeconomic unrest:

> Even as though one should saie unto you, my brethren of the poorer sort: these gentlemen and wealthier sort of the laitie do greatly abuse you: the children of God (you know) are heires of the world, and these things which the wicked have they enjoy by usurpation. . . . You have an equall portion with the best in the kingdome of God: and will you suffer this unequall distribution of these worldlie benefits? Consider how in the apostles time the faithful had all things common. . . . You can not but groane under the heavie burden which is laid upon you. Your landlords do wring and grinde your faces for the maintenance of their pride in apparell, their excesse in diet, their unnecessarie pleasures, as gaming, keeping of haukes & dogs, and such like vanities. They enhance your rents, they take great fishes, and do keep you in very unchristian slaverie & bondage. Why do you not seeke for your better releefe, to renue the use which was in the apostles times?[14]

Bancroft thus reiterates (and may even have been quoting) the ventriloquized grievances of those who did in fact participate in the rebellions of 1549, provoked, or rather encouraged, by Protector Somerset's anti-enclosure policies, grievances that were effectively recorded by Alexander Neville's Latin history of those occurrences:

> For, *said they*, the pride of great men is now intollerable, but their condition miserable. These abound in delights, and compassed with the fulnesse of all things, and consumed with vaine pleasures, thirst only after gaine, and are inflamed with the burning delights of their desires: but themselves almost killed with labour and watching, doe nothing all their life long but sweate, mourne, hunger and thirst . . . whatsoever fowles of the aire, or fishes of the water, and increase of the earth, all these doe they devoure, consume and swallow up; yea, nature doth not suffice to satisfy their lusts, but they seeke out new devices, and as it were, formes of pleasure . . . while we in the meane time, eate hearbs and roots, and languish with continuall labour, and yet [they] envie that we live, breathe, and injoy common ayre. Shall they, as they have brought hedges about common Pastures, inclose with their intolerable lusts also, al the commodities and pleasure of this life, which Nature, the Parent of us all, would have common, and bringeth foorth every day for us, aswell as for them? . . . Nature hath provided for us, aswell as for them, hath given us a body, and a soule, and hath not envied us other things. While we have the same forme, and the same condition of birth together with them, why

should they have a life so unlike unto ours, and differ so farre from us in calling?[15]

While the three editions of Neville's history (1572, 1576, 1582) may themselves have been timed to speak to the Admonition debates, Bancroft had adapted the locutions of the imaginary spokesmen, with the emphasis on an egalitarianism derived from primitive Christianity, to fit more closely with the ecclesiastical aspects of the controversy, and, perhaps, with the appearance of Martin Marprelate as an outrageous spokesman for change.

But his strategy is, nonetheless, to indicate, without any ambiguity at all, what is *wrong* with this argument, and in the process to indicate who, in fact, is his intended audience. Certainly not the dispossessed; and if the Puritans, primarily to the gentry and nobility, some of whom, as survivors of the Edwardian Reformation, were known to be secret sympathizers. To these Bancroft sharpened his address: "Now deerly beloved unto you of al sorts, but *especially to you of the richest,* I praie you tell me how you like this doctrine? Do you thinke it is true or meete to be taught? No surely it is not. The whole maner thereof is wholy Anabaptisticall, and tendeth to the destruction and overthrowe of all good rule and government." (italics added).[16]

We can now turn to some "literary" exhibits from this same historical juncture, the last quarter of Elizabeth's reign, during which, I am suggesting, the concept of the popular voice had acquired newly polemical force as a result of the intense campaign and countercampaign in the press for changes in the structure of the *church,* which implied to some an extension to changes in the structure of society at large. In 1575, George Gascoigne published among his *Posies* a long poem, *Dulce Bellum Inexpertis,* half military autobiography, half pacificist polemic, in which he first invokes the popular voice as a possible ally:

> Well then, let see what sayth the common voice,
> These old sayde sawes, of warre what can they say?
> Who list to harken to their whispring noise,
> May heare them talke and tattle day by day,
> That Princes pryde is cause of warre alway:
> Plentie brings pryde, pryde plea, plea pine, pine peace,
> Peace plentie, and so (say they) they never cease.
>
> And though it have bene thought as true as steele,
> Which people prate, and preach above the rest,
> Yet could I [never] any reason feele,
> To think *Vox populi vox Dei est,*

As for my skill, I compt him but a beast,
Which trusteth truth to dwell in common speeche,
Where every lourden will become a leech.[17]

At first sight these stanzas perform that turning toward and then turning away of the literary elite from popular culture for which I have made Hamlet the paradigm, that move, as in Bancroft's sermon, to ask the more privileged reader, "Do you thinke it is true or meete to be taught?" followed by the answer, "No surely, it is not." But (this being literature of a kind) there are complexities here that warrant further interrogation.

To begin with, the "olde sayde sawe" about the endless circularity of economic growth and militarism that Gascoigne attributes to popular culture is also to be found, thirteen years later, in George Puttenham's manifestly courtly *Arte of English Poesie* (1589), where it functions as a rhetorical example of "Clymax, or the Marching figure." It is there, however, attributed to "Jehan de Mehune, the French Poet":

Peace makes plentie, plentie makes pride,
Pride breeds quarrell, and quarrell brings warre:
Warre brings spoile, and spoile povertie,
Povertie pacience, and pacience peace:
So peace brings warre, and warre brings peace.[18]

According to Peter Burke's model of cultural interpenetration, this discovery implies either that a witty "saying" from the dominant culture has become a common proverb or, conversely, that the educated medieval poet has borrowed from popular wisdom. Yet the two versions of the "saying" are not identical; what is missing from the courtly version is the human suffering ("plea" and "pine") that redeems it from formal and social complacency. By the same token, Gascoigne's strategy of invoking the authority of a *Latin* proverb to equate the popular voice with the voice of God cannot simply be undone by his stated wish to disclaim it.

It was nevertheless part of Gascoigne's message to the commons that "pragmatic resignation" (in the phrase of James C. Scott[19]) is the best response to social inequality. Digressing to the problem of litigiousness at home, as a subcategory of militarism abroad, he advises: "Oh common people clayme nothing but right, / And cease to seeke that you have never lost," for the lawyers are the only ones who will profit.

Significantly, Gascoigne cites "Pierce the Plowman," who in 1381 had been appropriated as a symbol by the leaders of the Peasants' Revolt, reappeared in the contest of Robert Kett's midcentury uprising,[20] and was recuperated, as a reformer's tool, by Robert Crowley, who edited

Langland's poem with appropriate Reformation glosses.[21] Since what Langland's poem had *come* to represent (his own intentions notwithstanding) was so imbricated with popular protest, those who adopted a clearly antipopulist stand were obliged in some way to counter its effect. Puttenham would attempt to dispose of Langland as a satirist, "a malcontent of that time," one who "bent himselfe wholy to taxe the disorders of that age, and specially the pride of the Romane Clergy, of whose fall he seemeth to be a very true Prophet"; and he nailed down his critique with aesthetic disapproval: "his verse is but a loose meetre, and his termes hard and obscure, so as in them is little pleasure to be taken," (p. 50). In Gascoigne's poem Piers is adduced as an unfortunate advocate of "moving bounds," the model of petty disputes about landownership that leave the poor man worse off than he was; and, Gascoigne concludes:

> If common people could foresee the fine,
> Which lights at last by lashing out at lawe,
> Then who best loves this question, *Myne or Thyne,*
> Would never grease the greedy sergeants pawe,
> But sit at home and learne this old sayde sawe,
> *Had I revenged bene of every harme,*
> *My coate had never kept me halfe so warme.* (pp. 146–47)

Yet the overall effect is not to discredit but to maintain sympathy for those completely outmatched by the legal system.

   And as if to ensure that his opinions will be difficult to determine, Gascoigne *also* published in 1576 a satire of his own, *The Steel Glas,* which includes a defence of Piers Plowman as the spokesman "for the Comonaltie." "Stand forth Peerce plowman first," he wrote, "Thou winst the roome, by verie worthinesse":

> Behold him (priests) & though he stink of sweat
> Disdaine him not: for shal I tel you what?
> Such clime to heaven, before the shaven crownes.
> But how & forsooth, with true humilytie.

And whereas Bancroft parodied the arguments of popular spokesmen, Gascoigne repeats, in order to deny, the complaints made *against* the English peasantry by (one assumes) the gentry:

> Not that they hoord their grain when it is cheape,
> Nor that they kill the calfe to have the milke,
> Nor that they set debate betwene their lords,
> By earing up the balks that part their bounds:
> Nor for because they can both crowche & creep
> (The guilefulst men, that ever God yet made)

When as they meane mischiefe and deceite,
Nor that they can crie out on landelordes lowde,
And say they racke their rents an ace to high,
When they themselves do sel their landlords lambe
For greater price then ewe was wont be worth.
I see you Peerce, my glasse was lately scowrde.
But for they feed, with frutes of their gret paines,
Both King and Knight, and priests in cloyster pent:
Therfore I say, that sooner some of them
Shall scale the walles which leades us up to heaven,
Than cornfed beasts, whose bellie is their God.[22]

It was this poem, John King observes, that "kept the *Piers Plowman* tradition alive in the 1570s."[23]

Three years later, Edmund Spenser dispatched his *Shepheardes Calender* to the press with "a free passeporte," identifying its mission to circulate "emongste the meaner sorte," and also invoking the Piers Ploughman tradition. And in the *September* eclogue, Diggon Davie takes on, by ventriloquism, the role of spokesman for popular complaint against a corrupt and avaricious clergy:

They sayne the world is much war then it wont,
All for her shepheards bene beastly and blont.
Others sayne, but how truely I note,
All for they holden shame of theyr cote.
Some sticke not to say, (whote cole on her tongue)
That sike mischiefe graseth hem emong.
. . . .
Thus chatten the people in theyr steads,
Ylike as a Monster of many heads.[24]

Here is the rhetorical sign of ventriloquism, "they say" along with the catalogue of grievances; all, however, carefully qualified by that favorite trope of conservative thinkers, the many-headed Monster. Like Gascoigne in *Dulce bellem inexpertis* Spenser indicates that Diggon Davie stands for the speaker who, though sympathetic, retains some doubts about popular complaints: "Others sayne, but how truly I note (know not)"; he too has one of his "voices" appeal to precisely that "pragmatic resignation" defined by Scott: "Better it were, a little to feyne, / And cleanly cover, that cannot be cured. / Such il, as is forced, mought nedes be endured." But like Gascoigne in *The Steel Glas,* Spenser *also* invoked an unbracketed radical tradition. In the *May* eclogue a character named Piers articulates the Edenic claim (rejected by Bancroft a decade later) that social hierarchy, in church or state, was not ordained from the beginning but constituted a fall from original egalitarianism:

> The time was once, and may againe retorne,
> (For ought may happen, that hath bene beforne)
> When shepeheardes had none inheritaunce,
> Ne of land, nor fee in sufferaunce (p. 437).

One reader who deduced from this passage that Spenser was indeed opposed to church hierarchy was John Milton. In *Animadversions*, during his tirade against the Anglican bishops of his own generation, Milton remembered "that false Shepheard Palinode in the Eclogue of *May*, under whom the Poet lively personates our Prelates." Claiming that "our admired Spenser inveighs against them, not without some presage of these reforming times," Milton proceeded to copy out accurately the twenty-nine lines from the *May* eclogue that begin with this egalitarian premise.[25]

The acid test of Spenser's intentions with respect to populism must, however, be found in *The Faerie Queene*, where in Book V he personified it. Using the representational economy of allegory to give underclass protest a single head and mouth, Spenser introduced the figure of the Egalitarian Giant, who is permitted to speak the ancient tropes of cosmic fairness. The Giant plans first to weigh (literalizing the scales as the emblem of justice) and then to redistribute all the elements:

> For why, he sayd they all unequall were,
> And had encroched uppon others share,
> . . . .
> And so were realmes and nations run awry.
> All which he undertooke for to repaire,
> In sort as they were formed aunciently;
> And all things would reduce unto equality.

And, turning from reported speech ("he sayd") to dialogue:

> Were it not good that wrong were then surceast,
> And from the most, that some were given to the least?
>
> Therefore I will throw downe these mountains hie,
> And make them levell with the lowly plaine:
> . . . .
> Tyrants that make men subject to their law,
> I will suppresse that they no more may raine;
> And Lordings curbe, that commons over-aw;
> And all the wealth of rich men to the poore will draw.
>
> (5:2:32, 37, 38)

Of course, Spenser framed this episode, not only in an allegorical narrative that presumes that the Giant is the natural antagonist of justice, but also in a series of editorial comments. "Therefore," he remarks, "the vulgar did about him flocke / And cluster thick about his leasings vaine, / Like foolish flies about an hony crocke, / In hope by him great benefite to gaine, / And uncontrolled freedome to obtaine" (5:2:33). Yet in a hermeneutics of suspicion it is *possible* to see this not as an unequivocal attack on populism (and not, as some nineteenth century commentators did, in the wake of the French Revolution, as anti-Jacobinism *avant la lettre*[26]) but rather as a bringing into question the role of economic justice in a system that excluded it.

And, as in *The Shepheardes Calender*, Spenser complicated the task of any reader who has not predetermined what this episode *must* mean, by having his own narratorial voice support the Giant in advance of his appearance. Artegall (and many of Spenser's modern critics) rejects the Giant's premise that change has occurred since the first divine measurements were taken. Not only is the earth "immoveable" in the center of the universe, he claims, but all the other elements know "their certaine bounde. . . . And mongst them al no change hath yet beene found" (5:2:35, 36). From this premise, Artegall draws a sociopolitical conclusion. As part of his immutable plan, God "maketh Kings to sit in sovereignty; / He maketh subjects to their powre obay" (5:2:41). Yet this position flagrantly contradicts the narrator's clear statements in the Proem (stanza 4):

> Me seemes the world is runne quite out of square,
> From the first point of his appointed sourse,
> And being once amisse growes daily wourse and wourse.
> . . . .
> Right now is wrong, and wrong that was is right,
> As all things else in time are chaunged quite.

The result is, at the very least, an incoherent sign system, a problem only intensified when Artegall and Talus break the rules of debate and solve the intellectual dispute by using brute force:

> Like as a ship, whom cruell tempest drives
> Upon a rocke with horrible dismay,
> He shattered ribs in thousand peeces rives,
> And spoyling all her geares and goodly ray,
> Does make her selfe misfortunes piteous pray.
> So downe the cliffe the wretched Gyant tumbled; (5:2:50)

The simile patently *mourns* the Giant before the official, editorial comment ("So was the high aspyring with huge ruine humbled") can condemn him; more remarkably, the very choice of this image aligns the Giant with Spenser's own project, which at the end of Books I (12.42) and VI (12.1) is described as a feat of adventurous and often dangerous navigation, with the poem and its poet themselves represented as the "vessell" of the imagination.[27]

My third, and perhaps most telling example, shows us an inarguably courtly author, Sir Philip Sidney, not only investigating the ideology of popular protest but also *changing his mind* about the value of popular protest in his expanding political analysis. It is well known that Sidney began to rewrite his prose romance, the *Arcadia*, almost as soon as the first version was finished, and that one of the motives for rewriting was to cast the romantic plot in a large-scale narrative of political theory and relations, with the states of Asia Minor probably standing in allegorical relationship to those of early modern Europe. Less attention has been paid to the manner in which Sidney revised his account of a popular uprising, which in the *Old Arcadia* is simply related, and contemptuously, by the narrator. In so far as this episode has been scrutinized, it appears, as in the following account by W. D. Briggs, as the twentieth-century equivalent (though attributed to Sidney) of bishop Bancroft's position:

> It will not be supposed, of course, that I wish to accuse Sidney of any belief in democracy; only ignorance would expect to find evidence suggesting such a conclusion. His views on that subject are seen in the long, interesting, and minute account of the seditious riot which occupies an important place in the second book of the *Arcadia*. The mass of the people, the multitude, ignorant, fickle, passionate, and easily misled, are not to be trusted with power nor are they to have a direct share in the administration of public affairs, though government is to be carried on for their benefit and though they are the ultimate source of authority. Their duty is to obey.[28]

Briggs, however, was unconcerned by Sidney's revisions, the most important of which affect the causes of the uprising. In the *Old Arcadia*, the narrator informs us that "this tumult" originated with "Bacchus," or a celebration of the king's birthday that gets out of hand (a charge still repeated by social historians today); but it quickly develops into political critique:

> Public affairs were mingled with private grudge; neither was any man thought of wit that did not pretend some cause of mislike. Railing was accounted the fruit of freedom, and saying nothing had his uttermost praise in ignorance. At length the prince's person fell to be their table-talk; and to speak licentiously of that was a tickling point of courage to them. . . . Till at length . . . they descended to a direct dislike of the duke's living from among them. Whereupon it were tedious to write their

far-fetched constructions; but the sum was he disdained them, and what
were the shows of his estate if their arms maintained him not: who would
call him a duke if he had not a people? When certain of them of wretched
estates (and worse minds), whose fortunes change could not impair,
began to say a strange woman had now possessed their prince and
government. . . . If Arcadia grew loathsome in the duke's sight, why did he
not rid himself of the trouble? There would not want those should take so
fair a cumber in good part. Since the country was theirs and that the
government was an adherent to the country, why should they that needed
not be partakers of the danger, be partakers with the cause of the danger?
"Nay rather," *said they,* "let us begin that which all Arcadia will follow.
Let us deliver our prince from foreign hands, and ourselves from the want
of a prince. Let us be the first to do that which all the rest think. Let it be
said the Phagonians are they which are not astonished with vain titles
that have their forces but in our forces. Lastly, to have said and heard so
much was as punishable as to have attempted; and to attempt they had
the glorious show of commonwealth with them.[29]

Even if this were Sidney's final words on the subject, we might well
wonder whether this is a text from the dominant culture that ventrilo-
quizes the popular voice *only* to speak against it. The familiar charges
of drunkenness and malevolence are, of course, the editorial frame; and
at the other end of the episode, when precisely the figure the Phagonians
suspect of subverting the government, Pyrocles disguised as an Amazon,
successfully (for the moment) offers them pardons in exchange for
submission, the narrator produces the other great cliché of conservative
thought: "A weak trust of the many-headed multitude, whom incon-
stancy only doth guide at any time to well doing!" (p. 115). Yet the
complaint that the king has abandoned the task of government the
reader already knows to be justified; the perception that "vain titles" of
sovereignty depend in the last event on popular support ("have their
forces but in our forces") is evidence of the popular capacity to penetrate
ideology; and the penultimate statement that "to have said and heard so
much was as punishable as to have attempted" is an intelligent and
self-validating claim that the repression of social criticism is itself a
major cause of illegal action; more precisely, that a society that punishes
the word will have to live with the deed.

When Sidney revised his text, he paid extraordinary attention to this
section of the narrative. He increased both the violence and the black
humor with which the rebels are ultimately disposed of, recounting a
series of grotesque mutilations; and he complicated his account of the
grievances that led to the uprising, by showing the difficulty of creating
"common consent," the stock phrase of democratic theory, when eco-

nomic interests diverge. Each of those changes could point in more than one direction. But the same cannot be said of the two major alterations to the representation of the popular *voice*. For Sidney removed the discreditable account of the causes of the uprising from the omniscient narrator and put it in the mouth of the obviously unreliable speaker Clinias, now (in the revised plot) suborned by the king's sinister sister-in-law to incite the uprising. Concerned to explain its causes *to* the king so as to deflect all blame from himself, it is now Clinias, not "Sidney," who accuses the Phagonians of drunkenness and malice; and it is now Clinias, not the narrator, who uses the trope of the many-headed multitude. "O weak trust of the many-headed multitude, whome inconstancie onely doth guide to well doing. . . . So said a craftie felow among them, named Clinias, to himselfe."[30]

Moreover, Sidney changed the ventriloquized popular protest in certain crucial places not only to demonstrate Clinias's flattery and hypocrisy but also to increase the clarity and validity of the grievances.[31] Instead of pointing to the "strange woman" who had now "possessed their prince and government," the rebels (who are now called Enispians) "began to say":

> that your government was to be looked into; how the great treasures (you had levied among them) had bene spent; why none but great men & gentlemen could be admitted into counsel, that the commons (forsooth) were to plaine headed to say their opinions: but yet their blood & sweat must maintain all. . . . Since the Countrie was theirs, and the government an adherent to the countrie, why should they not consider of the one, as well as inhabite the other? Nay rather, (*say they*) let us beginne that, which all Arcadia will followe. Let us deliver our Prince from daunger of practises, and our selves from want of a Prince. Let us doo that, which all the rest thinke. Let it be said, that we onely are not astonished with vaine titles, which have their force but in our force. Lasting, to have saide & heard so much, were as dangerous, as to have attempted: & to attempt they had the name of glorious liberty with them. (pp. 322–223)

The mention of great taxes levied and spent, the dislike of gentlemen as having a monopoly of counsel, and the equation drawn between living in a country and "considering" of its government, taken together, amount to a program of limited monarchy and parliamentary process; while the change in the last sentence, from "the glorious show of commonwealth" to "the name of glorious liberty" is particularly revealing of Sidney's concept of popular protest's agenda.

In 1983, Stephen Greenblatt inaugurated the founding journal of the New Historicism in an essay entitled, "Murdering Peasants," which combines interpretations of Spenser's Egalitarian Giant and Sidney's treatment of the uprising of the commons in the *Arcadia,* along with Shakespeare's of Jack Cade's uprising in *Henry VI, Part 2.*[32] Greenblatt began his argument with characteristic flair by way of Dürer, as a sixteenth-century artist directly affected by the German Peasants' War of 1524–25, who in one of his notebooks described an imaginary "Monument to Commemorate a Victory over the Rebellious Peasants." Reading the description of the monument with late twentieth-century liberal sympathies, Greenblatt wrote, it seems to be the "commemoration not of a victory but of a vicious betrayal. . . . There, on top of it all, the peasant sits, alone, hunched over, unarmed, stabbed in the back. In his solitude, misery, and helplessness, he is the very opposite of the great ruling class nightmare in the Renaissance; the marauding horde, the many-headed multitude, the insatiate, giddy, and murderous crowd" (p. 5). Yet finding no evidence elsewhere in Dürer's work of populist sympathy, and accepting the statement of Panofsky that Dürer never wavered from his allegiance to Luther, who was explicitly hostile to the peasants, Greenblatt concluded that Dürer's monument expressed no ambiguity.

And he therefore delivered a manifesto of how we in the late twentieth century should understand this problem in interpretation: "The question then is how Dürer could have created a brilliant, detailed, and coherent design that could lend itself to a strong interpretation so much at odds with his own probable intentions, a design that has become in effect two quite different monuments." Constrained by a central premise of New Historicism—the irremediable alterity of the past—Greenblatt nevertheless found himself swaying to and fro between two incompatible hypotheses: the first, that the modern or postmodern critic merely *desires* to see in such complex forms the shapes of his own liberalism; the second, that Dürer had himself done something, perhaps not fully deliberately, to heighten the risk of misinterpretation—in this case, by "modelling his defeated peasant on the iconographic type of Christ in Distress." "This aesthetic decision," Greenblatt continued, "may signal a deep ambivalence on Dürer's part, a secret, subversive sympathy with the vanquished encoded at the very pinnacle of the victor's monument."

> I do not think we can rule out this possibility, one that satisfies a perennial longing since Romanticism to discover that all great artists have allied themselves, if only indirectly or unconsciously, with the oppressed and revolutionary masses. What is poignant and powerful about Dürer's design is that the identical signs can be interpreted as signifying both the radical irony of personal dissent and the harsh celebration of official order. This uncanny convergence is not . . . the theoretical

condition of *all* signs, but the contingent condition of certain signs at particular historical moments, moments in which the ruling elite, deeply threatened, conjure up images of repression so harsh that they can double as images of protest. (p. 11)

While implying that in the case of Dürer's monument the choice between liberal wishful thinking and authorial intention is undecidable, or at best mediated by some mysterious third alternative (the ambiguous condition of certain signs at particular historical momentes), Greenblatt turned from mid-sixteenth-century Germany to late sixteenth-century England, and proceeded to examine three literary instances of the representation of popular protest there: Shakespeare's Jack Cade, Spenser's Egalitarian Giant, and the rising of the commons in the *Arcadia*. In all three cases, Greenblatt surprisingly assumes that the state of creative ambiguity created by Dürer's monument no longer exists. All three simply share the aforementioned "great ruling class nightmare." The most ambivalence he will allow to Sidney is anxiety about a history of enclosures on the family estate (p. 16), and to Spenser, a "nagging sense of social marginality" (p. 21).

Further (and we can observe his predicament most clearly in the case of Spenser),[33] the New Historicist must steer between the Scylla of an old historical accounting for these courtly writers, which assumes *they* must all have been constrained by the prejudices of their class, and the Charybdis of a modernist allegiance to Freud. In relation to Spenser's Giant, Greenblatt acknowledged "the uncanny resemblance between the Giant's iconographic sign [the scales of Justice] and Artegall's" and "the still more uncanny resemblance between the Giant's rhetoric and Spenser's own." But this perplexity, we are told, "is not an embarrassment but a positive achievement, for Spenser's narrative can function as a kind of training in the rejection of subversive conclusions drawn from licensed moral outrage" (p. 22). Here, Freud's "uncanny" is made to substitute for the more complex social phenomenon of authorial ambivalence, let alone for a theory of conscious intention. Quoting with satisfaction Spenser's image of the Giant tossed over the cliff by Talus, Greenblatt decided that Talus's violence "exorcises" "the potentially dangerous social consequences—the praxis—that might follow from Spenser's own eloquent social criticism." It would be so much simpler, I aver, to imagine that Spenser's own eloquent social criticism was being expressed, all the more eloquently for its symptomatic evasions, in the enigmatic forms he thought he could get away with.

To deal with such elusive, ambiguous, *literary*, investigations of class consciousness with an elusiveness of our own does not, I suggest, make full use of the liberating power of the New Historical criticism Greenblatt has helped to unleash. The texts I have exhibited here speak to the responsibility felt by persons of means and letters to think and rethink the condition of those less well endowed. But whether I have succeeded better than my predecessors in elucidating their opinions will, to a very large degree, depend on the predisposition of *my* readers to believe this case, rather than those I have tried to refute. Naturally, I acknowledge my own predisposition. Criticism, like Nature, abhors a vacuum, and none of us is ideologically neutral when we embark on another attempt to recuperate the past. In an essay addressed to quite a different issue, Stanley Fish has written, "the practice cannot 'say' the Other but can only say itself, even when it is in the act of modifying itself by incorporating material hitherto alien to it."[34] Yet we do not need to conclude that what is difficult, epistemologically precarious, or imprecise should not be done at all; particularly when the practice offers us (like Sidney) the chance to change our minds.

NOTES

1. Robert Weimann, *Shakespeare and the Popular Tradition in the Theater* (Baltimore: Johns Hopkins University Press, 1978), pp. 130–31.

2. See Jean Howard, "The New Historicism in Renaissance Studies," in *Renaissance Historicism: Selections from English Literary Renaissance,* ed. Arthur F. Kinney and Dan S. Collins (Amherst: University of Massachusetts Press, 1987): "It seems to be that the historically-minded critic must increasingly be willing to acknowledge the non-objectivity of his or her own stance and the inevitably political nature of interpretive and even descriptive acts . . . since objectivity is not in any pure form a possibility, let us acknowledge that fact and acknowledge as well that any move into history is an *intervention"* (p. 33).

3. See Edward Pechter, "The New Historicism and Its Discontents: Politicizing Renaissance Drama," *Publications of the Modern Language Association* 1023 (1987): "For despite their protests about being open, new historicists tend persistently to fix and close their attention on the dominant institutions of Renaissance society, especially the monarchy. . . . Even when not directly concerned with royal power, new historicists still tend to locate the centers of plays by referring to the ideological interests of a dominant cultural force, such as the titled or monied classes, institutions of religious authority, or male power" (p. 296).

4. See, for instance, his revealing statement that the Elizabethan mind could not conceive of contestation as an inevitable, still less useful, part of the social process: "Such a way of thinking was abhorrent to the Elizabethans (*as indeed it always has been and is now to the majority*), who preferred to think of order as the norm to which disorder, though lamentably common, was the

exception" (E. M. W. Tillyard, *Shakespeare's History Plays* [London: Chatto & Windus 1961], p. 21 [italics added]).

5. Sir Thomas Smith, *De Republica Anglorum* (1583), ed. L. Alston (Cambridge: Cambridge University Press, 1906), p. 46.

6. Peter Burke, "Popular Culture in Seventeenth-Century London," in *Popular Culture in Seventeenth-Century England,* ed. Barry Reay (New York: St. Martin's Press 1985), p. 32.

7. Burke, "Popular Culture," p. 24.

8. Burke, "Popular Culture," p. 46.

9. Roger Manning, *Village Revolts: Social Protest and Popular Disturbances in England, 1509–1640* (Oxford: Clarendon Press 1988). For Manning, this concentration of disorder in the last two decades of Elizabeth's reign was primarily a crisis of urbanization. "It was not the harvest failures of the 1590s that precipitated outbreaks of disorder in London so much as the effects of war and the extraordinarily rapid population growth" (p. 187).

10. See "The Very Name of the Game: Theories of Order and Disorder," *South Atlantic Quarterly* 86 (1987), pp. 519–43.

11. Michael Mullett, *Popular Culture and Popular Protest in Late Medieval and Early Modern Europe* (London: Croom Helm, 1987), pp. 1–2. This paragraph is an instance of how social condescension pervades even the work of those with an apparent left-wing agenda.

12. Annabel Patterson, *Shakespeare and the Popular Voice* (Oxford: Basil Blackwell, 1989), pp. 39–51.

13. Pierre Macherey, *A Theory of Literary Production,* trans. Geoffrey Wall (London: Routledge and Kegan Paul, 1978), 265 (italics added).

14. Richard Bancroft, *A Sermon Preached at Paules Crosse the 9 of Februarie, Being the First Sunday in the Parleament, Anno. 1588* (London, 1589), pp. 25–26.

15. Alexander Neville, *De furoribus Norfolciensium Ketto Duce* (London, 1575), 1576, 1582; trans. Richard Woods (London, 1615), as *Norfolkes Furies, or A View of Ketts Campe,* Biv-B2r.

16. Bancroft, *Sermon,* p. 26.

17. George Gascoigne, *Complete Works,* ed. John W. Cunliffe, 2 vols. (Cambridge: Cambridge University Press, 1907), 1:142–43.

18. George Puttenham, *The Arte of English Poesie* (London, 1589) (Menston: Scolar Press, 1968), pp. 173–74.

19. In Patterson, *Shakespeare and the Popular Voice,* pp. 44–45, I adduced the anthropology of James C. Scott, in *Weapons of the Weak: Everyday Forms of Peasant Resistance* (New Haven: 1985), as an analogy of the representations of popular culture I was analyzing in early modern England. Scott maintains that it is an error to confuse "pragmatic resignation" when no practical alternatives are available with ideological acceptance of an repressively unequal socioeconomic system.

20. *Pyers Plowmans Exhortation, unto the lordes, knightes and burgoysses of the Parlyamenthouse* (c. 1550). According to John King, *English Reformation*

Literature (Princeton, N.J.: Princeton University Press, 1982), in this Edwardian complaint "the medieval plowman is almost unrecognizable . . . having become a radical spokesman for the commons against the enclosure movement and the misappropriation of monastic lands by the nobility" (p. 324). One is tempted to date this pamphlet *before* Kett's rebellion, as an instance of how popular protest could make use of the forms of literacy to spread its message. Compare the antienclosure tract, *Certayne Causes gathered together, wherin is shewed the decaye of England, onely by the great multitude of shepe, to the utter decay of householde keping . . . approved by syxe old Proverbes* (London, 1548).

21. For accounts of how the Piers Plowman tradition was used by sixteenth-century reformers, see Helen C. White, *Social Criticism in Popular Religious Literature of the Sixteenth Century* (New York: Macmillan, 1944), pp. 1–40; King, *English Reformation Literature* 322–57; and David Norbrook, *Poetry and Politics in the English Renaissance* (London: Routledge and Kegan Paul, 1984), 42–55.

22. Gascoigne, *Complete Works*, 2:169–70.

23. King, *English Reformation Literature*, p. 340.

24. Edmund Spenser, *Poetical Works*, ed. J. C. Smith and E. De Selincourt (Oxford: Oxford University Press, 1912), p. 453.

25. John Milton, *Complete Prose Works*, ed. D. M. Wolfe et al., 8 vols. (New Haven: Yale University Press, 1953–80) 1:722–23.

26. See, for instance, G. L. Craik, *Spenser and his Poetry*, 3 vols. (London: Charles Knight, 1845), 2:194–95: "If this had been published in the end of the eighteenth instead of the end of the sixteenth century—in the year 1796 instead of in the year 1596—the allegory could not have been more perfect, taken as a poetical representation or reflection of recent events, and of a passage in the political and social history of the world generally held to be not more memorable than entirely novel and unexampled. Here is the liberty and equality system of philosophy and government—the portentous birth of the French Revolution—described to the life two hundred years before the French Revolution broke out; described both in its magnificent but hollow show, and its sudden explosion or evaporation."

27. At the end of Book I Spenser wrote:

> Now strike your sailes ye jolly Mariners,
> For we be come unto a quiet rode,
> Where we must land some of our passengers,
> And light this wearie vessell of her lode.
> . . . . And then againe abroad
> On the long voyage whereto she is bent:
> Well she may speede and fairely finish her intent.

Book VI, Canto 12 begins with another version of the same simile:

> Like as a ship, that through the Ocean wyde
> Directs her course unto one certaine cost,

Is met of many a counter winde and tyde,
With which her winged speed is let and crost,
And she her selfe in stormie surges tost;
Yet making many a borde, and many a bay,
Still winneth way, ne hath her compasse lost:
Right so it fares with me in this long way,
Whose course is often stayd, yet never is astray.

28. W. D. Briggs, "Political Ideas in Sidney's *Arcadia*," *Studies in Philology* 28 (1930), pp. 37–61.

29. Sir Philip Sidney, *The Countess of Pembroke's Arcadia (The Old Arcadia)*, ed. Katherine Duncan-Jones (Oxford: Oxford University Press, 1985), pp. 111–12.

30. Sidney, *The Countesse of Pembrokes Arcadia* (London, 1590), in *The Prose Works*, ed. Albert Feuillerat, 4 vols. (Cambridge: Cambridge University Press, 1969), 1:318–19.

31. There is no way to deal with Gordon Zeefeld's assertion ("The Uprising of the Commons in Sidney's *Arcadia*," *Modern Language Notes* 48 (1935), p. 213, that "there is an emphatic repudiation in the revision, of the excuses the commons make for rebellion" except to state that it cannot be derived from the text.

32. Stephen Greenblatt, "Murdering Peasants: Status, Genre, and the Representation of Rebellion," *Representations*, 1 (1983), pp. 1–29. Though referring to the "New" *Arcadia*, and not taking into account the process of revision, Greenblatt in fact worked with the composite text as edited by Maurice Evans.

33. For a critique of Greenblatt's account of the *Arcadia*, see Richard Berrong, "Changing depictions of popular revolt in sixteenth-century England: the case of Sidney's two *Arcadias*," *Journal of Medieval and Renaissance Studies* 19 (1989), 15–33. While broadly noting the revisions I focus on, Berrong's main point is that Greenblatt ignored another major revision of Sidney's—the addition of an alternate description, and hence theory, of popular protest in the revolt of the Helots, which not only governs the Enispian revolt by preceding it, but which also exemplifies no "cruel laughter" at all. Rather it presents a serious account of how concepts of political liberty arise when the greed of the rulers forces the ruled to abandon their previous stance of accommodation.

34. Stanley Fish, "Being Interdisciplinary Is So Very Hard To Do," *Profession* 89 (1989), p. 19.

Robert Weimann

"Bifold Authority" in Reformation Discourse: Authorization, Representation, and Early Modern "Meaning"

In the course of the twentieth century we have witnessed a crumbling, not just of diverse types of authority, but of the social and intellectual foundations upon which authority as such, the very *idea* of authority, appears possible. This "crisis of authority" has, ever since the Protestant Reformation, led to "the attempt to internalize authority, that is, to shift the basis of its verification from external and public modes to internal and private ones."[1] This problematic shifting of credentials, I suggest, connects with a comparable change in the aims, the ways, the means and the media of authorizing discourse, especially the discursive forms of representation. The crisis of authority in our time appears to have much to do with the extreme vulnerability of legitimating representations, arising out of its ambivalence as a mode of linguistic and cultural production and value. Since we have heard so many voices raised against representation, there is little need for documenting the intellectual disaffection from its premises except perhaps to recall what, in our context, is the most characteristic charge of them all, namely the power of representation to order and to command language and constrain "the imperious unit of Discourse" (Foucault) by coercing upon us the incompatible link between language and humankind.

In raising the problem of authority in the context of Reformation discourse, I find it impossible to ignore the need for us to be aware of the historicity (and urgency) of our own perspectives on these problems. As we set out to redefine the relations between language and history, it would be reckless to assume that these relations can be discussed innocently today. There is abundant reason to believe that the hugeness of the problem of authority and the difficulties with the project of representation in our own postmodern or post-Enlightenment condition would stringently affect the presuppositions of our critical writing and thinking on the subject. The issue of authority in Reformation discourse may appear quite remote today, but the astonishing extent to which representations in the sixteenth century tend to interrogate both the institutionalized authority of office, law, and penalty and the internalized authority of epistemic or moral credentials[2] should give us pause to think.

The point, however, is not to be content with analogies between then and now. The establishment of similitude invites a critical pattern that at best is one of self-projection, at worst is one of affirmation or, even, self-congratulation. But this paper suggests that the Reformation crisis in authority appears to challenge but also to broaden the function and structure of representational discourse, thereby transforming the very conditions upon which "meaning" can be structured and signified. The question, then, which needs to be addressed to these discourses is one that goes against the grain of some of the most widely held poststructuralist positions of our own day. How to account for, and cope with, the culturally potent links between the crisis of authority and the simultaneous expansion of representational form and function in the Reformation and Renaissance?

In sixteenth-century Northern and Western Europe, the Reformation radically changed the conditions of discursive practice. There emerged in the social history of reading and writing a revolutionary potential for redefining the relations between the authority of power and an alternative source of authority that resides in conviction, knowledge, and the competent uses of language. Hitherto unknown contradictions among these different locations of authority developed in a context of momentous and rapid transformations—social, economic, religious, and cultural. Hence, the Reformation may be said to launch, or to be accompanied by, a series of far-reaching changes that, in England and Germany as well as in other European countries, mark the rise of modern conditions of authorizing public discourse. Henceforth the authority derived from power and the power of a new, subjective type of author-ity in the uses of discourse would engage far more profoundly and frequently in conflict and contradiction. And it is these conditions in early modern history that would affect signifying practices and reconstitute the structure of meaning itself.

If, in the words of the British historian Joel Hurstfield, the Reformation was "in the profoundest sense a crisis of authority,"[3] the implications of this for a new approach to representation in this period are worth pondering. In the study of literary history, the contribution made by the Reformation to Renaissance literature has only recently begun to be appreciated. In sixteenth-century England in particular, the Reformation became the catalyst of a flourishing national culture in which Protestantism and Renaissance Humanism merge in a unique alliance. The Protestant movement in England, unlike its counterpart in strife-ridden Germany, found its place in the framework of a centralized and jealously watchful absolutism under which the Reformation gradually and fluctuatingly became a constitutive element in the formation of early modern conditions of discourse and authorship. What is strikingly "modern" about this formation process, as distinct from its medieval components, is the expression of political motivations and intellectual arguments that, scarcely articulated under the conditions of lineage society, now gave way to ideologically reasoned modes of writing and thinking. At the same time the advent of print and the concomitant spread of discursive skills and activities made political, religious, and cultural processes accessible to incomparably larger numbers of people. In these conditions the reformers began to dispute unquestioningly accepted ways of administering grace and truth and power. As the previously infallible institution of the papacy and the rule of cardinals, bishops, and priests started to totter, as the immense power of the confessional began to crumble, the most basic levels of religious legitimation shifted away from the collective bodies and rituals of the church toward an altogether new emphasis, derived from the strength of personal faith, on the reading and interpretation of Scripture as the divine locus of a finished revelation.

While the early Reformation debate between William Tyndale and Sir Thomas More had brought out a good many irreconcilable positions in their respective modes of authorization, the line of division was to become more blurred than the hostile opposition between Protestantism and the old church might lead one to assume. For as soon as the issue of authority was viewed in relation to conflicting strategies of representation, there emerged a more complex awareness of the diverging uses of signs, images, and symbols. This at least was the case in the letters exchanged, in the spring and early summer of 1547, between the Lord Protector Edward Seymour, duke of Somerset, and Stephen Gardiner, then bishop of Winchester. At that time Gardiner, already under suspicion for his Catholic leanings, must have been cautious about airing them too freely. But looking back at the undisturbed

days of his bishopric ("as it was when I was in some little authority"[4]),
he went out of his way to recall how graciously the late sovereign
tolerated him when "I stooped not, and was stubborn" (Foxe p. 36).

Gardiner's appeal to the past was part of his policy of resistance to
any further change in church and state. As he bluntly put it, "I can
admit no innovations" (Foxe p. 42). Thus he admonished Somerset, "to
keep and follow such laws and orders in religion as our late sovereign
lord [Henry VIII] left with us" and not, during Edward's minority, "to
call any one thing in doubt . . . whereby to impair the strength of the
accord established" (Foxe p. 40). On that platform, Gardiner's position
on the unsanctioned uses of Protestant discourse remained quite inflexible.
Above all, he was anxious "not to suffer . . . to slip the anchor-hold of
authority, and come to a loose disputation" (Foxe p. 41). For the conservative bishop, "authority," far from being the *result* of discussion and
clarification, appeared to *precede* "disputation." It was important to
avoid the loose, that is, the uncontrolled, uses of public discourse,
especially about what Gardiner saw as the given meaning of Scripture.
Hence, the "authority" once and for all to fix such meaning was "the
anchor" to hold the "accord" on no further innovation. Such authority
was "to make for stay of such errors as were then by ignorant preachers
sparkled among the people" (Foxe p. 41). For although, as Gardiner
admits, "the ministration of the letter, which is writing and speaking, . . .
hath been from the beginning delivered, through man's hand," yet he
held "the setting out of the authority of the Scripture" (Foxe p. 40) to be
a matter of institutionalized privilege and not to be meddled with by
any curious preacher or layman.

While this of course could in no way obviate the conflict over
authorization, Gardiner's reformulation of the familiar contradiction
was noteworthy in more than one respect. In the first place, he was
concerned with what he called the authorization of the "setting out of
the authority of the Scripture" in religious as well as in other types of
discourse. In fact, by listing "preachers" together in one sentence with
"printers" and "players," Gardiner must have faced the problem of
authorizing a wider constellation of discursive activities. For what he
objected to in these discourses was that the "setting out" of the inscribed
agent of authority, the act of authorization itself, was not controlled or
even decided, and thus left subject to definition *and* appropriation.
Hence,

Certain printers, players, and preachers, make a wonderment, as though
we knew not yet how to be justified, nor what sacraments we should have.
And if the agreement in religion made in the time of our late sovereign

lord be of no force in their judgment, what establishment could any new agreement have? and every uncertainty is noisome to any realm. And where every man will be master, there must needs be uncertainty. And one thing is marvellous, that at the same time it is taught that all men be liars, at the selfsame time almost every man would be believed; and amongst them Bale, when his untruth appeareth evidently in setting forth the examination of Anne Askew, which is utterly misreported. (Foxe p. 31)

The context of this passage leaves no doubt that the setting out of authority in writing is here linked with both the question of power ("where every man will be master") and the issue of representation in cultural history. On the one hand, there are "books written without authority, as by Master Bale" (Foxe p. 30). But the element of "uncertainty" appears to be involved with greater complications than the absence of authority. What seems so "marvellous" (and contradictory) has to do with what is viewed, on the other hand, as some sort of flaw in the uses of representation: although quite unreliable ("all men be liars"), these uses "at the selfsame time" set forth claims upon truth ("every man would be believed").

It is interesting to note the barely concealed tension between the general reference to "all" and "every" and the sharper thrust toward those particular unsanctioned representations that are used as vehicles of power and "untruth." Obviously, it is the self-authorized uses of language that especially combine an "enterprise to subvert religion, and the state of the world" with that strange incongruity between "untruth" in discourse and the desire to "be believed." What is telling in his attack upon dissident writers such as John Bale is the underlying assumption that authority in truly authorized uses of language involves a stable or even fixed relation between signs and their meanings. This much at least appears to be confirmed by a letter written in the same month against "innovation" in the town of Portsmouth, "where the images of Christ and his saints have been most contemptuously pulled down" (Foxe p. 26). In his response to this incident, Gardiner puts forward what may well be called a semiotics of political stability:

For the destruction of images containeth an enterprise to subvert religion, and the state of the world with it, and especially the nobility, who, by images, set forth and spread abroad, to be read of all people, their lineage and parentage, with remembrance of their state and acts; and the poursuivant carrieth not on his breast the king's names written in such letters as a few can spell, but such as all can read be they never so rude, being great known letters in images of three lions, and three fleurs-de-luce, and other beasts holding those arms. And he that cannot read the

scripture written about the king's great seal, . . . yet he can read St. George
on horseback on the one side, and the king sitting in his majesty on the
other side; and readeth so much written in those images, as, if he be an
honest man, he will put off his cap. And although, if the seal were broken
by chance, he would and might make a candle of it, yet he would not be
noted to have broken the seal for that purpose, or to call it a piece of wax
only, whilst it continueth whole. (Foxe p. 27)

For Gardiner, the "destruction of images" involves, on the level where
signs and politics interact, an unforgiveable heresy. In terms of its
semiotic structure, such heresy occurs when the continuity between
material signifiers and social signification is illicitly disrupted. Social
stability and linguistic continuity are especially strong when religious
icons and their Christian symbolism appear indivisible; stability seems
equally guaranteed when social status symbols and the message of
subordination inseparably go hand in hand (as when the illiterate
"readeth so much written in those images, as . . . he will put off his
cap"). The semiotics of political order allows no instability between
signifier and signified. In dealing with the "king's great seal," an
honest subject would, as long as "it continueth whole," make no
distinction between the signifier and what it signifies: he would
not call the wax "a piece of wax only," even though its use-value
(as in a candle) is so self-evident. The "wholeness" of the sign involves complete continuity between what materially signifies and
what spiritually is signified by it. The "whole" nature of social symbols, then, presupposes closure in representation; stability in their
political function appears linked to stable relations in their semiotic
structure.

Here, Gardiner is concerned with the threat that derives from rupture and discontinuity in unauthorized representations. Writing against
the Lollard-Protestant distinction between "stocks and stones, in which
matter images be graven" and their spiritual meaning, he points out
how absurd would be a similar difference between the meaning of
"writing" and its signifiers "comprised in clouts and pitch."[5] Again, the
lesson is one of social subordination, suggesting, in the face of "Lollards'
idolatry," the need for royal ceremony and feudal symbols (those
"lendings" that will be so precious to Lear before he parts with them).[6]
Gardiner provides a somber warning against those who seem to him
unlawfully to "gather upon Scripture" the destruction of "due reverence":
"If this opinion should proceed, when the king's majesty hereafter
should show his person, his lively image, the honour due by God's law
among such might continue; but as for the king's standards, his banners,
his arms, they should hardly continue in their due reverence for fear of

Lollards' idolatry, which they gather upon Scripture beastly—not only untruly" (Foxe p. 27).

This reads like a report on an early crisis in representation. Such crises occur when preconceived continuity in the representational use of signs is challenged by the self-authorized stance of an intense subjectivity in reading and interpretation. In terms of speech-act theory, such discursive subjectivity has a strong "performative" that appears to thrive upon the critique of the unity of seeming and meaning. Such a performative is especially vigorous in iconoclasm, which "does not recognize any *necessary* linkage between signifier and signified," emphasizing as it does "the constitutive value of internal factors (belief, conscience)."[7] In Shakespeare, a disruption of this linkage occurs when Lear sheds his "lendings," when Henry V questions the use-value of "ceremony," and when Hamlet makes a distinction between the "seems," that is, the signs of "mourning," and his truly felt experience "within."[8]

At this point, to anticipate concurrence between players and preachers is to suggest that the issue of authority or of authority's opposite in representation cannot be reduced to an area of opposition between Catholic and Protestant writings. Even where Gardiner finds fault with Bale, there is a good deal of closure and stability in Bale's writing, whereas the most forceful energies of disruption obtain where the eye of orthodoxy may never have looked for them. Among Bale's dramatic figures of allegorical evil, it is the vice "Idolatry" that most disrupts stability, including any stable language of identity. While, for instance, in Bale's *Three Laws,* natural law's sincerity "had dictated that character, appearance, and name were one," identity becomes altogether fluid, in fact dissolves itself, when through the use of disguise the vice shifts his gender. In his amazement, Infidelity cries: "sometime thou wert an he!" Replies Idolatry: "Yea, but now Ich am a she, / And a good midwife, perde!"[9]

As this excursion suggests, Gardiner's linkage between lack of orthodox authority and crisis in the closure of representation has considerable implications for the cultural history of Tudor drama. Dramatic language could use but could also disrupt such continuity between signs and meanings. For Gardiner to insist on stable relations between the two was to buttress his distinction between wholesome and "false" representation. In our instance, the differentiation was between authoritative uses of "images and ceremonies" (Foxe p. 58) and mere "idolatry": "so hath 'idolum' been likewise appropriate to signify a false representation, and a false image" (Foxe p. 59).

As their correspondence showed, however, the bishop's poetics of stability and suppression did not fall in well with the Protestant inclinations of the duke of Somerset. Urged by the bishop not to use his authority to "command books to be bought" (Foxe p. 43), the lord protector did not respond neutrally. As his letters indicate, he chose to follow an altogether different notion of how to authorize discourses. Rather than divide discourses on the basis of a given authority into "false" and sanctioned ones, Somerset takes a considerably relaxed and much less coercive position when he writes:

> There be some so ticklish, and so fearful one way, and so tender stomached, that they can abide no old abuses to be reformed, but think every reformation to be a capital enterprise against all religion and good order; as there be on the contrary side some too rash, who, having no consideration what is to be done, headlong will set upon every thing. The magistrate's duty is betwixt these, so in a mean to sit and provide, that old doting should not take further or deeper rust in the commonwealth, neither ancient error overcome the seen and tried truth, nor long abuse, for the age and space of time only, still be suffered; and yet all these with quietness and gentleness, and without all contention, if it were possible, to be reformed. (Foxe p. 30)

Concerned with "good and politic order of the commonwealth" (Foxe p. 30), Somerset appears to follow the Tudor strategy of via media where he writes that "quiet may as well be broken with jealousy as negligence, with too much fear or too much patience: no ways worse, than when one is over light-eared the one way, and deaf on the other side" (Foxe pp. 35–36). To a certain extent, this recalls Henry VIII's position. It is worth noting in the present context, however, that Seymour, in arguing for a more balanced response, addresses himself to a newly relevant distinction between the authority of power and that different type of "authority" that derives from authorship and writing. On the one hand, there is the authority of "magistrates"; on the other hand, there are the institutions of printing, playing, and preaching, and those who are engaged in them "would set forth somewhat of their own heads":

> The world never was so quiet or so united, but that privily or openly those three which you write of, printers, players, and preachers, would set forth somewhat of their own heads, which the magistrates were unawares of. And they which already be banished and have forsaken the realm, as suffering the last punishment, be boldest to set forth their mind; and dare use their extreme license or liberty of speaking, as out of the hands or rule of correction, either because they be gone, or because they be hid. . . . In the most exact cruelty and tyranny of the bishop of Rome, yet Pasquill (as we hear say) writeth his mind, and many times against the bishop's tyranny, and sometimes toucheth other great princes; which thing, for the most part, he doth safely: not that the bishop alloweth Pasquill's rhymes

and verses—especially against himself; but because he cannot punish the author, whom either he knoweth not, or hath not. In the late king's days of famous memory, who was both a learned, wise, and politic prince, and a diligent executer of his laws—and when your lordship was most diligent in the same—yet, as your lordship yourself writeth, and it is too manifest to be unknown, there were that wrote such lewd rhymes and plays as you speak of, and some against the king's proceedings, who were yet unpunished, because they were unknown or ungotten. (Foxe pp. 34–35)

Although the lord protector objects to Gardiner' lumping together "goodly sermons" and "Jack of Lent's lewd ballad" ("which be evil in your letters joined together"), he does affirm a common mode of self-authorization on the part of all those discourses that "dare use their extreme license or liberty of speaking." Note how close the "license" of lewd ballads and the "liberty" of godly sermons remain, for all their obvious generic and functional difference. What they do have in common is the fact that they are "out of the hands or rule of correction." As against the authority of "rule," it was possible that the author in these discourses "writeth his mind." The authorization of the "license or liberty of speaking" was one thing; the "rule of correction," the authority of the "diligent executer of . . . laws," was another. From now on, their incongruity was to be reckoned with.

For Seymour to make a distinction of such consequence for centuries to come indicated a post-Reformation order of things. Already the medieval emphasis on the wholeness of hierarchical order must have appeared untenable. After the Great Schism, the grand scheme of universal harmony and unity implicit in the concept of "Christendom" tended to be superceded by "debate and discord." As Seymour put it, "the world" simply did not appear "so quiet or so united" that, amid the noise and strife, one type of authority could hold sway. In the absence of unity, those unified uses of representation that Gardiner continued to advocate could find no place. Though he rejected as "evil" a view in which all the different forms of unruly language were "joined together," Seymour did reformulate a vision of the most variegated discursive activities. But by returning to Gardiner's discursive outlets of heresy ("printers, players, and preachers"), he did not have in mind a suppression of the elements of nonconformity among them. Rather, he was making an early (possibly the earliest known) attempt to come to terms with differentiation of discourses—that process of *Ausdifferenzierung*, which, following Max Weber, sociologists such as Jürgen Habermas and Daniel Bell have considered as constitutive of modernity.

Clearly, this early emphasis on diversity was incompatible with a unifying approach to the uses of representation. Correcting the bishop in his "reading" of the king's great seal, the duke of Somerset finds an embarrassing reason for reconsidering the meaning of signs, "when your lordship (as appeareth) hath not truly read a most true and a most common image" (Foxe p. 29). Correcting Gardiner's confusion of St. George with the image of royalty, an error often made by "the rude and ignorant people," Somerset refers to the validity of the seal's inscription: "as the inscription testifieth, the king's image is on both the sides." He reminds Gardiner that "not . . . what is commonly called so, is always truest" (Foxe p. 29). Emphasizing such difficulties with the true uses of representation, though not relinquishing the notion of "true uses," Somerset altogether rejects a black and white approach to signification:

> What you mean by true images and false images, it is not so easy to perceive. If they be only false images, which have nothing that they represent, as St. Paul writeth, "An idol is nothing," (because there is no such god,) and therefore the cross can be no false image, because it is true that Christ suffered upon it: then the images of the sun and the moon were no idols, for such things there be as the sun and the moon, and they were in the image then so represented, as painting and carving doth represent them. (Foxe p. 29)

In this view, the charge of idolatry cannot be proved on the basis of the representational content of an image. Indeed, according to a strictly Protestant poetics and semiotics, mimesis cannot serve as a reliable register of "true" meaning. "True" and "false" thus emerge as highly problematic categories. This remarkable piece of theorizing suggests that the meaning of representations is not a question of epistemology. Such meaning cannot be gauged by the extent to which what is represented corresponds to what exists prior to the act of representation. The "meaning" of representations, then, is not a matter of "true images and false images," but has to do with how and to what effect these representations are used.

Remarkably, in setting forth these positions, the writer of this letter is so much more subtle and balanced than its editor. Even so, it seems possible for John Foxe once more to return to the uses of unauthorized discourses, presumably with an eye to directing their shattering impact on the archenemy, the pope. When we keep in mind the limits of Foxe's reliability as a chronicler,[10] we should not be surprised to find him endeavoring to unify the various types and sources of self-authorized discourse under the exclusive rubric of their antipapal slant. Thus he all too easily accounts for the act that Gardiner "thwarteth, also, and wrangleth much against players, printers, preachers. And no marvel why: for he seeth these three things to be set up of God, as a triple bulwark against the triple crown of the pope, to bring him down; as, God be praised, they have done meetly well already" (Foxe p. 57).

Despite his inevitable bias, John Foxe in his *Acts and Monuments* documented the two dominant positions in the mid-Tudor debate on authority with admirable clarity. To use John N. King's convenient phrase, this debate was over "the relative merits of internal and external authority."[11] Whereas the latter appeared to be established on traditional institutionalized grounds, the former, as Christopher Hill notes, was "an internal authority, whose validity he [the believer] can test in discussion with other believers." And he adds: "That distinction is what the Reformation had been about."[12]

In its centrality, this debate continued well into the seventeenth-century political revolution, culminating in Thomas Hobbes' paradoxical solution whereby the absolute natural rights of individuals necessitate the constraining authority of the sovereign.[13] But even at the height of the Elizabethan settlement, when the threat of anarchy arising out of the self-authorizing Protestant conscience must have appeared somewhat weaker, the controversy continued unabated. This was the case especially with those writers who zealously responded to what they perceived as highly dangerous parallels between the revolutionary fringe of the German Reformation and the potential (or actual) insubordination among English Puritans. For an illustration, we have only to glance at Richard Cosin's *Conspiracie for Pretended Reformation: viz. Presbyteriall Discipline* ("Published now by authoritie," 1592) or at Oliver Ormerod's *The Picture of a Puritane* (enlarged edition, 1605). Cosin's lengthy subtitle asserted the "resemblance" between Puritan dissent and what "happened heretofore in Germanie"; Ormerod's advertised "A Relation of the opinions, qualities, and practices of the Anabaptists in Germanie, and of the Puritanes in England," and claimed that in the following text "that the Puritanes resemble the Anabaptists, in above four score several things" was "firmly prooved."[14]

In this context, the clash between internal and external positions of authority became most pronounced. The antagonism between the two positions was turned into a spectacular theme; indeed, it was sensationalized in the sense that behind this antagonism sinister patterns of contamination were seen at play. When, for instance, Ormerod attacked those that "are become scalding hot in desire of innovation" (using the very same phrase that Cosin had used before),[15] he made it plain that the revolutionary "opinion of equality of authority and dignitie," as Cosin had described Thomas Müntzer's position,[16] involved internal questions of conscience as well as external considerations of power.

Addressing himself to the English Puritans, Ormerod argues that they desire "this equalitie . . . because you condemne and disdaine to be ruled, and to be in subjection. Indeed your meaning . . . to rule and not to be ruled, to do what you list in your several cures, without controlement of Prince, Bishoppe, or any other. And therefore pretending equalitie, most disorderly you seek Dominion."[17] The emphasis on "rule" was unambiguous enough. The powers that be were challenged on the level of the appropriation of spiritual authority: "are all Prophets? are all teachers? . . . do all interpret?"[18] At the same time, the self-authorized, internally justified claim to read and "interpret" aimed at a "meaning" by which questions of textual exegesis and the issue of political power were inextricably entwined.

While these pamphlets were more concerned with wild denunciations of the specter of Anabaptist anarchy than with any balanced assessment of the actual state of crisis in authority, there is at least one late Elizabethan text that provides a truly remarkable epitome of post-Reformation divisions on authority. This is Richard Bancroft's *A Sermon Preached at Paul's Cross.* At the time of its publication (the same year when, February 9, 1588, the sermon was preached), Bancroft was chaplain to Sir Christopher Hatton, lord chancellor of England; he soon was to become bishop of London, and before taking over England's highest ecclesiastical office, he served as the right hand and closest confidant of Archbishop Whitgift. The *Sermon* may well be read as a strategic statement made by one of the most promising high-ranking representatives of the Elizabethan settlement.

To say that Bancroft's utterance had strategic significance appears as no exaggeration as soon as we recall that, on the highest levels of church and state, the issue of authority tended to be defined pragmatically as well as ideally. But while the uses of authority (except in Richard Hooker's *Laws*) were usually considered in negative reference to both the Catholic church and the Puritan movement, Bancroft, from his high Elizabethan position went one step further. Attempting to define the grounds for what was to become the Anglican position on authority, he provided a carefully worked out, coherent context to the left and right of his own orthodox via media position. In his concern not simply with authority as such but also with diverse modes of authorizing discourse, Bancroft rejected any facile caricature of positions hostile to the state church. Whereas Cosin had reduced both the old-church and the Puritan concepts of authority to a theological justification of diverging aspirations to power, in his *Sermon* Bancroft sees the opposition between the two as constituting a wider cultural and political pattern of antagonistic discourses. On the one side are the "false prophets" of Rome:

The Popish false prophet will suffer the people to trie nothing, but do teach them wholie to depend upon them . . . First they forbid them the reading of the scriptures. And the better to be obeied therin, they will not permit the scriptures to be translated into their vulgar toong . . . The second shift which these false prophets of the Romish church do use, is this: Now that they perceive the scriptures to be translated into the language almost of every nation; and that the bookes are now so common in every mans hands, as that with their former devise they are no longer able to cover their nakedness: they labor with all their might to bind us to the fathers, to the councels, and to the church of Rome, protesting verie deeply, that we must admit of no other sence of place of the scriptures, than the Romish church shall be pleased to deliver unto us: . . . If a man have the exposition of the church of Rome touching any place of scripture, although he neither know nor understand, whether and how it agreeth with the words of the scripture, yet he hath the word of God.[19]

Once again the old-church authority is seen as located *at the beginning* of exegesis: the meaning of discourse, the Biblical "sence," is delivered by and through the religious institution. Diametrically opposed to this is the opposite extreme of radical Protestant self-authorization:

Another sort of prophets there are, (you may in mine opinion call them false prophets) who would have the people to be alwaies seeking and searching: and those men (as well themselves as their followers) can never finde wherupon to rest. Now they are caried hither, now thither. They are alwaies learning (as the apostle saith) but do never attaine to the truth . . . They wring and wrest the Scriptures according as they fancie. It would pittie a mans hart considering what paines they will take in quoting of places, to see how perversely they will apply them . . . To represse therefore this boldnes, first I say with *Tertullian* . . . that it hath ever been noted as a right property of heretikes and schismatikes, alwaies to be beating this into their followers heads: *Search, examine, trie, and seeke:* bringing them thereby into a great uncertainty.[20]

The radical Protestant position is taken to task on opposite grounds: inscribed authority is not given, but rather needs to be appropriated by the reader through scrutinizing the text for its truth value. "Meaning," in this view, appears to be not nearly as determined as in the case of preordained authority. Rather, the biblical text is "searched," "examined," and "tried" for what it truly means. As a result, Christian doctrine itself is tried "by private men, and privately"—which "trial of doctrine" has grave dangers. For "if authoritie and libertie of judging shall be left to private men, there will never be any certaintie set downe, but rather all religion will whollie become doubtfull."[21]

The point, of course, is for Bancroft to reject both procedures in favor of a more balanced position. Authority as inscribed in the biblical text is neither preordained nor "delivered" ready-made by the councils or by the church; nor can it be sought freely by "private men." Instead, Bancroft attempts to sanction the via media position of the state church through rejecting both extreme modes of authorization: "The meane therfore betwixt both these extremities of trieng nothing and curious trieng of all things, I hold to be best." The irony of this position was not that it recommended a sort of hermeneutical halfway house ("Read the Scriptures, but with sobrietie,"[22]) but that in repudiating "unlawful authoritie" on the part of both popes and heretics, Bancroft would do so on the behalf of and "according to the lawful authoritie which is united unto hir [Elizabeth's] crowne."[23]

This was a desperate strategy to develop in these circumstances, and Bancroft seemed to know as much. Wherever he looked, "debate and discord" had not abated in the wake of the Reformation. In much the same way that Henry VIII had been before him, Bancroft was confronted by "the laie factious" and "the clergie factious." "I warrant you," he noted, "they are not toong-tied on their own behalfe":[24] not tongue-tied by their own self-fashioned authority. In the post-Reformation context, outside of the theater, there were few means to bridge the divided uses of discourse. Richard Hooker had first cited the telling metaphor in his *Laws* and was to use the same again in his *Two Sermons upon Part of S. Judes Epistle:* "Thy breach is great like the sea, who can heale thee?" (Lamentations 2.13).[25] Bancroft, from his own position, contented himself with a fainter echo: "who . . . would ever have dreamed of such division?"[26] The division was to become so deep that players, more deftly than preachers, could render the politics and the semiotics of authority in terms of a "bifold authority" in the representation of speaking, thinking, and doing: "there doth conduce a fight / Of this strange nature, that a thing inseparate / Divides more wider than the sky and earth" (*Troilus and Cressida* V.2.151–53). In Shakespeare's play, the crisis of authority has to do with the "bifold" direction of "reason" and perception. In "the spacious breadth of this division," the uses of discourse find themselves in maddening contradiction between the order of "the bonds of heaven" and the "fragments, scraps, the bits, and greasy relics" of sensory experience. But such "madness of discourse," which Troilus has in mind, makes representations questionable when some bewildering rupture between visible signs and transcendental meanings upsets whatever continuity was possible in representational utterances. This, although not unrelated to, goes much beyond the Reformation crisis in authority. Unlike the pulpit or the pamphlet, the Elizabethan theater itself projected two types of a divided site, one in dramatic thought and one on an ununified platform stage. Here, finally, authority—having shed its innocent claim upon unity and validity—emerges into the modern world as conflictual and contestatory.

NOTES

1. Editor's "Introduction" to *Authority: A Philosophical Analysis,* ed. R. Baine Harris (University: University of Alabama Press, 1976), p. 1.

2. See E. M. Adams, "The Crisis of Authority," in *Authority: A Philosophical Analysis,* pp. 3–24.

3. Joel Hurstfield, "Introduction: The Framework of Crisis," *The Reformation Crisis,* ed. Joel Hurstfield and A. F. R. Smith (London: Edward Arnold, 1965), p. 1.

4. John Foxe, *Acts and Monuments,* ed. Stephen Reed Cattley, 4th ed. rev. by J. Pratt, 8 vols. (London: Seeley and Burnside, 1877), 6:39. All further references to this edition will appear in the text.

5. Gardiner here seems to go back on certain positions of the Henrician Reformation, when royal policy was behind the "dismantling of the gilded shrines of Canterbury, Walsingham and elsewhere." See Margaret Aston, *Lollards and Reformers: Images and Literacy in Late Medieval Religion* (London: Hambledon Press, 1984): "Image-breaking became official and entered a new era" (p. 192).

6. Stanley Wells and Gary Taylor, eds. *William Shakespeare: The Complete Works* (Oxford: Clarendon Press, 1986); *King Lear* (III.4.102).

7. James R. Siemon, *Shakespearean Iconoclasm* (Berkeley: University of California Press, 1985), pp. 143, 178. In his suggestive treatment of the problem, Siemon on p. 143 cites Victor and Edith Turner, *Image and Pilgrimage in Christian Culture: Anthropological Perspectives* (New York: Columbia University Press, 1978), p. 144 (Turner's emphasis).

8. David Bevington, ed. *The Complete Works of Shakespeare* (Glenview, Ill.: Scott, Foresman, 1980); *Henry V* (IV. 1.237–281); *Hamlet* (1.2.76–86). Further quotations from Shakespeare's plays will refer to this edition.

9. John Bale, *A Comedy Concerning Three Laws of Nature, Moses, and Christ,* in *The Dramatic Writings of John Bate,* ed. John S. Farmer (New York: Barnes & Noble, 1966), p. 17. On Bale's "universe of stark antinomies," see Ritchie D. Kendall, *The Drama of Dissent: The Radical Poetics of Nonconformity, 1380–1590* (Chapel Hill: University of North Carolina Press, 1986), p. 131; on Bale's dramatic figure of "idolatry", see p. 104.

10. See for example, John A. F. Thomson, "John Foxe and Some Sources for Lollard History: Notes for a Critical Appraisal," *Studies in Church History* 2 (1963), pp. 251–54.

11. *English Reformation Literature: The Tudor Origins of the Protestant Tradition* (Princeton: Princeton University Press, 1982), p. 84; see also King's article, "Freedom of the Press, Protestant Propaganda, and Protector Somerset," *HLQ* 40 (1976), 1–9. My debt to Professor King's work is obvious and should be acknowledged.

12. "The Problem of Authority," *The Collected Essays of Christopher Hill*, Vol. II: *Religion and Politics in 17th Century England* (Amherst: University of Massachusetts Press, 1986), p. 47. For a definition of external authority in relation to "the poetic text," see Jacqueline T. Miller, *Poetic License: Authority and Authorship in Medieval and Renaissance Contexts* (New York: Oxford University Press, 1986), p. 5.

13. See *Leviathan*, part 1, chap. 14 and part 2, chap. 18.

14. For modern historical perspectives, see chap. 7. Oliver Omerod, "The Anabaptists and the Reformation," in *Enthusiasm: A Chapter in the History of Religion*, ed. R. A. Knox (New York: Oxford University Press, 1950), pp. 117–138, for special emphasis on links to medieval heresy; see also Irvin B. Horst, *The Radical Brethren: Anabaptism and the English Reformation to 1558* (Nieuwkoop: De Graaf, 1972) for a revision of Foxe's approach to the radical Reformation (pp. 57–58).

15. Oliver Ormerod, *The Picture of a Puritane*, Enlarged ed. (1605), p. 8; Richard Cosin, *Conspiracie for Pretended Reformation: viz. Presbyteriall Discipline* ("Published now by authoritie," 1592), p. 1.

16. Cosin, *Conspiracie for Pretended Reformation*, p. 83.

17. Ormerod, *The Picture of a Puritane*, p. 25.

18. Ibid., p. 70

19. Richard Bancroft, *A Sermon Preached at Paul's Cross* (London, 1588), pp. 33–36.

20. Ibid., pp. 38ff.

21. Bancroft, *A Sermon Preached at Paul's Cross*, p. 45. The Protestant urge to "search and read" has to do with what Alan Sinfield calls the "Reformation belief of contradictories," insisting "on the need for grace whilst denying any means to obtain it." See *Literature in Protestant England, 1560–1660* (London: Croom Helm, 1983), p. 11. Cf. in this connection Robert Burton, *The Anatomy of Melancholy* (III.419): "the more they search and read Scriptures, or divine treatises, the more they puzzle themselves, as a bird in a net" (cited in Sinfield, p. 18).

22. Bancroft, *A Sermon Preached at Paul's Cross*, pp. 41, 42.

23. Ibid., pp. 79, 80.

24. Ibid., pp. 23, 25

25. Oxford, 1614; rpt. Amsterdam: Da Capo Press, 1969, p. 40.

Marguerite Waller

Historicism Historicized:
Translating Petrarch and Derrida

The explosion in Renaissance literary studies of "historical" readings of canonical, noncanonical, and not yet canonical early modern
texts bespeaks a passionate commitment to a critical praxis explicitly,
as well as implicitly, located in relation to the social forces and political
agendas of both the early modern period and our own era. This "new
historicism" has been described, defended, attacked, and theorized in
ways as heterogeneous as its practitioners, but new historicists seem to
be relatively united in writing against the grain of an earlier "literary
history," that tended to search its canonical texts for the literarily and
morally exemplary, for nonideological models of verbal mastery and
social and political comportment.[1] Noncanonical texts, visual material,
archival records, and demographics have, meanwhile, begun to figure
more prominently in the literary scholar's field of reference, as Marx,
Foucault, feminist theory, gay theory, and other analyses of social relations have been introduced to show how implicated the linguistic forms
we have called "literature" are in the cultural codes within which
subjectivities, values, and epistemologies are constantly being renegotiated. As characterized by Louis Montrose, "its [New Historicism's]
collective project is to resituate canonical literary texts among the
multiple forms of writing, and in relation to the non-discursive practices and institutions, of the social formation in which those texts have
been produced—while, at the same time, recognizing that this project
of historical resituation is necessarily the textual construction of critics
who are the themselves historical subjects."[2] Some of the excitement
generated by this reconceptualization of the object of study has to do
with the new role it seems to offer the scholar-critic. Relieved of the

possibility of being authoritative in the old literary historical sense, the New Historicist's reflections on discursive positions and position-taking seem to authorize a rather appealing "new good guy" role—that of the politically engaged scholar-teacher who can use history to convince readers and students that as Montrose puts it, "history is always now," and there continue to be "possibilities for . . . agency" within our contemporary regime of power and knowledge."[3]

Although this role appeals to me, too, I am troubled by its reinscription, however subtle, of the pedagogue as moral guide, the very role a rigorous historicism would, it seems to me, necessarily preclude. (That is, it should go against their own grain for historicists, who claim to be as discursively and negotiably put together as their objects of study, to perform unironically the role of moral or political seer.) My disquiet with this reinscription has led me to reconsider one aspect of New Historicism's historiography, for which I would like to sketch an alternative.[4] I want to call attention to the binary relationship that, in practice, New Historicism seems to set up between the historian and "the past," between, let us say, the present and Tudor England. It seems to me that once the historian's relationship to his or her material is structured this way only two plots are possible. Either the past will turn out to be like the present or it will turn out to be other than, different from, the present. But in both cases "we," the present, remain the principle of intelligibility, the point of reference. This way of knowing ourselves historically repeats the binary logic of "othering" or "saming" that, as Naomi Schor has brilliantly argued, conspires in the very oppressions that many Renaissance literary scholars wish to historicize.[5] Texts and readers, furthermore, are stabilized by this structuring relationship, short-circuiting from the outset the scholar's impulse toward change, and, incidentally, laying the groundwork for the moralism I noted above.

By contrast, to write, to think, to "know" historically could involve finding a way to allow all the positions at play in our historical investigations mutually and continuously to transform one another. There are, no doubt, innumerable ways of doing so. What seems required in one form or another, though, is a departure from the binary arrangement between present and past. Italianist Juliana Schiesari, for example, in an essay entitled "The Gendering of Melancholia," locates her own position as feminist Renaissance scholar in relation to Freud, also reading Renaissance texts in the formulation of his theory of melancholia, and to two Italian poets, one male and one female, Torquato Tasso and Isabella di Morra. While Tasso's construction of the melancholy subject meshes with Freud's, di Morra's differs strikingly; the relationship between the two brings the male orientation of Freud's analysis into focus. As Schiesari outlines the project, it has to do with the psychoanalysis of Renaissance texts, the better to understand historical relationships between power and subjectivities, *and* the historicizing of psychoanalysis, with respect to both feminist criticism and the Renaissance material to which Freud was indebted. "If the very conditions of the patriarchal subject were first made possible in the Renaissance," she writes, "then the combined feminist and psychoanalytic criticism of texts from that period is urgent, not only for a greater understanding of the Renaissance, but also for the radicalization of psychoanalysis itself" (and, she might well have added, for feminist criticism).[6] Though none of the positions in this investigation remains stable, we are not, therefore, disoriented, but continuously and variously reoriented. Positions (if that is still the appropriate term) are remapped in dynamic relation to each other, so that the project neither falls into indeterminacy nor requires that we privilege one point of reference, not even, or especially not, that of theory.

The kinds of cul-de-sac into which New Historicists sometimes suggest a too self-conscious theorizing would take them presents itself, consequently, as a function of New Historicism's own historiographical model, with its implicit binarism and demand for stability. They are not created, in other words, by the theoretical analysis, which merely foregrounds such historicism's narcissistic structure.

What I propose to do in the following pages is a good deal less complicated than Schiesari's project but begins with the same fundamental moves: an abandonment of the binary approach to figuring historical relationships and a strategy for denaturalizing and reorienting in relation to one another my own position and those of the texts I am reading. I will call your attention to a pattern I have noticed in the rhetorical construction and modus operandi of the subject in the English translations of two Romance language texts. My question is, what might we make of the fact that a similar rhetorical sleight of hand occurs on the occasion of each translation, that in each case there is an occlusion of the instability of the (male) subject as he is represented or constructed in the source text and a concomitant change in the way the female subject is figured. By juxtaposing Petrarch's fourteenth-century sonnet 140 with Sir Thomas Wyatt's and Henry Howard, earl of Surrey's sixteenth-century "translations" of it, and by similarly juxtaposing a passage from Derrida's essay "La Différance" with its translation by Alan Bass, I propose to create a "historical" context that gives me a way of thinking about any number of issues—including the historical and cultural specificity of gender identities, the sixteenth-century English appropriation of Italian culture, and the twentieth-century North American appropriation of French theory—without having to portray myself as a suprahistorical knower. I do not wish to disguise, but rather to emphasize, the complex intertextual cross-referencing that the writing of history always involves—in this case, how Derrida's writing has informed my reading of Petrarch's, Wyatt's, and Surrey's poetry and vice versa how the poetry has motivated the readings and uses I have made of Derrida's writing and how it has shaped my reading of Bass's translation. But if the framing perspective offered by this context is admittedly an effect merely of the arrangement of texts, it will the more readily reveal what, as a would-be historian of subjectivity, I am looking for—that is, significant variations in the rhetorical construction of the subject. Paradoxically, as we will also be able to see from this perspective, rhetorical difference is precisely what escapes analysis, what cannot be seen, when one's historiography depends upon ignoring its own constructedness.[7]

For strategic reasons, let me begin with a brief sketch of the poetic subject in Wyatt's "The longe love, that in my thought doeth harbar."

> The longe love, that in my thought doeth harbar
> And in myn hert doeth kepe his residence,
> Into my face preseth with bolde pretence,
> And therein campeth, spreding his baner.
> She that me lerneth to love and suffre,
> And wills that my trust and lustes negligence
> Be rayned by reason, shame and reverence,
> With his hardines taketh displeasure.
> Wherewithall, unto the hertes forrest he fleith,
> Leving his entreprise with payne and cry;
> And ther him hideth, and not appereth.
> What may I do when my maister fereth
> But in the felde with him to lyve and dye?
> For goode is the liff, ending faithfully.[8]

Wyatt's subject, the lover, tends to structure his experience as a narrative of temporally unfolding, relatively discrete events, beginning with his reference to "the longe love." The phrase in line 8, "With his hardines *taketh* displeasure," for example, represents love's pressing into the face as an event that causes an effect, the negative reaction of the beloved, which is another event. Cause and effect may be repeatable and repeated, but they are presented as occuring in sequence, occupying separate temporal moments. Similarly, the phrase in line 12, "when my maister fereth," suggests a repeated occurrence but not necessarily a continuous or constant state. All these narrativizing terms, including the "when" in line 12, allow the narrator who asks "What may I do" to face an apparently real choice. He may choose whether or not to accommodate such moments (harbor them, so to speak). That is, regardless of which choice he makes, these moments do not define him; he defines them.

By structuring the effects of desire as a series of events, the text constructs a perspective apart from, and unconditioned by, the perspective of any one moment it describes. That is, Wyatt's historian displaces the generative element *of* his narrative (desire or "love") into a temporal series of advances and reversals *in* a narrative that conceals (or, if analyzed rhetorically, reveals) Love as the constitutive condition of the narration. The autonomous subject implied by the rhetorical form of the narrative, the agent conceptually separate from his actions and passions and therefore capable of interpreting and directing them, is not commensurable with the desiring subject. Desire, whether defined as a lack, or less theologically, as a certain openness to contingency, signals a subject's positioned status.[9] So positioned, the subject cannot also be autonomous and "know" itself and the world in the authoritative way implied by the narrative of Wyatt's lover. The nontranscendent position of the desiring subject implies as well that its perspective will be temporally contingent. Time, instead of figuring as the continuum within which the autonomous subject could be known and represented, presents itself as the discontinuity between one moment and another that precludes the possibility of their synthesis.

In Wyatt's poem, then, we confront a narrative that presents a situation (active desiring) antithetical to the situation it performs (stable being). The brilliance of the sonnet, from a rhetorical, theoretical perspective, has to do, not with the greater truthfulness, authenticity, or complexity for which English literary historians have ranked it above its Petrarchan source, but with the deftness with which it conceals and exploits its conceptual *aporias*.

Here, let me put as many of my cards as possible on the table. English-speaking literary historians over the past forty years have consistently told a story in which Petrarch's "artifice" is superseded by Wyatt's and/or Surrey's superior "realism." Arguments then focus on whether Wyatt or Surrey is the superior realist. E. M. W. Tillyard in 1949 and Thomas M. Greene in 1982, despite their different styles and approaches, exemplify the gist and conceptual homogeneity of Wyatt/Surrey criticism during the era they bracket. Tillyard writes of Wyatt's "air of unaffected self-expression" and contrasts his "drama" to "Petrarchan convention."[10] Greene offers a highly sophisticated account of Wyatt's exemplification of a certain historical consciousness, a richly nuanced argument to which I cannot do justice here, in which, nevertheless, Wyatt still comes out distinctly better than Petrarch, morally as well as poetically. "If in the *Canzoniere* the poetic consciousness repeatedly fails to make authentic contact with an external presence, if it constitutes a closed, circular system, in Wyatt our sense of an external presence in any given poem . . . is very strong. . . . Thus the etiological passage from the Italian text to the English can be described as an *engagement* of the closed system with its human surrounding, an opening up to the noneself, an involvement, a contextualization." And, a few pages later he writes, "This suppression of ornament and Petrarchan decorative richness, this imagistic asceticism, is essential to Wyatt's language because it strips the word of its esthetic pretentiousness and leaves it as a naked gauge of integrity."[11] Such claims, I will argue, are not supported by rhetorical readings of the sonnets. The investment of either Wyatt's or Surrey's translations with such attributes as presence, transparency, and authenticity may be seen as indicative of a similar investment by the reader in his own interpretive position. That is, if either Wyatt or Surrey can be directly and unproblematically in touch with experience, as an autonomous, authoritative subject, then the critic's position in relation to his material is similarly secure. The result of this literary history, which would tell the story of the progress of poetry toward experience (and of criticism toward poetry) would be the effective concealment of the terms, processes, and structures of its own interpretive position.

The transparency of this kind of critical discourse is already belied, without recourse to deconstructive theory, by the disagreement chronic to the project of assessing the relative merits, or even the substance, of the poetry of Wyatt and Surrey. In this context, the unorthodox response of a woman critic to what has been described by her male colleagues as "rationality" and "empiricism" is worthy of note. Patricia Thomson comments coolly: "The first thing to do in considering Petrarch's influence on English poetry is to disregard the stock notion that he is flattering, unpsychological, artificial, superficial, and unrealistic, and that, in consequence, sixteenth-century English love poetry suffers under these disabilities. If these are found in English Petrarchan poetry . . . their presence proves something about the Tudors, but not about Petrarch."[12] As for English verse forms, an important element in Greene's and others' analyses, Thomson's impression is that especially Surrey's " 'advances' were made at considerable cost" (p. 93). In both the article from which I have been quoting and the corresponding chapter of her book, *Sir Thomas Wyatt and his Background,* she clearly considers Petrarch the master poet, both technically and conceptually. The article concludes, with barely concealed alienation from the whole ethnocentric Wyatt/Surrey debate:

> Wyatt's divergence from Petrarch appears to be a perfectly conscious and deliberate thing, an open act of repudiation in favor of opposite values. Surrey, on the other hand, is not aware of clashing values; and he is not a rebel because, for him, there is nothing to rebel for or against. Again, Wyatt was, I think, fascinated by much in Petrarch's imagery, rhythm, and phraseology; but Surrey's literalness and his decasyllabic treadmill suggest the contrary. (p. 105)

Note, though, that Thomson's dissenting opinions operate, however ironically, from within the terms of the problem to be investigated. She does not force the question of the necessity or possibility of judging these poems' "historical importance, intrinsic value, and comparative merits" (p. 86), nor does she question the status of her own critical representation of his poetry.

To conduct an analysis of the representational processes that constitute the positions these critics variously agree or disagree with, I am appealing to an alternative model of historical reading, a "literary" history that is not chronological and does not take the form of a narrative. It would not appear to be definitive or even "historical" in the conventional sense, but it could be revealing of historical significance in the variations and distinctions among texts that it discloses. What I find in Wyatt's and Surrey's sonnets by means of this analysis are poetic subjects no less rhetorically constituted than the poetic subject of Petrarch's sonnet. The rhetorical processes constitutive of the poetic subjects are nonetheless different in all three sonnets, as are the ways in which the subjects' purely rhetorical status is revealed or concealed, accepted or denied, in the appearance of the product of these processes: the represented subject.

When we take a closer look at the lexical and grammatical changes Wyatt has made in translating Petrarch's sonnet, it becomes more apparent that there will be no real contest between desiring and being and that the figure of the female, the beloved, will be exploited to guarantee the privileged status of that being whose gendering as male now comes to seem not coincidental, but constitutive. Here, for comparison, is Petrarch's sonnet 140:

> Amor, che nel penser mio vive et regna
> e'l suo seggio maggior nel mio cor tene,
> talor armato ne la fronte vène;
> ivi si loca et ivi pon sua insegna.
> Quella ch'amare et sofferir ne 'nsegna.

e vòl che 'l gran desio, l'accesa spene,
ragion, vergogna et reverenza affrene,
di nostro ardir fra se stessa si sdegna.
Onde Amor paventoso fugge al core,
laciando ogni sua impresa, et piange, et trema;
ivi s'asconde, et non appar più fore.
Chè poss'io far, temendo il mio signore,
se non star seco infin a l'ora estrema?
Ché bel fin fa chi ben amando more.[13]

Love, who lives and reigns in my thought and keeps his principal seat
in my heart, sometimes comes forth armed into my forehead, there lodges
himself (or is lodged) and there sets his banner. She who teaches us to love
and endure, and wishes that reason, shame, and reverence rein in great
desire and kindled hope (or, who wishes that great desire and kindled
hope would rein in reason, shame, and reverence) at our boldness is angry
within herself. Wherefore Love flees terrified to my heart, abandoning his
every enterprise (also device, motto), and weeps and trembles; there he
hides and no more appears outside. What can I do, my lord being afraid
(also fearing my lord), except stay with him until the last hour? For a
good end he makes who dies loving well.[14]

In the opening line of "The longe love," Wyatt virtually reverses
Petrarch's representation of a hierarchical relation between love and the
self. Where Petrarch's *amor* lives and reigns ("vive et regna"), Wyatt's
Love merely "harbars." Actually, Wyatt's poem effects more than a
reversal in the sense that Wyatt's touristic Love, consequently, is at the
mercy of his host, who does not reciprocally depend upon him the way
Petrarch's ruler depends upon that which he rules. Love in Wyatt's
version is not simply a subordinate; he is a subordinate *alien*. Nevertheless, nothing would be gained by simply dismissing such a visitor.
Wyatt's harborer is given a legitimate place, a residence, in the poet's
heart. This heart, though, unlike Petrarch's, is not the capital of a
kingdom that includes the intellect. Wyatt's term "residence" is one
possible translation of "seggio," but it loses the technical sense of
"seggio maggior," a center of government or governing center, and the
change is telling. It splits head and heart into different domains. On the
face of it, this is an ingenious strategy for acknowledging desire while
dissimulating the contradiction between desire and autonomy. But this
strategy also raises a secondary problem. Once the affections and the
intellect have been separated or alienated from one other, the repression
of one by the other becomes possible. In the next line, just such a
repression manifests itself in Love's need to press "with bold pretence"
into the lover's face. That the narrator describes the attempt as bold

suggests that Love is not likely to have his claims recognized in the ordinary course of events. That he calls it a "pretence" confirms the suspicion that Love, having first been included, has then been more subtly excluded as constitutive of the subject. This may seem like an antithetical reading of a movement that looks at first like the very opposite of repression, but once again the poem's deviation from the Italian is instructive. The violence of the attempt, greater than in Petrarch's poem ("preseth" rather than "comes"), suggests a love pent up. "Campeth," in the following line, works like "pretense" to subvert Love's title to the territory of the face—a title that Petrarch's neutral "si loca" does not contest.

Having posited a split and alienated subjectivity in the interest of presenting a coherent subject (a fundamentally stable or coherent "face"), Wyatt's lover may now exercise some repressive tolerance toward Love. He may show off the generosity and forebearance with which the autonomous subject deals with such internal rebelliousness, though, by the way he does so, notice, his superiority to and distance from his unruly cohort are ever more surely established. In line 6, for example, as he shoulders half the blame for the disruption Love causes ("*My* trust and *lustes* negligence") his role in Love's insurrection appears to have been a passive one, virtually the antithesis of Petrarch's "great desire" and "kindled hope." The beloved's displeasure is similarly construed, in lines 5 and 8, to the lover's ontological advantage: "She that *me* lerneth to love and suffre. . . . With *his* hardines taketh displeasure." "She" not only is made to distinguish between the lover and his actions, but, here identified as the source of the demand on the lover to display both desire and the appearance of completeness and autonomy, she also takes the blame for the contradiction we have seen displaced along the narrative axis. Her femininity is constituted precisely, to borrow Naomi Schor's terms, of "the refuse of masculine transcendence."[15] In fact, as happens in other Wyatt translations, too, the figure of woman is the lynchpin in a rhetorical operation that constructs a male subject whose status over the course of fourteen lines is made to appear ever more secure.[16]

The sestet presents a thematically brilliant recuperation of the schisms and slippages we have so far discovered in the narrative formulation of that position. In lines 9 through 11 the beloved's displeasure alone is made responsible for the suppression and concealment of Love's claims— "Wherewithall, unto the hertes forrest he fleith, ... And there him hideth, and not appereth"—leaving the lover free to propose that *his* course of action is to heed Love's "payne and cry." Though he refers to love as "my maister," it is at this point that the lover most decidedly displays his own ascendancy and imperial design, reintegrating the previously segregated wilds of the "hertes forrest," reclaiming the territory previously reserved for Love, in order to emerge "in the felde," as what looks like a whole and undivided agent, living and dying with Love. This move prepares the way for the final gesture of line 14, where we find the lover making an authoritative declaration vis-à-vis Love that leaves Love not only rhetorically subjugated, but absent as well. "For goode is the liff, ending faithfully" quite literally equates "the subject" with "life" while consigning Love to a lesser, nonlinguistic existence, which the linguistic subject seems both grammatically able and morally obligated to regulate.

One final observation, about the mode of address of this sonnet to the reader or auditor, will prove relevant to the question of how these moves do not at all correspond to the course of the poetic subject in Petrarch's sonnet. Because the poem does not explicitly open to question the status of the narrating subject, it threatens to place us in the same double bind the lover occupies. Just as the lover who has "liberated" himself from the discontinuities that call his narrative position into question could be considered either a momentary victor over the inherent indeterminacy of the subject, or a victim of the rhetorical strategies of concealment and displacement fundamental to the mode of narrative representation through which he would achieve this illusory victory, so we can either ally ourselves with the lover in the construction of the narrative, or participate in the narrative mechanism with an awareness of our own subjugation to its laws of exclusion and displacement. We seem to be offered a choice between performing as misogynist mimetic readers or as resisting rhetorical readers. Either we can treat the subject as "autonomous," capable of knowing and writing history, or, alternatively, we can see in the poem's constitutive narrative a definition of the subject as a kind of nonexistence, a subjectivity so-called, that would simply be incapable of self-representation and "self-knowledge" and therefore incapable of even entertaining notions of individual will and choice. Those Renaissance scholars who would see historicism and rhetorical theory, or even selfhood and rhetorical theory, as antithetical, are, I would argue, caught within precisely this view of the alternatives. But readers who find themselves caught in this kind of discursive trap could conceivably strike out in a third direction. Confronted with such discourse, they may realize that between an illusory subject and an awareness of the properties of that illusion, both of which preclude a historicist epistemology, there is no reason to choose because there is no choice to be made.

I would also like to dwell for a moment upon the way in which the pseudochoices presented to us here are linked to the semantic displacement onto a different sex (which could just as well be a different race or class) of that which, recognized as the self's own, would threaten its assumed integrity and completeness. Thematically the beloved provides the occasion upon which the lover can appear to "act." Because it is the beloved, not the lover, who appears indeterminate and contradictory, this occasion has built into it the possibility or necessity of there being other occasions as well, on which the subject may continue to reinscribe his mastery. (Recall that the narrative structure of Wyatt's poem suggests a repeated and repeatable process.) The rhetorical manipulations both demanded and allowed by the positing of an autonomous, authoritative subject can, in fact, be supported only by the continued repetition (or invention) of such occasions, which remain, however, as epistemologically fruitless as the first.

I find it significant from a feminist, as well as from a deconstructive and/or historicist, perspective that the subject in Surrey's sonnet performs just such a repetition, pushing the strategy, if anything, somewhat further. Certain formal features of the poem suggest that its lover-narrator assumes a position of still greater detachment from the problems of narrative representation and desire than did Wyatt's narrator:

> Love that doth raine and live within my thought,
> And buylt his seat within my captyve brest,
> Clad in the armes wherein with me he fowght,
> Oft in my face he doth his banner rest.
> But she that tawght me love and suffre paine,
> My doubtfull hope and eke my hote desire
> With shamfast looke to shadoo and refrayne,
> Her smyling grace convertyth streight to yre.
> And cowarde love than to the hert apace
> Taketh his flight, where he doth lorke and playne
> His purpose lost, and dare not show his face.
> For my lordes gylt thus fawtless byde I payine;
> > Yet from my lorde shall not my foote remove.
> > Sweet is the death that taketh end by love.[17]

The use of past and future tenses—"And buylt his seat," "with me he fowght," "But she that tawght me," "from my lord shall not"—more definitively than Wyatt's indications of sequence, implies a fixed point or perspective from which the past can be known and the future decided. The couplet, which reverses the direction in which the three quatrains appear to have been tending, serves to reinforce the impression that this poem sets forth an authoritative, self-determined subject. This impression is threatened, on the other hand, by the initial portrayal of Love's sovereignty over the self whose story is being told. If

Surrey's narrator appears to out-do Wyatt's, so does Surrey's Love, who is not a mere harbourer, but who lives and reigns in the Lover's thought, *and* has "buylt his seat" in the lover's breast. In Surrey's poem we confront a narrative that presents a situation (active desiring) absolutely opposed to the situation it performs (stable being). If the gap between the two situations is still greater here than in Wyatt's poem, the apparent elimination of that gap promises to be no less dissimulating.

With deceptive simplicity, the first three lines of the opening quatrain display this gap as a paradox. Narrative form and narrated content render mutually exclusive subjects. The subject who is completely dominated by Love cannot describe this domination in retrospective narrative terms. The subject who assumes a position of narrative authority cannot claim that he is ruled in every aspect by Love. Nevertheless, the poem suggests, these subjects coincide. The lover's claim in line 4 that Love often appears in his face, freely and against none of the resistance confronted by Wyatt's lover—"*Oft* in my face he doth his banner rest" (emphasis mine)—suggests, for example, that they are related as container to contained. As the lover's face is to the Love that appears there, so, it might be supposed, the face or appearance of his language is to the account of Love that it embodies. This positioning of the narrative voice vis-à-vis Love, though, is not allowed to disrupt the narrative structure. The paradox is not resolved but decided, as in fact it has been from the beginning, at the expense of the desiring subject and Love. As this line in particular illustrates, narrative structure is not at all a container-like form that can be disinterestedly filled with a content at odds with itself. It is, instead, the set of verbal relationships from which any and all self-images emerge.[18] What remains in question, even (or especially) after the thematic statement in line 4 "makes sense" of the paradox of the three preceding lines, is the authority on which this sense is being made.

The same question is raised differently by the disposition of certain thematic elements in the quatrain. We are told that the lover retains for himself no territory, no "ground," so to speak, on which to base his narrative authority. But his concession of all vulnerable territories and features (head, heart, and face) to a Love characterized chiefly by the material constructions ("And buylt his seat") and defenses ("Clad in the armes wherein with me he fowght") that constitute and support Love's own authority also effects a separation or distinction between Love and his domain, on the one hand, and the narrating subject on the other. This separation or distinction, like the one we are encouraged to make between form and content, works like a kind of Moebius strip in which what appear to be two sides are always already only one. It defers (or conceals for the time being) the coherence-threatening contradiction between the situation being described and the discursive mode of the description, but this deferral and the mode of discourse it allows depend in turn upon the distinction (between Love's and the lover's authority) having already been made. The problem we are left with, if we are not to have the voice that makes the distinction already compromised, is to find from where else, other than from the subject-governed-by-Love, it could be coming. If Love governs the entire being of the lover, can the substance or status of the narrative voice be recuperated?

It falls to the beloved (not surprisingly) to provide the occasion on which the narrative may exercise a strategy that would grant the voice the status of an existential being. It follows from the first quatrain that if the narrative voice, separate from the subject whom Love rules, is nevertheless to *represent* that subject, its position separate from the territories governed by Love must be subsumed within a larger unity. The description in the second quatrain of the beloved's authority over the lover works to establish this unity. Although the lover speaks in line 6 of "*My* doubtfull hope and eke *my* hote desire," the grammar of the clause in which this line is embedded short-circuits this gesture toward assimilating Love to the verbal construction of the subject. Because Surrey's lover omits the distinction made in the other two poems between what "she" teaches and what "she" wills, lines 6 and 7 become either an appositive or a correlative to "love and suffre paine." Whichever way one reads these lines, it appears that the beloved has taught him everything he does—doubtfully hoping and hotly desiring, as well as shadowing and refraining—and it is therefore she who appears to be responsible for the situation in the opening quatrain where there was a separation or gap between the lover's mode of discourse and his position in relation to Love.

This position itself is recast by the positing of a beloved who makes such large claims for herself. Love's power over the lover is subsumed by her greater authority over the lover, making Love or desire appear to derive entirely from her. By the same stroke, the lover is endowed with the possibility or capacity he did not yet have in the first quatrain, to perform as if his desire were the nonconstitutive, acquired (from the beloved) characteristic it now appears to be. What the beloved "teaches"— not that the lover repress desire (rein it in both outwardly and inwardly, as in Wyatt's poem), but that he dissimulate ("shadoo and refrayne") it with an outwardly "shamfast" look—is a manifestation of this capacity. It reconstitutes the same subject who was ruled by Love as, here, a disinterested, governing (vis-à-vis Love) being, who conceals his non-constitutive desire legitimately and at will, and who in this sense appears to have coincided with his narrative self-representation from the beginning. The trick of this poem, the symmetry whereby it would neutralize and discharge the threat of dissolution posed by desire, is this reconstitutive demand by the beloved that would have us efface, that attempts to make us forget, the narrative voice's previous lack of any substantial status.

The large task remaining to the poem is to effect a final reversal in the relationship between lover and beloved. The authority of the beloved must finally be shown to work in the service of the subject it reconstitutes, the subject whose ultimate narrative authority still stands, at this point, in the beloved's shadow. This final recuperation begins in the third quatrain where the strategy whose structure I have been describing surfaces narratively. Love is defeated by the beloved, and the lover appears to be what he claims to be, an innocent bystander to their quarrel. The lover is not moved to sympathy for Love's plight because he does not have to be in order, like Wyatt's lover, to demonstrate his freedom or recuperate some displaced part of himself. Because Love appears to be external to him, he need only sit back and let the battle take its course. Significantly, in this regard, the lover can make a statement in line 12, at the point where there is a question for the lovers of both Petrarch and Wyatt. Surrey's subject, having assumed a more authoritative disentanglement than either of them, neither faces a realization nor confronts a choice. He appears simply to *be*, to "byde," as he puts it, in a godlike "fawtless" state. Only the expression of extreme contempt for "coward Love" gives away, perhaps, this disinterested, dissimulating pose. The narrating voice holds Love in contempt precisely because, and to the extent that, Love's constitutive role in the production of a position from which it is possible to be contemptuous threatens to unmask the lover's appearance of transcendence.

This thematic rendering of the lover's independence from Love provides the context for the poem's striking last turn. In the couplet the narrator reappropriates Love to his own position, not as a constitutive element of that position, but as a kind of aesthetic addition to it. One sense, at least, of "Yet from my lorde shall not my foote remove. / Sweet is the death that taketh end by love," is that the otherwise disinterested subject can choreograph desire's disruption as something to be enjoyed, and that the lover is he who knows how to enjoy it. By means of this reappropriation, the narrating voice usurps even the beloved's authority, for the self previously subordinate to her now appears to make a choice, to act, apart from her, and even against her wishes. The situation masked in the couplet by the pose of the aesthete is, nevertheless, coordinate with the situation presented at the beginning of the poem.

Although the last line of the poem provides a thematic motive—aesthetic pleasure—for the lover's "choice" to remain with Love, the choice *qua* choice otherwise seems odd, a gratuitous recasting of the lover's original complaint that he is consumed and victimized by Love. Furthermore, what is presented as a present and future action is not an action at all, but a continuation of the kind of inaction ("Yet from my lorde shall *not* my foote remove") that in the beginning characterized the lover ruled by Love. Once we understand that the narrator who makes these distinctions—between staying with Love by necessity and staying with Love by choice, between not being able to remove the self from Love's power and choosing not to do so—is the illusory product of a narrative that conceals the constitutive role of Love in its production, the distance or difference between the beginning of the poem and its ending, between the aesthetic "choice" of a subject and the structure of its desiring, collapses. As in Wyatt's poem, then, the narrative places us within a double bind. Our only alternatives are to accede or not to an image of independent choice that itself precludes the possibility of either independence or choice.[19]

Traditionally, English-speaking readers have tended to fault the series of three hundred and sixty-six *canzoni, madrigali, sestine,* and sonnets that make up Petrarch's *Rerum vulgarium fragmenta,* or *Canzoniere* for not achieving the kind of closure presented by the images of the subject we find in Wyatt's and Surrey's translations of Sonnet 140. Read from a position that assumes that readers and writers are, and poems should represent, the kinds of subjects constructed by Wyatt's narrative, Petrarch's poem appears to offer only an image of disequilibrium, uncertainty, and impotence. In the same way that I have been reading Wyatt and Surrey through a Petrarchan lens, though, it is possible to read Petrarch in (nonnarrative) relation to Wyatt and Surrey, whose poems I will use here to bring the specificity of Petrarch's poetics into focus. Such a comparative rhetorical reading will show that Petrarch's subject and the representational processes that produce it constantly and transformatively put each other in question. The status of the speaker as a desiring subject is not dissimulated in the service of creating an illusion of authoritative discourse, nor does the discourse of the poem, which itself is not structured as a narrative, produce the illusion of a stable subject. Instead, at each step of the way, recognitions are generated that retroactively modify the significance of the assertions, recognitions, or questions from which they follow. The text is constantly "changing," implying and helping to produce both a poetic subject and a reader whose nature and status are also being constantly renegotiated.

The opening quatrain:

Amor, che nel penser mio vive et regna
e'l suo seggio maggior nel mio cor tene,
talor armato ne la fronte vène,
ivi si loca, et ivi pon sua insegna

Love, who lives and reigns in my thought and keeps his principal seat
in my heart, sometimes comes forth all in armor into my forehead, there
places himself, and there sets his banner, flag, insignia

immediately presents us with the same *aporia* that structures the opening quatrain of Surrey's sonnet. The subject who claims unequivocally that love governs both heart and head should not be in a position so to describe the movements and gestures of Love, to position Love in relation to himself as if Love were merely an attribute of an essential subject. But Petrarch's sonnet neither insists that these two versions coincide nor demands that the disposition of Love and the lover in these lines be confirmed or given greater coherence by what follows. The paradox is neither resolved nor decided, but is thematically and grammatically acknowledged in the next quatrain:

Quella ch'amare et sofferir ne 'nsegna
e vòl che 'l gran desio, l'accesa spene,
ragion, vergogna et reverenza affrene,
di nostro ardir fra se stessa si sdegna.

She who teaches us to love and to endure and wants reason, shame, and reverence to rein in great desire, kindled hope, with our boldness within herself is angry. Or, equally plausibly, she who . . . wants great desire and kindled hope to rein in reason, shame, and reverence, with our boldness within herself is angry.

The lines may be read either way, Petrarch's dazzling double zeugma very precisely imaging what the beloved is said to want—a subject who both exists and desires. In calling the discourse of the opening quatrain into question, though, the second quatrain does not settle the further question of its own authority. Who or what can we infer to be producing this account of the beloved's criticism? In the tercet that follows, where Love is said to go into hiding, this problem is thematized:

Onde Amor paventoso fugge al core,
laciando ogni sua impresa, et piange, et trema;
ivi s'asconde, et non appar piú fore.

Wherefore Love flees terrified to my heart, abandoning his every enterprise-emblem, and weeps and trembles; there he hides and no more appears outside.

Such a description—Love concealing itself and no longer appearing "outside"—could characterize equally well either the discourse of the desiring subject who does somehow control or lend order to its language through reason, shame, and reverence, or the deceptive discourse produced by the dissimulation of the subject as a desiring being. The beloved's reported disdain toward the lover's initial faux pas notwithstanding, the nature of language is such that it cannot be made the ground for such moral or epistemological distinctions. Language itself always displays desire in the sense that the representing subject is always caught in its own indeterminacy—and at the same time this indeterminacy is also concealed by the simulacrum of coherence that language gives to the representing subject.[20] Even in the act of calling attention discursively to the disruption of discourse by the condition of its production, language, it seems, can "make sense" only by dissimulating this disruption. Love or desire no longer *appears* outside at the very moment of, or as a corollary to, *any* attempt to represent the subject. As the represented action of Love in this tercet dramatizes, though not what the lines themselves can tell directly, however, desire still lies at the heart of what its enterprise or sign ("sua impresa"—about which more in a moment) can only betray—betray in the sense that the sign is untrue to desire and that it nevertheless gives desire over or makes it accessible to representation.

Further symptomatic of the poem's semantic, syntactic, and grammatical instability—and the way in which instabilities migrate from one dimension of the poem to another—is the way the term *impresa,* embedded within this tercet, also comments upon the behavior of the tercet, and, retroactively and proleptically upon the behavior of the sonnet, or, to put a little more pressure on the case, upon the *Canzoniere* (and textuality) in general. *Impresa* can mean "emblem" or "motto" as well as an action, undertaking, or enterprise. The *impresa,* that is, can be seen or read as referring not only to an action that Love apparently undertakes only to abandon, but also to an emblem—perhaps the previously mentioned *insegna* of line 3, a visual figure left where it can be seen, even though its owner cannot make good on its signification. This emblem or figure, embedded in the midst of a literary structure, the sonnet, can function, as I shall explain, to refocus our attention on the unhidden and purely rhetorical structure of the entire poem.[21] In the line immediately following, Love is said to appear no longer. More precisely, it is *here (ivi)* that Love ambiguously either hides himself or is hidden. Love is no longer either active or passive, as the Italian construction *"s'asconde,"* which can be translated into English either way, indicates, because we now see that "he" has been (is?—tense begins to make less and less sense as we go on) implied by a discursive structure. Consistent with the course that the language of the poem appears to be taking in this first tercet are two instances of its echoing, and in the process rereading or rewriting, the opening quatrain—the source, so to speak, of the character-like figures that may seem to have governed our reading of the poem thus far. *"Impresa,"* first of all, sends us not only on to the disappearance of Love *"ivi"* or here in line 11, but back to the first appearance of Love's *"insegna,"* his banner or sign *"ivi,"* in line 4. If once it seemed possible for Love to be represented within the poem by such a sign, and hence to emerge from and stand free of the poem's rhetorical structures as a figure of a different order, it now seems that this disposition of figure or image in relation to the poem was a misleading appearance. That banner is rewritten now (or here) as not only the emblem of an undertaking but also as the undertaking of a different kind of emblem.

Actually, the *impresa* of line 10 operates like a very extreme instance of emblem making known as the rebus. The rebus has been described as a kind of visual pun in which a picture stands for words that make up a motto, which, in turn, may refer to some unpicturable concept or circumstance. A picture of an artichoke juxtaposed to a picture of the top of a Greek column, for example, can be read as "artichoke capitol" or, in other words, Castroville, California. In Sonnet 140, the picture itself is also a word—*"impresa"*—which, in its oscillation between pictorial and verbal figuration represents the possibility of a turn or a shift in the figural mode in which the poem might be read. This image, that is, enacts or displays the possibility of seeing/reading the story of the lover, Love, and the beloved as itself a riddle that is always already rewriting itself (and by extension other such stories) as an account of the present moment of its narration. Furthermore, it now becomes arguable that such rhetorical readings can be more "historical" (that is, grounded in temporality) than an epistemologically double-binding historiography that implies and depends upon an illusory, atemporal, essential subject.

The lines we have been working with immediately reward an attempt to respond to this shift in figural mode. Line 4, *"Ivi si loca, et ivi pon sua insegna,"* reread now, or here, from the perspective of line 10, may be taken to mean, not simply "here" in the visage or appearance of a poetic subject, but "here" in this poem, "here" in this line, "here" in the poetic circumstances under which Love and the poetic subject may appear to so position themselves in relation to each other. If *"ivi"* is taken to mean "here" in the latter sense, then the ambiguously reflexive or passive form of the verb to locate, *"si loca,"* becomes, not ambiguous at all, but rigorously precise. It is entirely appropriate and perfectly accurate for the verb to display the passive positioning of Love *by* the poem *as well as* the appearance of active self-positioning that the text, read mimetically, makes possible.

By the final tercet the poem has thus raised a whole series of issues having to do with textuality, desire, and the subject—the subject as both representer and represented. It is to these issues, and to the situation of the subject, that the deceptively simple-looking interrogative *"Che poss'io far"* (What can/may I do?) seems to refer. Unlike Wyatt's poem, where this same question appears to present a choice, but, in so doing, merely provides an occasion for the lover to entrench himself in the illusory position that he has implicitly claimed from the beginning of the poem, Petrarch's contextualization of this simple line presents us with a real, if startling, alternative to the (illusory) autonomous subject. Here grammar is, as usual, significant. The deployment of a simple subject (*io*), verb (*posso fare*) and object (*che*), which is a structure avoided throughout the rest of Sonnet 140, can seem to imply a stable hierarchy of relationships and functions. Grammarians speak of subjects "governing" their verbs and direct objects. Grammatical subjects are usually taken to differ in kind from verbs, the former function usually being performed by a noun or pronoun, which is understood to name an entity, the latter function being performed by words that are understood to indicate the kinds of processes, movements, actions of which such an entity is capable. Here there is no reason not to read the question "What can I do?" as a question about the nature and status of these grammatical structures. How, for example, does an understanding of the operation of the shifter "I" influence our understanding of a question that seems to be about the course of action to be taken by a human subject? Is it safe to assume that the attributes of a grammatical category correspond to those of a human subject? These questions about what "I" can "do" are logically prior to, and very much to the point of, any moral or philosophical inquiry concerning the subject. And, at least in Petrarch's poem, a different kind of subject, different from the illusory ontological subject of Wyatt and Surrey, emerges from its asking.

Reading this line in the context provided by the sonnets of Wyatt and Surrey will clarify the trajectory of the Petrarchan conversion to grammatical and syntactical aspects of textuality. Both English sonnets substitute the direct pronoun "me"—"She that me lerneth" and "But she that tawght me" for Petrarch's *"ne"* (us) in line 5—"Quella ch'amare et sofferir *ne* insegna"—giving the "I" in their respective line 12s an antecedent and apparent referent. "I" refers to "me," which, in turn, names a subject defined as initially and ultimately separate from desire

(desire deriving entirely from the beloved), and therefore unproblematically coincident with the autonomous subject implied by the poem's
narrative form. As we have seen, though, this subject puts us in a
double bind vis-à-vis the language that produces it, which can neither
be believed nor disbelieved. The absence of a simple, grammatical
antecedent to the "I" in Petrarch's sonnet, conversely, refers us either to
the poetic subject that it appears to name, or simply, to itself, to the
grammatical function of the pronoun "I." The phrase, *"Che poss'io far,"*
then, could be read as a question, not only about what kinds of action
either the grammatical or the poetic subject is capable of performing,
but also, about whether the categories of action and agent, implied by
the use of the subject pronoun, are appropriate to the poetic subject as it
has been displayed thus far in the poem.

It is not that the possibility of an epistemology of the subject is
suddenly opened up, but rather that its possible impossibility and the
reasons for this impossibility are beginning to surface in the text. This
is not the kind of information or knowledge that a text can state openly
or directly, for, as this half line demonstrates, the grammar and syntax
of the language in which it would be told are fundamentally unreliable.
The function of the grammatical subject and the characterization of the
poetic subject are at odds with one another. But even as the question is
posed, it displays a space between what it asks and how it asks it that
performs a kind of answer, a "doing," or "making" by means of which
the grammatical subject and the lover can be distinguished. In this
sense *"io"* works analogously here to the way *"amor"* did earlier in the
poem. As the signs of Love or "Love" the sign appeared to be "untrue" to
desire, and yet necessary to desire's representation, so here, *"io"* fails to
signify, but helps to trace in language, the course of an unrepresentable
subject. Not just analogical, Petrarch's text goes on to suggest, *"amor"*
and *"io,"* desire and the subject, could be considered interchangeable
and indistinguishable. In the perfectly ambiguous phrase *"temendo il
mio signore,"* following the question *"Che poss'io far,"* the affinity of
the two personnae is made explicit by the destabilization of the grammatical boundaries that have kept them separate. The syntax of line 12
becomes indeterminate at this point, lending itself to either a conventional, colloquial reading—"What may I do, my lord being afraid?"—or
the more literal "What may I do, fearing my lord?" Or rather both the
one reading and the other, though mutually contradictory and nonsense making on a narrative, thematic level, together continue to pose
the form of an answer to the poem's question. If, and only if, a conversion is made from reading what one takes to be the story of a life to
reading what one takes to be the story of a text, or, as it is put subsequently,

only if the subject who might appear to act, to choose, to narrate, independently of the text, "dies" out of it, can the means of the production or construction of just such a life or subject be glimpsed.

In the remarkable closing line this death finally finds its grammatical enactment. Subjects, verbs, and objects no longer function as separable, stable categories. Lover and love in the form of the relative pronoun "*chi*" and the present participle "*amando*" function as mutually constitutive elements forming the grammatical subject of the verb "*more*" (dies), and the whole clause, verb included, then becomes the grammatical subject of "*fa bel fin*" (makes a good end). Significantly, at this point language no longer presents a problem. It now appears that the ambiguities, indeterminacies, and contradictions encountered along the way could be read as a function of the notion of the autonomous subject rather than as an inadequacy of language. Once the lover no longer tries to write himself as an autonomous subject, the linguistic subject is at last able to perform semantically, syntactically, and grammatically like a lover, which is to say like a contingent, "historical" being, whose "subjectivity" is from moment to moment constantly being renegotiated.[22]

To round out this argument, now, we need to return to the figure of the beloved and to the way this poem addresses or positions the reader. What difference to them does it make for the poetic subject, the lover, to be figured so differently from the way he is in the sonnets of Wyatt and Surrey? The beloved, significantly, does not appear unreasonable or irrational. On the contrary, she figures as that which keeps the lover from maintaining an unreasonable, irrational, self-contradictory, delusional subject position. If this version of the beloved does not necessarily bespeak Petrarch's feminism, it nevertheless gives Laura (the name given the beloved throughout the *Canzoniere*), no less than the lover, the status of a relational figure. Indeed, sexism and misogyny as we know them, involving the objectification and exploitation of women to maintain the illusion of the sovereign (male) subject, cannot come into being when subjects are written and read as Petrarch reads and writes them. As a pun often made in the *Canzoniere* between Laura and *lauro* (between Laura the beloved and the laurel wreath of the triumphant poet) suggests, she functions as language itself does in the sequence, as a complex figure for the figurality of all subject positions.

The reader's position, of course, must be included among these. It has been difficult to offer an exegesis of this poem because the reader is never offered a stable position from which to read. As we have seen, lines and stanzas are not linked by the indications of temporal sequence that would bind together (though ultimately undo) the sonnets of Wyatt and Surrey. On the other hand, Petrarch's reader is not being entrapped in, and epistemologically disempowered by, the image of an essential, if illusory, subject. Nor is that reader, by implication, gendered male. On the contrary, as the *laura-lauro* device emblematizes, not even gender—especially not gender—escapes the problematic of the construction of the subject.[23] When, at every step of the way, the process of reading Petrarch's sonnet involves taking responsibility for the way one necessarily rewrites it, this rewriting also necessarily becomes a rewriting of the subject who reads. "Male" and "female" reading subjects, in this instance, are alike permitted the pleasure, or anxiety, or both, of occupying a kind of rhetorical space in which their own "positions" are anything but fixed. In this sense, too, text and subject (whether the subject is understood as the writing subject or the reading subject) are not separable and are open at any and all moments to change.

What can we make "historically," then, of these differences between Petrarch's sonnet and Wyatt's and Surrey's renditions of it? Before trying to answer that question, I would like to detour for a moment through one of Jacques Derrida's best-known essays "La Différance." I do so, not necessarily to find a philosophical account of what we might mean when we talk about differences, though something like that may turn up, but to offer a third example of translation that repeats, in a curious way, the examples of Wyatt's and Surrey's translations of Petrarch. In a paragraph a few pages into the essay, Derrida's text goes to great lengths to enact rhetorically as well as to discuss thematically, a problem posed by the task of writing about writing, a task not unlike, we are now in a position to see, writing about the subject:

> Comment vais-je m'y prendre pour parler du *a* de la différance? Il va de soi que celle-ci ne saurait être *exposée.* On ne peut jamais exposer que ce qui à un certain moment peut devenir *présent,* manifeste, ce qui peut se montrer, se présenter comme un présent, un étant-présent dans sa verité, verité d'un présent ou présence du present. Or si la différance est (je mets aussi le "est" sous rature) ce qui rend possible la présentation de l'étant-présent, elle ne se présente jamais comme telle. Elle ne se donne jamais au présent. A personne. Se réservant et ne s'exposant pas, elle excède en ce point précis et de manière reglée l'ordre de la verité, sans pour autant se dissimuler, comme quelque chose, comme un étant mystérieux, dans l'occulte d'un non-savoir ou dans un trou dont les bordures seraient déterminables (par exemple en une topologie de la castration). En toute exposition elle serait exposée à disparaître comme disparition. Elle risquerait d'apparaître: de disparaître.[24]

The paragraph begins with a version of the very question, "What may I do?" upon which both Petrarch's and Wyatt's sonnets hinge. Derrida's text draws the question out—"Comment vais-je m'y prendre" or, literally,

"How am I going to take myself . . . ?"—in a way that emphasizes the issue of the subject's representation in language raised in Petrarch's poem. The subsequent description of the relationship between *différance,* which, in French is gendered feminine, and the masculine *l'étant-présent,* strikingly resembles the description I have developed of the relationship between lovers and beloveds in all three sonnets. In all four cases it is "she" who enables the presentation of a masculine being or presence. The differences among them have to do with the status of that "she." In Wyatt's and Surrey's sonnets, of course, "she" *is* dissimulated as some being (*un étant*), who does not exceed the order of truth, whereas in Derrida's text the trajectory of the gender play seems closer to that in Petrarch's sonnet. To speak of the "a" in *différance* necessarily involves the philosopher (a lover of wisdom) in a betrayal of "her" that might make her look as if she is the one playing coy games (*"Elle ne se présente jamais comme telle. Elle ne se donne jamais au présent"*), but that also betrays this appearance and the enunciating subject, the "je," who takes recourse in it, as themselves functions of the operation of *"différance"* (another name for "desire" as I have been using the term).

This philosopher also signals with his gender game something about a difference (spelled with an "e") enabled by, but not coincident with, *différance.* The game is identified as one invented and played by a heterosexual male, not, in other words, by a universal, subject. This representing subject, that is, presumes to speak neither for nor from the perspective of, all other subjects. It represents itself as partial and indeterminate simultaneously with its attempt to speak of the *"a"* of *"différance,"* which, it claims, underwrites the appearance of being. Thus, by implication, this very account of the problematic of *différance* is itself doubly qualified as contingent, conditional, and positioned—on the one hand, by the philosopher's performative account of the impossibility of representing that which enables representation, on the other hand, by his self-representation as a subject caught in one particular illusory subject position. It signifies "historically" that this is the same gender position occupied by the "sovereign" male subject, who has tended in some Western philosophical *and* historical discourses to indulge in a rhetoric of authority, a practice for which neither Derrida nor Petrarch seems to find language at all well-suited.

Both these levels of rhetorical activity are obscured in Alan Bass's English translation of this paragraph from "La Différance." Beginning with the nonreflexive question "What am I to do?" little, if any, attention is given to the precise and layered performance of the French text. Indeed, gender and sex are completely eliminated from view. As one consequence, I think the paragraph in English reads, by comparison, as precious rather than playful, reductively doctrinaire rather than rigorously and continuously in motion:

> What am I to do in order to speak of the *a* of *différance?* It goes without saying that it cannot be *exposed.* One can expose only that which at a certain moment can become *present,* manifest, that which can be shown, presented as something present, a being-present in its truth, in the truth of a present or the presence of the present. Now if *différance* is (and I also cross out the "is") what makes possible the presentation of the being-present, it is never presented as such. It is never offered to the present. Or to anyone. Reserving itself, not exposing itself, in regular fashion it exceeds the order of truth at a certain precise point, but without dissimulating itself as something, as a mysterious being, in the occult of a nonknowledge or in a hole with indeterminable borders (for example, in a topology of castration). In every exposition it would be exposed to disappearing as disappearance. It would risk appearing: disappearing.[25]

It seems an affectation for Bass's "I" to cross out "is" after *"différance"* since this *"différance,"* referred to invariably as "it," has been transformed grammatically into precisely the kind objectified concept that does appear to "be" and whose function here seems to be to aggrandize the unproblemetized "I" who so cleverly puts it through its paces. This *"différance"* has no will of its own—it passively suffers itself to be "never offered to the present, never presented as such," rather than reflexively not presenting herself as such or not offering herself to the present—so it/she does not seem to activate any real anxiety about the structural limits of mastery, and there does not seem to be much reason for all the fuss. I sympathize with all the readers, New Historicist and otherwise, for whom this is "theory" and who find it apolitical or politically reactionary and tedious to boot.

It appears from the vantage we have constructed here, when I include Derrida and Bass in my textual configuration, that American New Historicism and the American translation and assimilation of Continental theory may be in cahoots (unbeknownst to themselves) conceptually in the way they construct their objects of study—be it texts from the past or textuality per se. Whatever the conscious politics of its practitioners might be, what we might call the essentially realist epistemology of American academia's notion of knowledge (identifiable in "old" literary history as well as in New Historicism and American deconstruction) has built into it a denial of difference, including sexual and gender difference. The kind of unproblematized universalizing of the subject position that we see taking place in the difference between Derrida's text and Bass's tacitly privileges and perpetuates, rather than locates, the universalizing, autonomous (male) subject.

In the trajectory of my own readings and arguments, my intention has been to locate that subject in relation to contrasting presentations of male subjects. In so doing, I have necessarily complicated our assurance that we *know* where anyone is or was, but this complication, I trust, rather than bringing in its wake impotent confusion, will point toward other ways that a historicized historicism, not necessarily at odds with, or even separable from, deconstructive theory, can (dis)place us in a transforming relation to the past.

NOTES

1. See, for example, Robert Langbaum's introduction to the Signet edition of Shakespeare's *The Tempest,* ed. Robert Langbaum (New York and Scarborough, Ontario: New American Library, 1964), xxi–xxxiv, to offer a random instance of the moralizing style of literary history commonly found in U.S. English departments until a post–Viet Nam generation of scholars, including feminists and theorists of colonialism, began to challenge this view of a unified and readily accessible "history of ideas." Langbaum writes:

> There is no question as to which view of nature Shakespeare adheres to. He presents here, as in the history plays and the tragedies, a grand vision of order in nature and society. . . . Caliban's crime in conspiring against Prospero is a sin against degree—like the plot of Antonio and Sebastian against Alonso, and Antonio's usurpation of Prospero's throne. Prospero erred in attempting to educate Caliban, just as he erred in allowing Antonio to play the duke in Milan. In both cases, he blurred distinctions of degree and helped create the disorder that followed. (p. xxvi)

And further on he writes: "With its bias against realism, and its interest in symbolic art, our time is better equipped than any time since Shakespeare's to appreciate the last plays. The seventeenth and eighteenth centuries liked best of all Shakespeare's early comedies. The nineteenth century liked the tragedies best, and on the whole we still do. But it may be that the last plays—and especially *The Tempest,* which is as I see it the best of them—will in future have most to say to us" (p. xxxiv). Note the emphasis on judgment. The student is asked to judge (or rather to accept the critic's judgment of) the morality of characters' behavior and the aesthetic success of the text in representing that behavior. Neither these judgments, nor the ideas and dramatic strategies of "Shakespeare" are ever portrayed as positional except insofar as they seem to belong to different "centuries," which have arbitrarily, but conveniently, different tastes from one another.

2. Louis Montrose, "Renaissance Literary Studies and the Subject of History," *English Literary Renaissance* 16 (1986), p. 6.

3. Ibid., p. 12.

4. In her introduction to this volume, Janet Smarr has already ably reviewed

208   Marguerite Waller

the evolution over the last two decades, largely initiated by Hayden White, of historiographical theory, a field that has received surprisingly little attention from New Historicists. Here, though space does not permit me to discuss their work, I would also like to call attention to the implications for historiography of such feminist works as Joan Kelly's *Women, History, and Theory,* (Chicago and London: The University of Chicago Press, 1984), and Joan Wallach Scott's *Gender and the Politics of History,* (New York: Columbia University Press, 1988), as well as the work of theoreticians/historians/readers of colonialism such as Homi Bhabha and Gayatri Spivak. See, for example, Homi Bhabha, "Articulating the Archaic: Notes on Colonial Nonsense," Talk delivered at "History/Event/Discourse" conference, UCLA, January, 1989. Also see Gayatri Spivak, "The New Historicisms: Political Commitment and the Postmodern Critic," in *The New Historicism,* ed. H. Aram Veeser (New York: Routledge, 1989), and *Selected Subaltern Studies,* ed. with Ranajit Guha (New York: Oxford University Press, 1988).

  5. As Schor explains in "This Essentialism Which Is Not One: Coming to Grips with Irigaray," *differences* 1 (1989):

> If othering involves attributing to the objectified other a difference that serves to legitimate her oppression, saming denies the objectified other the right to her difference, submitting the other to the laws of phallic specularity. If othering assumes that the other is knowable, saming precludes any knowledge of the other in her otherness. If exposing the logic of othering—whether it be of women, Jews, or any other victims of demeaning stereotyping—is a necessary step in achieving equality, exposing the logic of saming is a necessary step in toppling the universal from his (her) pedestal.
>
> Since othering and saming conspire in the oppression of women, the workings of *both* processes need to be exposed. (pp. 45–46)

  6. I am working from a long manuscript, entitled "The Gendering of Melancholia: Torquato Tasso and Isabella di Morra," part of which was delivered at the 1989 MLA. Since then a briefer version of Schiesari's argument has appeared as "Mo(u)rning and Melancholia: Tasso and the Dawn of Psychoanalysis," *Quaderni d'italianistica* 11 (1990), pp. 13–27. The passage I quote is on page 3 of the longer manuscript.

  7. Dominick LaCapra's contention, in *Rethinking Literary History: Texts, Contexts, Language* (Ithaca: Cornell University Press, 1987), pp. 31–32, that the performative aspects of "literary" works themselves constitute an object of historical study is highly compatible with my interest in differences among what I am calling rhetorical constructions of the subject. My project here is also related conceptually to the dialogical, intertextual reading, advocated by Jean Howard and Leigh DeNeef, from which one derives a "historical" record not otherwise available. See Jean Howard, "The New Historicism in Renaissance Studies," in *Renaissance Historicism,* ed. Arthur Kinney and Dan Collins (Amherst: University of Massachusetts Press, 1987), p. 19, and

DeNeef, "Of Dialogues and Historicisms," *South Atlantic Quarterly* 86:4 (1987), pp. 511–12.

8. This version of "The longe love" is to be found in the excellent edition, Sir Thomas Wyatt, *Collected Poems,* ed. Kenneth Muir and Patricia Thomson (Liverpool: Liverpool University Press, 1969), p. 3.

9. Jacques Lacan is our major contemporary theoretician of desire as lack. St. Augustine, most notably and accessibly in *The Confessions,* spells out the theological significance of so defining desire. This definition is contested by a range of French and American feminists and gay and lesbian theorists who criticize its implicit model of identity as substance or essence and its implicatedness in the binarism of (hetero)sexism. See, for example, Sue Ellen Case's introduction to her edited volume *Performing Feminisms: Feminist Critical Theory and Theater* (Baltimore and London: The Johns Hopkins University Press, 1990), p. 6.

10. E. M. W. Tillyard, *The Poetry of Sir Thomas Wyatt: A Selection and a Study* (London: Chatto and Windus, 1949), pp. 48, 33.

11. Thomas M. Greene, *The Light in Troy: Imitation and Discovery in Renaissance Poetry* (New Haven and London: Yale University Press, 1982), pp. 247–48, 256. Other critics who have written in the same vein include Hallett Smith, "The Art of Sir Thomas Wyatt," *The Huntington Library Quarterly,* 4 (1946), pp. 323–55; and Douglas Peterson, *The English Lyric from Wyatt to Donne: A History of the Plain and Eloquent Styles* (Princeton: Princeton University Press, 1967).

12. Patricia Thomson, "The First English Petrarchans," *The Huntington Library Quarterly* 22 (1959), p. 86. All further citations are quoted from this article and identified by page number. See also Thomson's book, *Sir Thomas Wyatt and his Background* (Palo Alto: Stanford University Press, 1964).

13. I use the edition, Francesco Petrarca, *Canzoniere,* ed. Gianfranco Contini with notes by Daniele Ponchiroli (Torino: Einaudi, 1968), p. 195.

14. This translation is partly adapted from Robert M. Durling's dual language edition, *Petrarch's Lyric Poems: The Rime sparse and Other Lyrics* (Cambridge: Harvard University Press, 1976), 284. Durling, however, does not attempt to indicate the syntactical reversibility and the lexical polyvocality of Petrarch's sonnet.

15. Schor, "This Essentialism Which Is Not One," p. 45.

16. I present a fuller discussion of this dynamic, discussed in the context of Wyatt's "Whoso list to hunt," in "Academic Tootsie: The Denial of Difference and the Difference it Makes," *diacritics* 17 (1987), pp. 2–20. See esp. p. 12.

17. This version of Surrey's sonnet is quoted from Henry Howard, Earl of Surrey's *Poems,* ed. Emrys Jones (Oxford: At the Clarendon Press, 1964), p. 3.

18. Laura Mulvey and Teresa de Lauretis have both provocatively argued that, in fact, linear narrative "fits in," as Mulvey puts it, with the construction of a sadistic subject. In her 1975 *Screen* article, "Visual Pleasure and Narrative Cinema," reprinted in *Visual and Other Pleasures* (Bloomington: Indiana University Press, 1989), pp. 14–26, she suggested that "Sadism demands a story,

depends on making something happen, forcing a change in another person, a battle of will and strength, victory/defeat, all occurring in a linear time with a beginning and an end." (p. 22) De Lauretis, in *Alice Doesn't: Feminism, Semiotics, Cinema* (Bloomington: Indiana University Press, 1982), p. 132, considers how the formula works in reverse: "Story demands sadism."

19. Lauro Martines's essay, "The Politics of Love Poetry," in this volume suggests that the figure of the beloved, the way sexuality is conceptualized, and the structure and reproduction of political power are all interrelated. Such relationships were also the subject of a conference sponsored by *Genders* on "Nationalisms and Sexualities" held at Harvard University in June, 1989. The proceedings of this conference were published in *Nationalisms and Sexualities*, ed. Andrew Parker, Mary Russo, Doris Sommer, and Patricia Yaeger (New York: Routledge, 1992). In "Academic Tootsie," p. 12, I have sketched out the relationship between male sexuality and the structure of Henry VIII's court that I see displayed in Wyatt's "Whoso list to hunt," but space does not permit me to pursue this fascinating issue here.

20. This problematic has been formulated many times in both deconstructive and psychoanalytic theory. See, for example, Paul de Man's essay "Allegory (*Julie*)" in *Allegories of Reading: Figural Language in Rousseau, Nietzsche, Rilke, and Proust* (New Haven: Yale University Press, 1979): "Like 'man,' 'love' is a figure that disfigures, a metaphor that confers the illusion of proper meaning to a suspended, open semantic structure. In the naively referential language of the affections, this makes love into the forever-repeated chimera, the monster of its own aberration, always oriented toward the future of its repetition, since the undoing of the illusion only sharpens the uncertainty that created the illusion in the first place. In this same affective language, the referential error is called desire" (p. 198). Lacan places desire at the center of his psychoanalytical theory and represents it as "a perpetual effect of symbolic articulation," to borrow Alan Sheridan's phrase in his translator's introduction to *Ecrits: A Selection* (New York and London: W. W. Norton, 1977), p. viii. About one of Derrida's many formulations of this problematic, I will have more to say at the conclusion of this essay.

21. In both the *Canzoniere* and the *Trionfi,* I have come to believe, Petrarch is often engaged in literary experiments that enact conversations between "writing" (as defined and practiced within the hegemonic, imperial Latin tradition) and the semiotically different oral, visual, and performative textualities of vigorous vernacular cultures. I discuss what I take to be the political and historical import of one of these experiments, in "Petrarch's *Triumphs* and the Spectacle of Society," in *Petrarch's Triumphs: Allegory and Spectacle,* ed. Konrad Eisenbichler and Amilcare A. Iannucci (Ottawa: Dovehouse Editions, 1990), pp. 349–358. See also Domenico Pietropaolo's "Spectacular Literacy and the Topology of Significance: The Processional Mode," in Ibid., pp. 359–368.

22. This death of the subject might be related to Foucault's discussion in *The Order of Things: An Archeology of the Human Sciences* (New York: Pantheon, 1970) of a similar demise of the subject in what has come to be known as the

postmodern episteme. I find it easier to think of the subject in question as an ideological chimera that corresponds to and is one aspect of the history of absolutist power in western European cultures. Gayatri Spivak and Homi Bhabha have both illuminated, from various colonial perspectives, how open to renegotiation subjectivity can be and how constantly it is being negotiated. See Spivak, *Selected Subaltern Studies* and Bhabha, "Colonial Nonsense."

23. It is tempting to compare Petrarch's gender play in the *Canzoniere* to the excellent work of Judith Butler on the deconstruction of gender identities. See her book *Gender Trouble: Feminism and the Subversion of Identity* (New York and London: Routledge, 1990). Though Petrarch and Butler make several of the same moves, these moves do not necessarily "mean" the same thing, of course. On the other hand, Butler's work, allows me to give Petrarch's gestures a significance they did not have before, while, from the perspective of Petrarch's poetry I find that Butler's work has an unexpected and exciting historical resonance. The feminist deconstruction of gender does not seem such an isolated, isolating activity. This is one kind of history that can be made when positions remain permeable to one another.

24. Jacques Derrida, "La Différance," in *Marges de la philosophie* (Paris: Les Editions de Minuit, 1972), p. 6.

25. Jacques Derrida, "Différance," in *Margins of Philosophy*, trans. Alan Bass (Chicago: The University of Chicago Press, 1982), p. 6.

Discussion

MICHAEL THURSTON: This is addressed to Lauro Martines. In your book on English Renaissance poetry and society, the thrust seems to be that we can look at history through poetry, and that posits a priority for social history over literature; this paper seems to have the same thrust. I am wondering if there is a possibility that sometimes—or any time—they can work the other way: I mean if literary change can cause social change, if a change in the semiotic system can lead to a change in "real" history.

MARTINES: I don't suggest or admit as much in the book, but since having finished it, because of some of the things that have gone on in theory since then, I think that I have at the very least to admit the possibility.

PETREY: Let me follow up that question, which I like very much. I was most impressed by the way that you brought social practice into what seemed to be the highly stylized and conventional form of love poetry. Would you be willing to go along a step further and say not just that poetry or literature produces social change, but that social and literary expression, one taking the form of material practice, the other of verbal expression, are one and the same thing? At one point you say, "We move from one semiotic system to another." Would you be willing to see a sociosemiotic system as a whole in which the way you talk to the lady and the way you deal with the lower class is part of a single experience of existing?

MARTINES: The way you talk to your servants, to peasants in the countryside, to your lady or your prince or the leading oligarch—clearly in language there has to be a bond, a relationship there, something that snakes through all those discourses.

PETREY: At one point you say, "The lady stands in for courtly civilization." Couldn't you say the other: courtly civilization stands in for the lady? That is, why are you putting the priority on social practice rather than on symbolic form?

MARTINES: Well, I'll put my cards on the table: 1) because I am a historian; 2) because I think of myself as a social historian; and 3) because as I look over time, over history, while it may be true that there are moments from time to time when high culture—let's put it that way—is so efficacious that it can bring about political and social change, one tends in history to see that far less often than movement the other way. That is why you detect some reluctance here.

To pick up on something else you were saying, there was something deeper here that made talking to one's lady, one's servant, or one's prince part of the same discourse, and that was the new system of humanistic education that wins the day by 1400, 1420 at the latest. Nearly all these men have had that education. Even though they are writing in the vernacular, many of them can write Latin and do (certainly Bembo does). And in their education oratory, rhetoric, has been stressed; that is, what has been primary, and they have been prepared to use oratory with anyone: slave, prince, or my lady. So perhaps one should look to one aspect of the social system here, namely the new educational program.

BRENKMAN: I want to encourage Lauro to respond somewhat differently to Sandy. I think one way to come at this is to avoid here a kind of false homology. I think we falsify the problem by making this homology in which literature comes to stand in for the symbolic, because first of all it cannot bear the weight of that. Some several hundred love poems cannot be socially causal in a meaningful fashion. If you put the question that way, it looks silly. But if you look at the interaction of what are distinguishably the symbolic and social practices in a way that that interplay is applicable both to the analysis of literature and to the analysis of politics, which seems to me the direction you are going, then you are not making that categorical choice at the outset. The whole form of causation then has to be refashioned into a different sort of problem of explanations. I want to move the controversy in that direction rather than back to what is really a kind of controversy—if we are not careful—about which twentieth-century Western intellectual discipline has its finger on the pulse of causation.

PETREY: To go back to the question of how you do representational criticism, I think one of the things that came out very strongly of Lauro's paper was that there is a general move away from the sense of direct representation—for example this is what the Restoration looked like—to indirect representation: how did the forms of literature manifest the structures of society in one way or another? How do the forms of literature become part of the structures of social coexistence? You'd think that one of the most exciting ways to do this indirect representation or this productive representation, where you can see social reality in literature, would be the formation of the canon.

MARTINES: A thing I would love to see, which I think you won't see, is the walls between history and literature being knocked down altogether and the two faculties being brought together into one. The institutional conventions, barriers, habits, interests, are such that this will not happen. First of all, it would present funding problems. We have at UCLA a cross-disciplinary Ph.D. program that is handled out of the central administration building; but when a student goes there and says, "I would like to work on a special Ph.D., completely interdisciplinary," right then they have to talk her or him out of it because the claim straightaway is, "But you've got to think about your career. Who will hire you?"

COHEN: That's right. This pertains to the success of the division of labor in Western society. The whole academia is one more illustration of the overall segmentation of work processes. Why not do geography in the history department? Unfortunately, all too many professors, as they move through the profession, come to represent themselves as if they were members of the corporate world. The idea of the eccentric, weird, strange, uncontrollable, wild professor is not part of the representation of the profession to the public any longer. So we have a safe professorial image. That to me is all part of the containment of representation. It's all part of the segmentation of labor that I tend to see as the real evil demon in the constant grinding of more and more divisions that make it more and more difficult to introduce change.

MARTINES: But at the same time clearly there are lots of people in the profession who are making plans to cross over and to take in more and more. It's interesting and I think revealing that the attempt by lots of New Historians now to make the historic experience something much richer is coming about not in the first instance by going through literature but by going through anthropology—maybe because we think,

"Social science: we're on firmer ground here." I think that's false myself, but it's one of the reasons behind it. By richer historical experience, I mean taking things from anthropology such as the New Historical study of ritual, also of the whole notion of what a neighborhood is, and a city, a parish church, and what people met and what they did. It's an attempt to fill up the whole texture of social life. And I think the time is coming when historians will be forced to look at the kind of literature that makes them uneasy, because for a historian to be thrust into the middle of a group of critical theorists can be very unnerving and queasy making.

COHEN: I tend to see the historical discourse in general, from the nineteenth century on, as nothing but a series of appropriations of other discourses. When historians took over psychoanalysis, they stripped it of its radical implications. When historians took structuralism, they stripped it of its radical implications. And unfortunately, E. P. Thompson and writers like that, when they took in Marxism, stripped it of its radical implications. And so I tend to see the discourse as a constant stabilization. I don't think there is a radical history writing or representation in that sense.

BRENKMAN: I think these are the wrong questions; or rather that Sande asked the right first question and then the wrong second question. The right first question said: what are the uses of history? What are the uses to which historical investigation and interpretation are put—not simply contained within its academic framework but in the broader social sense? I think that's something very important for us to explore, but I don't think we can explore it via this sort of totalizing critique in which the whole discipline of history is to be charged with this, that, and the other sort of social integration. Rather, we need to look at it as a much more multifaceted set of questions and problems about the competing uses of historical investigation. What we might object to is this or that task, or this or that past, rather than saying that the problem is a false concept of history. For example, let's take Lauro's paper. Now we can raise the question: what are the uses built into this particular practice of historical investigation? of this interest in Florentine literature and power structures and symbolism, and in trying to situate those in a particular way? And I think the answers would not have to do with the justification of what I consider the old historicism, that is: "because it's important to understand Florence in the 1500s, for its own sake." That's not what organized or motivated that talk. It's something about trying to understand power relations, the interplay between the history of heterosexuality and the role of men in hierarchical structures, and so on.

COHEN: But John, this presupposes the absolute continuity and transference of a situation from the Renaissance to today.

BRENKMAN: No, no, but it doesn't presuppose that it's irrelevant either. In fact, it opens that question. You might be able to criticize particular argumentative moves or conceptualizations that Lauro made on the grounds that they establish a false relation between that past and this present; but then you have to argue that out.

COHEN: You made a good distinction, which I should probably pay more attention to, between the critique of philosophies of history and the critique of particular works. What I would want to know about every particular work is: who's the implied reader? who's the implied audience? When I look at Braudel, in my book *Capitalism and the Material Life,* I constantly ask myself, for example: who's the implied reader for the statement that the Aztecs were too free and therefore deserved to get wiped out? And over and over again the implied reader was obviously somebody who had internalized Western notions such as: you have to live by dying—in other words, you have to work for a living—someone who had already internalized our whole social system. So I agree with you.

BRENKMAN: But you don't expand the audience by ceasing to address those who have been integrated into our social system. I think a difficulty in the stuff you quoted in your paper is that I see in it a hyperbolic interpretation of integration, a completely undifferentiated idea in which all aspects of social reproduction are technically qualified as bad because there is no distinction between cooperation among a group of humans and social control. In other words, if you use that vocabulary, you have no way of ever making a meaningful distinction between a good social control and a bad social control. And that tends to expand into the other critical categories in a way that makes the kind of utopian solution that particularly Deleuze and Lyotard propose look like the only alternative.

PETREY: One of the things that really struck me, especially here, is that historical criticism in the age of deconstruction is centered in the Renaissance. The whole New Historicism certainly started as Renaissance studies. Lauro, Annabel, and an immense number of people I've met from Illinois are also Renaissance people. I wonder if anybody has a historical explanation as to why that is.

SMARR: There has already been some commentary on this. The Renaissance is a moment in which people became very conscious of their construction of social identities and the construction of social systems in a way that we identify with; and therefore that has been picked up as a moment of kindred interest, in which we find people and texts doing the same kind of self-deconstruction and construction, very self-consciously, that we're interested in thinking about.

PALENCIA-ROTH: It's in the Renaissance, I think, that we have the first really modern anthropology—the first really modern historiographical works. And this is because of the discovery of America and the great disjunction that that brought into the course of Western history as it had been known up to that point.

RICHARD WHEELER: Insofar as most of the modern influences on literary criticism have been French driven, there was a tendency not to reach back in history as far as the sixteenth century, and I think that that is probably part of the problem. Foucault really was the only link up. If you read Derrida, you start with Descartes and come on down, as if Montaigne did not exist. And even if you read Foucault, you get a very skewed kind of sixteenth century: there's no Machiavelli, no Martin Luther; but at least there was a gesture back in that direction. The corresponding phenomenon is that Renaissance studies were very, very slow to absorb the thrust of the modern theoretical criticism at all. If you look back to the New Criticism, it was obligatory to establish the power to write a Shakespearean essay as well as to go on and say something intelligent about John Donne; and that just dropped out of the picture with the new wave of criticism in the '70s. It lost its hold. The New Historicism is the ladder it took to find that again; and the measure of what success it had, I suppose, is that at a conference like this people are wondering why the Renaissance has taken over again.

BRENKMAN: It has to raise a skeptical question too, I think: the possibility that one of the reasons why the Renaissance has been attractive to this kind of work is that it's a situation where one can make the relationship between political powers, social class, intelligible in a particular way. The question has to be raised whether that form of intelligibility interests us because it correlates with or because it does not correlate with the intelligibility or unintelligibility of those rela-

tions within our own context. This would be another way of talking
about the question: what are the uses of historical investigation? It's a
past-present issue. This is terrific work and I'm learning a tremendous
amount, but one lingering skeptical question I have is whether or not
it's the sort of situation where from these investigations we acquire a
certain illusion of now understanding the dynamics of power and
symbolization in a way that we yearn to in our own contemporary
situation; but we don't know what those coordinates are, of representational power and so on. That interplay between the unintelligibility of
something about the present and the intelligibility of something
akin—hypothetically anyway—in the past has to be one of the driving
forces of historical research in the first place.

I'm reminded of an interesting debate when Foucault's work on the
prisons came out. I heard in a space of a few weeks two different papers,
both by Europeans. One criticized *Discipline and Punish* because it
projected into the nineteenth century a view of social control that could
only have emerged to be of pertinence in the twentieth century. That's
what really motivated Foucault's argument: he wanted to understand
how control works in the disciplinary society we live in, and to do that
he conjured up this image out of the nineteenth century, though that's
not how control worked at all in the nineteenth century. The other
argument was just the opposite: that what's wrong is that this is something very specific to the nineteenth century, but the argument is being
made in a way that makes it seem to have relevance to political problems today, though it really is completely anachronistic for today. Now I
think those are wonderful moments when the whole question of the use
of historical investigation comes to the fore.

SMARR: I was wondering to what extent existentialism has been a
belated impetus in the new ways of thinking: ungrounded but committed,
responsible, unrepresentative but socially active.

COHEN: I think this goes back to the nineteenth century. It's no accident
that in many of the major novels of the nineteenth century the villain
in the piece is a historian. In Ibsen, for example, the historian is a fool
who is constantly seducing people to their own self-destruction. There's
a continuance in the anti-Hegelian mode from Kierkegaard through
Nietzsche and then into the literary people. In George Eliot, for example,
the historian is seen as a fool, as a destructive sorcerer, as a negative
seduction. This idea comes to an additional modernist crisis in *Nausea*,
where Sartre, speaking through Roquentin, argues: I can't write history
any more; it's all true; there are at least four or five stories I could tell.

That's his version of Eliot's multiple consciousness in the *Waste Land*. And I think in some sense we're still stuck in that moment in terms of historical theory.

Notes on Contributors

SANDE COHEN teaches courses in cultural criticism and the history of philosophy at the California Institute of the Arts, having previously taught at Brown University and UCLA. He is the author of *Historical Culture: On the Recoding of an Academic Discipline* (1986) and *The Academic Thing: Essays on Criticism and Historiography* (forthcoming).

LAURO MARTINES is professor of history at the University of California, Los Angeles, and the author of, among other books, *The Social World of the Florentine Humanists* (1963), *Power and Imagination: City-States in Renaissance Italy* (1979), and *Society and History in English Renaissance Verse* (1985); the editor of *Violence and Civil Disorder in Italian Cities, 1200–1500* (1972); and coeditor with Julia O'Faolain of *Not In God's Image: Women in History from the Greeks to the Victorians.* He is writing a book on politics and society in the poetry of the Italian Renaissance.

JULIO ORTEGA is professor of Hispanic studies at Brown University, author of many volumes of criticism and fiction, and editor of Latin American texts. His critical works include *La contemplacion y la fiesta* (1969), *Relato de la Utopia* (1973), *La imaginación critica* (1975), *La cultura peruana: experiencia y conciencia* (1978), *Texto, Comunicación, y Cultura: "Los ríos profundos" de J.M. Arguedas* (1982), *Poetics of Change: The New Spanish American Narrative* (1984), *La teoría poética de César Vallejo* (1986), and *Critica de la identidad: La pregunta por el Perú en su literatura* (1988).

ANNABEL PATTERSON is professor of English and the graduate study of literature at Duke University. She is the author of *Hermogenes and the*

Renaissance: Seven Ideas of Style (1970), *Marvell and the Civic Crown* (1978), *Censorship and Interpretation* (1984), *Roman Images* (1984), *Pastoral and Ideology* (1987), and most recently *The Hermeneutics of Censorship and the Politics of Genre* (1991).

SANDY PETREY is professor of French and comparative literature at SUNY, Stony Brook. His publications include *History in the Text* (1980), *Realism and Revolution* (1988), and *Speech Acts and Literary Theory* (1990).

MARY POOVEY is professor of English at the Johns Hopkins University. She is the author of *The Proper Lady and the Woman Writer: Ideology as Style in the Works of Mary Wollstonecraft, Mary Shelley, and Jane Austen* (1984) and *Uneven Developments: The Ideological Work of Gender in Mid-Victorian England* (1988).

JANET LEVARIE SMARR is professor of comparative literature and interpretive theory at the University of Illinois at Urbana-Champaign. She is the prize-winning translator of *Italian Renaissance Tales* (1983) and of *Boccaccio's Ecloques* (1987), and author of *Boccaccio and Fiammetta: the Narrator as Lover* (1986), as well as of articles on Italian and English Renaissance literature.

MARGUERITE R. WALLER teaches Renaissance literature, feminist theory, and film at the University of California, Riverside, where she is professor of English. She is the author of *Petrarch's Poetics and Literary History* (1980), as well as articles on Dante, Petrarch, Wyatt, Shakespeare, Fellini, Lina Wertmüller, and George Lucas. Her current research in Renaissance studies draws upon poststructuralist and feminist theory to perform ideological analyses of early modern texts and their late modern readings. Her forthcoming book on film compares different cinematic traditions from a feminist perspective.

ROBERT WEIMANN is professor of English and American studies at the Akademie der Künste, Berlin, and an honorary member of the Modern Language Association. His works include *Drama und Wirklichkeit in der Shakespeare-zeit* (1958), *New Criticism und die Entwicklung Bürgerlicher Literaturwissenschaft* (1962), *Tradition in der Literaturgeschichte* (1972), *Shakespeare and the Popular Tradition in Theater* (1978), *Shakespeare und die Macht der Mimesis: Repräsentation und Autorität* (1988), and *Structure and Society in Literary History* (1976, rev. 1984).

Index